HUNTER

a novel by

Andrew Macdonald

Second Edition

NATIONAL VANGUARD BOOKS

Library of Congress Catalog Card Number 89-69872

ISBN 0-937944-09-2

First edition, first printing, December 1989
First edition, second printing, March 1994
Second edition, first printing, March 1998
Cumulative total: 61,000 copies

Cover by D B Graphics

Published by National Vanguard Books
POB 330 • Hillsboro • WV 24946

PRINTED IN THE UNITED STATES OF AMERICA

I

As he pulled into the parking slot near the edge of the huge, asphalt lot an empty beer can crunched under one of the front wheels of the car. He turned off his lights and surveyed the area. Yes, this was a good spot; he had a clear view of each automobile turning from the lone entrance driveway into the lot, where it had to slow almost to a stop under the bright, mercury-vapor lamp there, and he also was well situated for seeing which row of the lot each vehicle eventually turned into. He pulled his coat more snugly around his neck, turned the radio dial until he found an FM station which was broadcasting his favorite Schubert sonata, and settled down to wait.

It was nearly 20 minutes before he spotted what he was looking for. A brown sports van barely slowed as it came bouncing up the entrance ramp. Its tires squealed as it made the turn at the top. For a single instant the faces of the two occupants were visible to Oscar: the driver, a mulatto with a bushy Afro, and the woman beside him, dark haired and with a rather broad nose, but still clearly White.

The van's tall antenna with the orange ping-pong ball on top made it easy for him to follow the course of the vehicle with his eyes after it turned into the fourth lane down from where he was parked. Oscar waited until the van stopped, then he started his engine and swung out of his parking space, following the route taken by the other vehicle. He wanted another look at the couple before they went into the supermarket, just to be certain. Then he would choose another parking slot, as near the van as possible, and wait for them to return.

As he rolled cautiously along the asphalt between the two lines of parked cars, he did not see the couple in his headlights until he was nearly opposite their van. They were both standing near the passenger side of their vehicle, apparently arguing about something.

A sudden, reckless impulse struck Oscar: why not do it now, instead of waiting for them to go into the store and then come back? There were no other cars moving in the lane and no other pedestrians in sight, except at the far end, near the store entrance. Unfortunately, though, the brown van and the couple were on his right, and his passenger-side window was rolled up. It seemed to him too awkward to have to lean across the seat and roll the window down while they were watching.

Would he be able to turn his car around and drive back up the lane before anyone else came or before the couple moved? Perhaps he should get out of the car now and hit them on foot. His palms became sweaty, and he felt his muscles tighten as the possibilities flashed through his mind with lightning speed.

Just as he came fully abreast of the van he spotted a vacant slot three cars down, also on the right. Good! He would pull in there. If no one else had appeared he would back out and move down the lane in the opposite direction, with the van on his left this time.

In the cold night air the perspiration rolled down his cheeks in rivulets as he fought to calm his nerves. It was always this way just before an operation. Even back in 'Nam, every time he'd had to take his F4 up on a run through that deadly North Vietnamese antiaircraft fire, he'd had to fight this jittery, sweaty feeling. Once he was in the thick of things, the fear disappeared; it was *just before* that was always the bad time—the time when it was still possible to back out.

His grip tightened convulsively on the steering wheel, and the motion of the car became jerky as he maneuvered into the parking space. An instant glance to the rear, and then he put his vehicle into reverse and backed it quickly around.

In another five seconds he was opposite the couple again. He stopped the car with a jerk, inadvertently killing the engine. Damn! And in the rearview mirror he saw a fat woman, two bags of groceries in her arms and a small child trailing her, walking down the lane, about 60 yards away. Both the bushy-haired mulatto and his rather dumpy, pasty-faced female companion stopped talking and turned to look directly at him. They were about eight feet from his open window.

An instant calm fell over Oscar, the expected calm for which he had been waiting. With a smooth motion, neither too hurried nor too slow but precise and deliberate, he lifted the rifle from beneath the blanket on the seat beside him, raised it to his shoulder, and, left elbow braced against the door, carefully squeezed off two shots.

The ear-shattering reports echoed through the huge lot, but Oscar remained calm as he put the rifle down, restarted his engine, and accelerated smoothly toward the exit ramp. As he turned at the end of the lane, he paused to glance back toward the van. The mulatto's body was sprawled out into the roadway; the woman apparently had fallen backward, beside the van, and was not visible. Both shots had been head shots, and Oscar was quite certain both the man and the woman were dead. He had seen their skulls literally explode into showers of bone fragments, brain tissue, and blood as the high-velocity projectiles struck them.

The icy calm stayed with Oscar all the way home. Not until he had put the car in the garage, entered the house, and taken off his coat did it give way to the euphoria he always felt afterward. He whistled contentedly to himself as he gave his rifle a quick cleaning and then returned to the garage to change his license plates. It took him only two minutes to remove the special plates and replace them with his regular ones.

He carefully checked the adhesive-backed plastic letters and numerals which he had pressed onto the flattened plates. He had been worried about the adhesive not holding the thick plastic pieces to the metal, especially in this cold weather. He pried gently at the edge of a letter with the blade of his pocket knife. The adhesive resisted, then gradually yielded, so that he was able to work the blade between the plastic and the metal and, with a few seconds of effort, peel the entire letter loose. That was reassuring, but he was still mindful of the time, a few days ago, when he had arrived at home and found a number missing from the plate altogether! After that he had done some experimenting with different adhesives. It took him nearly 20 minutes to peel loose all of the plastic pieces and rearrange them into a new pattern this time, but he did not begrudge the extra effort required.

How fortunate, he thought, as he turned out the garage light, that his automobile was such a common model. There must be 10,000 tan Ford sedans practically indistinguishable from his in the Washington metropolitan area. Still, he was pressing his luck to keep using the same *modus operandi*. Six times in a little over three weeks—22 days to be exact—with the same car, the same rifle, the same routine, just different parking lots and different license numbers, was really too much, he thought to himself.

But more than two weeks ago he had made up his mind that he would not vary his style until the news media broke their silence on the killings. There had been a big news splash after the first double shooting, three weeks ago. "Interracial couple gunned down in parking lot," the *Washington Post* headline had screamed, and the other media also had stressed the fact that the two victims were a Black male and a White female, even though the newsmen had no way of knowing then that the gunman had a racial motive. The naughtiness of the notion that he *might have* apparently was too titillating for them to resist.

When the second double killing came four days later, it had been mentioned briefly on the inside pages of the *Post* and then quietly dropped. The third, fourth, and fifth pairs of shootings had been greeted with total media silence. The reason was clear: at some time between the second and third shootings it had dawned on the media people that the killings *were* racially motivated, and the realization frightened them. They didn't want to encourage any would-be imitators, or even give hope to a great many Americans who would cheer anyone who might be going around picking off racially mixed couples.

By now the bastards really must be bursting at the seams trying to keep the lid on this, Oscar thought, grinning. They couldn't hold out much longer. He had a strong hunch, approaching certainty, that tonight's work would crack them wide open.

In the passageway between the garage and the house Oscar hesitated. He had some paperwork in the study to finish, if he were to have the new proposal ready in time for his meeting with Colonel Ericsson Thursday. But he couldn't stomach the idea of any more paperwork tonight, and it already was a bit late for calling Adelaide. He decided to put in a couple of hours in the shop before bedtime. Happy with his decision, he snapped his fingers and began whistling again as he turned down the stairs to the cellar.

Oscar Yeager was a consulting engineer by profession, a tinkerer and occasional inventor by inclination. After leaving the Air Force in 1976, he had gone back to school and earned graduate degrees in both electrical engineering and computer science. He had begun hiring out as a consultant even while finishing his graduate work at the University of Colorado. After that he had set up shop in the San Francisco area and, through an Air Force acquaintance from his Vietnam days, now a contract officer in the Pentagon, had acquired a series of design contracts. It was these contracts which had led him to move to Washington four years ago.

Actually, Oscar didn't have to work at all; the royalties coming in on one of his antenna patents were quite sufficient to meet his rather modest needs. He worked, not so much because he was eager to pile up more money in the bank, but because he thought it a good idea to keep his hand in. Furthermore, the extra income made it possible for him gradually to increase his stock of laboratory equipment, which was damned expensive. Anyway, the work fitted in nicely with his own tinkering inclinations, he did it all at home on his own schedule, and he almost never spent more than 20 hours a week at it.

Oscar moved easily between the racks of electronic equipment, carefully avoiding tripping over interconnecting cables, as he made his way to the corner where the computer quietly hummed and chittered to itself. He glanced at the sheaf of fanfold paper which the printer slowly had been disgorging all evening and noted with satisfaction that the calculations for the new antenna system were nearly finished. If things continued to go well, he just might have all the work done for which he was seeking another Air Force contract even before the contract was signed Thursday.

He wouldn't tell Ericsson that, of course. He would dribble out results over the next six months. That would keep the Air Force happy and give Oscar plenty of opportunity to justify expenses to pay for the new spectrum analyzer he wanted.

If it weren't for the damned paper shuffling, this government contract work would be ideal, Oscar reflected. But every contract required filling out literally hundreds of pages of absolutely asinine forms, for which the instructions were maddeningly obtuse. What percentage of his suppliers and subcontractors during the past three years were Blacks? the government wanted to know. How many were Spanish surnamed? How many were American Indians, Asiatics, or Aleutian Islanders? Were his percentages in each of the above cases at least equal to the percentages of the corresponding minorities in the work force in the county or municipality where the contract work was performed? Had he ever knowingly used contract funds to purchase supplies from a company not in compliance with regulations 148 c.(4) or 156 a.(1) of the Equal Employment Opportunity Commission? If so, why? Give full particulars. And on and on and on.

And the bastards actually checked all the answers! Once Oscar had tried to shortcut the paper work by scrawling "not applicable" across a whole page of questions which asked what percentage of the contractor's advertising budget went to media oriented specifically toward minority markets, whether the pictorial or photographic material used in the contractor's advertising depicted the contractor's employees/customers as racially mixed (and if not, why not?), and the like.

The forms came back to him with an eight-page letter from one of the Pentagon's regiment of Equal Opportunity compliance officers, full of unctuous cant about the essential nature of the government's program for "racial justice" and demanding that each question be answered fully. Oscar finally had had to submit copies of his itemized balance sheets to convince the sanctimonious oaf that he did not advertise and had neither employees nor customers and could not, therefore, be expected to explain why his nonexistent illustrated advertisements did not show the required racial mix of smiling Black, Brown, Oriental, and White faces among his "employees/customers."

He felt his temper rising as he remembered the paper work still facing him on the new contract. Well, perhaps he could coax Adelaide into doing all of it tomorrow evening. He put the thought of paper work out of his mind and flipped on the light in the shop. Oscar had converted his entire basement, originally consisting of two bedrooms, a recreation room, and a bath, to his special needs.

The computer and the electronics laboratory were in the recreation room, a chemical laboratory was in one of the bedrooms, a small but well-equipped machine shop was in the other, and the bathroom doubled as a photographic darkroom. Altogether he had more than half a million dollars worth of modern scientific instruments and tools at his disposal, and they served him well, both at work and play, with the border between the two types of activity often becoming quite fuzzy.

Tonight, for example, he intended to put the finishing touches on a project that had nothing to do with his Air Force contract work or with any other remunerative enterprise. And yet this was hardly a plaything, Oscar thought as he opened a cabinet and took out a tubular, metal device, carefully examining the threaded portion in one end. Satisfied, he put the device on a work table beside the smaller of his two precision metalworking lathes.

He reached into a drawer in the lower portion of the cabinet and removed an object wrapped in an oily rag. Discarding the rag, Oscar held a new, .22 caliber semiautomatic pistol with a long, cylindrical barrel in his hand. He quickly and expertly disassembled the pistol, returning everything but the barrel to the drawer.

An hour and a half later Oscar grinned with satisfaction as he blew away the last of the metal chips with an air hose and then screwed the tubular device smoothly onto the new threads he had just turned on the outside of the pistol barrel: a perfect fit! The threaded end of the aluminum-alloy tube snugged up tightly against the freshly cut shoulder on the steel barrel as the ball detent clicked into place. He could see no indication of misalignment between the barrel and the silencer when he sighted carefully down the bore. Now for the test.

Oscar reassembled and loaded the pistol and walked back into the electronics lab. A touch on a button concealed above the door frame caused a four-foot-wide section of the far wall to swing smoothly out at a right angle. Flipping a switch in the exposed recess turned on a floodlight at the far end of a long, horizontal tunnel lined with sections of 30-inch sewer pipe. Oscar ran a target down the wire to the end of the tunnel and seated himself comfortably beside the spotting scope at the firing bench. This basement target range, which he had built himself, was known only to him. With the concealed door to the recess closed behind him, he could fire even the largest of his rifles without a sound being heard in the house above him—or in his unsuspecting neighbor's yard, beneath which the bullets impacted in the target area.

Tonight, however, noise was no problem, and he left the door open. He squeezed off ten rounds, each one making a sound about like a champagne bottle being uncorked, but not half so loud. The shots were grouped nicely inside a three-inch circle on the target, which was almost as well as he had been able to do before modifying the pistol. Oscar was satisfied; now he could change his *modus operandi*.

II

Last night's shootings had been too late to make the morning paper, but the television news was full of them as Oscar fixed breakfast. As he had guessed they would, the masters of the media finally had decided to lift the curtain of silence with which they heretofore had shrouded his nocturnal parking-lot activities. The newscaster excitedly barked out the details: ". . . 12 known victims of a mad killer . . . apparent racial motivation for the shootings . . . more than 200 FBI agents working on the case for the last two weeks . . . a tall, blond man sought as a suspect . . . ."

At this last item Oscar became thoughtful. So someone had gotten a glimpse of him; it must have been the fourth shooting, when he had left his car and fired from a standing position. He strolled into the bathroom and looked searchingly at his reflection in the mirror: the deep-set gray eyes; the craggy lines of jutting nose and chin; the yellow stubble on his broad, heavy jaw; the somewhat oversized ears; the thin scar running diagonally across his left cheek, the consequence of a skiing accident some years ago; the high, smooth forehead beneath his uncombed, golden-blond hair. It was an easy face to spot in a crowd, unfortunately.

Well, it was almost certain that no one had gotten a clear view of his face, or there would have been more of a description, probably even an artist's sketch. Still, he would have to be much more careful in the future. He had been almost deliberately reckless the first few times. Defiance of the authorities had been as much a motive as the abhorrence he felt for those selected as targets. There had been another motive too, he reflected, and it had weighed at least as much as the others: the therapeutic motive, the need to purge himself of the spiritual malaise which had been afflicting him increasingly in the last few years.

How had that begun? Oscar tried to remember. Was it after he moved to Washington, or had it started earlier? Probably earlier; he thought he could trace it all the way back to Vietnam. He just became much more aware of it in Washington.

In Vietnam it was basically the Vietnamese which had bothered him. He had arrived there with no particular prejudices, but he quickly acquired a strong distaste for Vietnamese of both sexes and all ages. He didn't like their looks, their smell, their values, their behavior, or their company. He couldn't see that it made the slightest difference whether they were ruled by a gang of communist gooks in Hanoi or a gang of capitalist gooks in Saigon. He would have been just as happy if the South Vietnamese and the North Vietnamese had been left alone to kill each other indefinitely.

Oscar certainly was no pacifist; on principle, he was opposed neither to wars in general nor to the Vietnamese "police action" in particular. He thought of his job in Vietnam as dangerous, but also challenging and exciting. Nevertheless, there were certain things which began to worry him, certain nagging ideas.

One was the utter hypocrisy and falseness of the U.S. government's position. The South Vietnamese supposedly were America's "allies," and American forces were there in fulfillment of "treaty obligations." But that was clearly nonsense. These were not the sort of creatures anyone would choose for allies; if America ever got in a jam and needed military assistance, there would be none forthcoming from this quarter.

The better he had gotten to know the Vietnamese, the more Washington's self-righteous cant about "helping to preserve freedom" in Southeast Asia grated on his sensibilities. These gooks couldn't care less about "freedom"—but even if that weren't so, giving it to them wasn't worth the life of a single one of his comrades. This was something Oscar thought about every time one of the fliers in his squadron failed to return from a mission, and every time he saw the rubber body bags being unloaded from a chopper.

If the government had told everyone that the action in Vietnam was simply a war game—Spartan-style practice to keep the U.S. military machine on its toes—and all the phony target restrictions imposed on the U.S. forces were part of the game, it would have been easier for him to accept. But to maintain the pretense that they were fighting for vital national objectives, and at the same time to do everything possible to avoid the military victory which could have been won: that turned Oscar's stomach and left him with a deep bitterness toward the politicians, the masters of the controlled news media, and all the others who made up the "System" back home.

One other thing his Vietnam experience had given him was a deeper appreciation for people of his own kind. All the fliers in his unit were White—in fact, as fliers they were a highly selected group of Whites, an elite—and Oscar could not help contrasting them with both the ARVN troops and the Black GIs in the heavily integrated U.S. ground forces. It was not just his instinctive xenophobia responding to differences in appearance and speech; it was something deeper and more fundamental. The vibrations were different.

The Blacks felt it, and they used the word "soul" to express it: a good word, meaning the individual's spiritual roots to all the past and future generations of his race. From these roots come everything: physical, mental, and spiritual. They determine not only what an individual looks like and the way he thinks and behaves, but his entire relationship to the world.

Take the word "pride," for instance, another word much used by Blacks. It was manifested in wholly different ways by the various races. To Oscar and the other pilots it meant, essentially, self-respect, and it was based on the individual's sense of achievement or accomplishment—most of all on his achievement of mastery of himself; it came across as an aura of dignity or, one might even say, of honor.

To Blacks, on the other hand, "pride" meant a sort of swaggering insolence, a pugnacious determination to get one up on "Whitey." It manifested itself in the way of a barnyard pecking order. As for the Vietnamese, it was hard to say whether or not their language even had a word for such a concept. Probably the closest they came was something translated as "face." As with the Blacks it was primarily a social thing, depending upon relationships with other individuals, while with the Whites it was much more a private, inner thing.

Oscar hadn't personally liked all his fellow White fliers; there were a couple for whom he hadn't even had much respect. He recognized the personal failings of his fellows: the weaknesses, the stupidities, the meannesses—military life bares a man's true nature as no other life—but they nevertheless formed a natural community. Oscar understood them, and they understood him. They could work together on a common task and feel right about it, despite their individual differences. With the Blacks and the Vietnamese, neither Oscar nor his fellows could ever form such a natural community.

Oscar did not hate either the Vietnamese or the Blacks while he was in Vietnam, but he did become fully conscious that they were races apart. He became conscious of their innate differentness, as well as the differentness of their life-styles. He saw their folkways and their attitudes as products of race-souls wholly alien to his own, and this gave him a greater sense of racial self-awareness than he had felt before.

He did a lot of reading between missions, trying to understand better the significance of his newly heightened consciousness, trying to see it in a historical perspective. What began emerging in Vietnam and developed more fully in graduate school after he left the Air Force was a realization of the racial basis of history and of all human progress. Previously Oscar had seen history as a mere succession of events—battles, revolutions, technological advances—associated with dates and names, and he had a vague notion of progress as a sort of concatenation of events, with one political happening leading to another, one inventor or artist building on the work of a predecessor. His new conception placed the events in their human context, all the intimate details of which were essential for an understanding of the *meaning* of the former.

Take the Vietnam war as an example. Oscar could imagine himself as a history student reading about it in the 25th century. The account in the history book, if it were written the way most history books have been written, would tell of two countries, one rich and powerful, the other poor and backward and struggling to maintain its independence in the face of internal subversion and external aggression. It would relate a series of political and military developments in the poor country, as the rich country sent soldiers to help it against its enemies; it would describe the political reactions in the rich country to these developments; and it would analyze the way in which these political reactions prevented the rich country from utilizing its soldiers effectively to help the poor country, so that eventually the former had to withdraw its forces from the latter and leave it to be defeated by its enemies. The dates and places of every major battle, the numbers of troops involved, and the names of the leaders of the various political factions in both countries could all be set down without error or omission. Yet the whole account would be essentially meaningless.

The 25th-century history student could not possibly understand the Vietnam war unless he knew what the Vietnamese were like and what the Americans were like; unless he had already learned about the values, behavior, attitudes, and life-style of the Vietnamese the way Oscar had; unless he had a thorough comprehension of the decadent condition of American political life in the 20th century: of the hypocrisy, the cant, the concealed motives, the total irresponsibility of the leadership, the general ignorance and alienation of the citizens, the role of the media, the effects of the civil-rights movement on military morale, and a dozen other things.

History is a record of the thoughts and actions of people: not just political leaders and artists and inventors as individuals, but as members of the communities—racial, cultural, and religious—with which they share values and motivations, attitudes and tendencies, capabilities and aptitudes, specific strengths and weaknesses. It is, therefore, a record of the development and interaction of various human *types*: of races and ethnic groups, above all else. The record only has meaning when it is read with a comprehensive, detailed knowledge of the physical and psychical characteristics of the particular human type or types involved.

From the time that Oscar had understood this simple truth, the disturbing things which were happening around him after his return from Vietnam began to make some sort of sense. The growing use of drugs by young Whites; the open displays of homosexual behavior by an increasing number of them, with the blessing of the news and entertainment media; the appearance in public of more and more interracial couples—all of these things began to fit into a pattern which Oscar could understand. Understanding that the civilization of which he had felt himself a part was losing its sense of identity and therefore its ability to sustain itself was not only disturbing and depressing to Oscar, but also deeply frustrating, because he wanted to do something about it.

If he had been more of a political creature, Oscar might have thought about running for public office, perhaps even organizing a new political party. But he did not have the stomach for that sort of thing. He held a deep, visceral loathing for the whole democratic political process, as well as for every politician he had ever met in person or given notice to on the television screen. He could not, without a shudder of revulsion, imagine himself becoming a habitual liar and doing all of the other dishonorable things required to curry favor with a degraded and ignorant public and a corrupt media establishment, just so that he might win an election and the opportunity to attempt to reform the System from the inside.

Nor, he thought, was he the type to become a pamphleteer, so that he could rail at the System from the outside. Oscar was not only a man of few words, he was a man of action. His inclination was to *do* something about a problem, not talk about it.

What he did, when he finally decided to act, was begin shooting racially mixed couples in shopping mall parking lots. Not that he hadn't given the matter quite a bit of thought first: he had considered many possibilities, from using his electronic expertise to "break into" commercial television broadcasts with a pirate transmitter and deliver his own message, to renting an airplane at a nearby airport and using it to bomb the Capitol building during a session of Congress.

He settled on the shootings for three reasons. First, they were highly symbolic of America's sickness and of the danger threatening his race. Everyone would understand immediately their significance and the motivation behind them. Second, they were personal and direct actions; they had more therapeutic value for him than a more impersonal blow against the System would have had. Third, and most important, they were acts that could easily be imitated by others. Very few men were capable of operating a pirate broadcasting station or carrying out an aerial bombing raid on the Capitol, but many could shoot down a miscegenating couple on the street.

The media masters obviously were aware of this third consideration, and that was the reason for their previous blackout on his activities. Now that the blackout was over they were attempting to forestall any would-be imitators by pouring on the venom. Before he had finished his breakfast, Oscar already had heard newsmen on three channels represent the shootings as the most depraved and reprehensible crimes imaginable. He grimaced as he listened to a fourth commentator grimly describe the gunman as "obviously a very sick person." Clearly, there wouldn't be much glory for him in this business.

III

Adelaide was still busily typing at the keyboard of the word processor in the corner of the living room when Oscar came up from the basement. He paused behind her for a moment, admiring the smooth grace of her neck and shoulders. She was, he reflected, one of the most attractive benefits of his relationship with the Air Force. He had met her four months ago in the Pentagon office of his Vietnam buddy Carl Perkins, where she worked as a civilian analyst. She had grown up in a tiny town in Iowa, earned a B.A. in mathematics from Iowa State University, and been in the Washington area a little longer than a year.

Although at 23 she was 17 years younger than Oscar, the two of them had been strongly attracted to one another, and he had made a date with her on that first meeting. The relationship had developed very nicely, and lately she and Oscar were together three or four times a week. She was bright, generous and helpful, and always cheerful, a refreshing antidote to his own tendency toward gloominess.

He would have asked her to move in with him by this time—and she certainly was waiting for him to ask—except that he hadn't been able to reconcile his anti-System activities with that close a relationship; how could he hope to keep such things secret from a wife? Already it was awkward explaining to her why he was unavailable sometimes.

Impulsively, he leaned over her, slipped his arms under hers, and cupped both of her full breasts in his hands. She continued typing, but leaned back against his body as he began gently squeezing her nipples. He felt them hardening through the fabric of her blouse.

"Hey, you want me to finish this proposal for you, or what?" Adelaide giggled, still valiantly trying to type, but now also rubbing the back of her head provocatively against Oscar.

"What," Oscar answered emphatically, with a grin. "It's already nine o'clock, and I've been fantasizing about you all day. I don't think I can wait any longer. Stay here tonight, and we'll get up early enough tomorrow for you to finish the last page before you have to leave for work." He moved his hands back under her shoulders and lifted her from her chair.

On her feet, she turned and flowed smoothly into his arms. He hungrily kissed her mouth, her neck, her ears, her mouth again. His hands fumbled briefly with a button and a zipper at the side of her skirt, and it fell to the floor about her ankles. He slid both hands into her panties.

She snuggled against him and whispered into his ear, "Hey, fella, don't you think we should either close the drapes or go into the bedroom?"

"Oops! I forgot about the drapes." Oscar blushed and hurried to the window, while Adelaide scooped up her skirt and disappeared into the hallway.

It was just after midnight when Oscar next glanced at his watch. He stood in the doorway to the bathroom for a few moments, hesitating with his hand on the light switch. Adelaide was asleep on the bed, lying half on her back and half on her side, uncovered, and the light streaming over Oscar's shoulder from the bathroom cast the soft contours of her body into sharp relief. She was a beautiful woman, one of the most beautiful he had ever seen, long and lean and lithe, with silky-smooth skin, perfect thighs surmounted by a luxuriant bush of reddish hue, a flat belly, magnificent breasts, a graceful neck of extraordinary length, and a face so lovely, so pure, so childishly peaceful and innocent, that looking at it nestled gently there in the pillow, half obscured in the tangle of her long, golden-red hair, made his heart ache with desire, the way it ached when he watched an unusually spectacular sunset in the desert or came upon an especially glorious vista while hiking in the mountains. Adelaide was really a marvel of Nature, he thought.

Instead of turning out the light Oscar stepped over to the bed, gently brushed aside her hair, and kissed her softly on the lips, trying not to waken her. Despite his care, her lids opened wide as soon as Oscar's lips touched hers. He gazed silently into the clear, blue depths of her eyes for a moment, and then he felt her arms pulling him down against her. He made love to her again, more vigorously this time than before, almost brutally, and then he turned and lay back against his pillow, while she snuggled into his arms and fell asleep again, with her head on his shoulder. The bathroom light was still on.

Oscar was very sleepy himself now, but he remained awake a few more minutes, thinking. Adelaide was a bright spot in his life, and he was extremely fond of her. But she had a meaning to him which went beyond personal affection. She was a symbol of everything that really mattered to Oscar. She was beauty and innocence and human goodness personified. She was the prototypal woman of his race. She was Oscar's ultimate justification for his private war against the System.

Nothing was more important, it seemed to him, than to ensure that there always would be women like Adelaide in the world.

Anything which threatened to preclude that possibility must be stamped out.

Oscar mused on the difference between his own system of values and that which seemed to be the norm—or at least that which was enunciated by the media spokesmen. They talked about individual rights and equality and the sanctity of life. To them, a flat-nosed, mud-colored, wiry-haired mongrel spawned by one of the mixed-race couples he had been shooting down was as precious as a golden-haired, blue-eyed little girl who might grow up to be another Adelaide. More precious, actually. Despite their prattle about "equality," it was clear to Oscar that their vision of the future was one in which the mud-colored mongrels would inherit the earth. He shuddered involuntarily.

He remembered something he had witnessed in Washington a few years ago, during a period when crowds of White university students, Christian clergymen, Black activists, show-business per-sonalities, and politicians formed outside the South African Em-bassy nearly every day to carry placards and chant slogans against *apartheid*. He happened to be walking past the embassy quite by chance when two South African women who worked there were going inside. They had stopped to show their passes to one of the policemen who formed a cordon on the sidewalk, keeping the demonstrators away from the entrance. One of the women was a tall, striking Nordic beauty, the other a rather plain brunette of average height.

Several of the demonstrators pressed forward to heap invective on the two. He noticed one young White woman in particular, probably a university student and probably not unattractive herself under normal circumstances, whose face was contorted with hatred as she shrieked, over and over, "Racist bitch! Racist bitch! Racist bitch!" It was clear that she was directing her spite specifically toward the tall blonde, almost as if that woman, more than her shorter and darker companion, represented everything the demon-strator had been taught to hate. A White clergyman standing a few feet away smirked approvingly. The clergyman was holding a placard which read, "All of God's children, Black and White, are equal." But some, apparently, were more equal than others!

It was the same with all of the tears the media people were spilling for Oscar's victims. They blathered on and on about the sanctity of all human life, and about how no one had the right to judge another and take his life. Oscar thought about how few tears these commen-tators had to spare for the victims of ordinary criminals—rapists, muggers, armed robbers—who killed scores of people in the United States every day. In truth, they cared about some victims much more than others. He was sure, for instance, that they would all enjoy seeing him torn limb from limb or roasted over a slow fire.

It was entirely normal, of course, to care more about some people than others, to want to protect some and to see others destroyed. The difference between him and them was that he didn't try to deny that fact—and that he wanted to protect his own and to destroy those who threatened them, while they seemed to hate their own and to love those who were utterly unlike themselves.

He had read enough literature from the 18th and 19th centuries—even from the first half of the 20th century—to be quite certain that his own values used to be the norm. How had the inversion of values taken place? He shook his head drowsily. That was something he never had been able to puzzle out, even when he was wide awake. Well, the answer could wait. He knew what he had to do, and tomorrow he intended to strike another blow.

IV

"More coffee, sir?"

"Yes, please," Oscar told the waiter, as he placed the money for his check on the tray, mentally flinching at the amount. He leaned back in his chair and continued to survey the other tables in the restaurant, while a busboy approached to clear away the last of his dishes. He had chosen his table well for the purpose. It was in a dark alcove, partly screened from the main dining area by a large potted plant, so that Oscar could see without being seen. The restaurant was a pretentious, trendy one, just five blocks from the Capitol and frequented by the city's power seekers, as well as by a fair number of real power wielders: legislators, upper-echelon bureaucrats, lawyers, newsmen, lobbyists.

During the course of his dinner Oscar had spotted several interesting prospects at other tables. He recognized Congressman Stephen Horowitz in a boisterous, noisy group just two tables away. Horowitz had been much on television recently, as his committee held hearings on a new bill to bring 100,000 Haitian immigrants per year into the United States. In an emotional speech just a week before, he had denounced those who opposed his bill as the very same "racists" who had been against his earlier bill, since enacted into law, to ban White South Africans from immigrating into the country. What a hideously ugly little man he was, Oscar thought, feeling a distinct itch in his trigger finger as he studied the legislator's ratlike face, with its darting, beady, close-set black eyes and wide, leering mouth. But, really, shooting was too good for Horowitz. Oscar would much rather wait for a chance to catch the man alone and work him over with an ice pick, slowly.

Besides, he didn't want to change targets that radically yet; he wanted to keep hitting mixed couples for a while, except now he intended to pick them from a higher tax bracket, in order to make an even bigger splash in the news media. And there was an excellent possibility at a table on the other side of the room, which Oscar unobtrusively had been keeping an eye on for the last half hour: a tall, light-skinned mulatto with two White women, both of whom seemed to be on intimate terms with him. Oscar had no idea who the women were, but he had seen the mulatto on the television news several times—once, in fact, with Horowitz, in a news conference held in the street in front of the South African Embassy. He headed an organization which lobbied for punitive legislation against South Africa and economic aid for Black-ruled African countries. Perhaps the women were employees of his organization, or perhaps just a couple of power groupies, a species all too common in this city.

Finally the mulatto paid his bill, then sauntered over to Horowitz's table to pay his respects, one of the women hanging on each arm. Oscar rose and left the restaurant without looking again toward his intended targets. Outside he paused at a coin-operated newsrack and purchased a *Washington Post*. From the corner of his eye he saw the mulatto and his White companions emerge from the restaurant and turn to the left, down a tree-lined and imperfectly lighted sidewalk. Oscar followed at about 30 paces.

As soon as he was out of the brightly lighted area in front of the restaurant, he slipped his silenced pistol out of his coat and into the folded newspaper he was holding in his right hand. The trio in front of him turned the corner. By the time Oscar reached the corner they were entering a late-model, white Cadillac parked at the curb. He quickly scanned the area and sized up the situation, feeling the familiar tension in his muscles, the icy perspiration in his armpits. Although there was a moderate amount of traffic on the street with the restaurant, there were no moving vehicles on the side street. The nearest pedestrians were a group of five persons he had just passed on their way toward the restaurant; they were at least 100 feet away now, their backs to him.

Oscar increased his stride and drew abreast of the Cadillac as the mulatto closed the front passenger door on the two women. Oscar turned sharply to the right and intercepted him at the curb behind the automobile. As the mulatto looked up with surprise and annoyance at the large White man suddenly blocking his path, Oscar raised his pistol, still covered by the newspaper, and shot his victim between the eyes. The mulatto fell back heavily against the vehicle without uttering a sound, then sprawled into the gutter. Oscar fired two more carefully aimed shots into his head, then stepped forward and jerked open the door of the Cadillac. The women had not realized what was happening, and Oscar quickly and precisely shot each of them in the head once, then twice more. Then he turned and strode briskly back toward the main street.

Oscar glanced at his watch as he drove back across the Potomac into Virginia: just eight o'clock—still not too late to see Adelaide. He had told her he would be having dinner with some contract officers at Andrews Air Force Base that evening and would give her a call if he got away early. It hurt him to lie to her, but he could see no other way of dealing with the situation. The girl was intelligent and had basically good instincts, but he had no intention of burdening her with the knowledge of—and therefore the moral responsibility for—his private war. She had not been through the experiences in Vietnam he had, nor had she shared his prolonged soul-searching for an understanding of the meaning of many of the things happening around them—such as miscegenation. He was not at all sure that he would be able to make her accept the moral necessity of his actions. Like all women, she was much more likely to focus on the personal aspects—on what was happening to the individuals Oscar chose as targets—than on the impersonal justification for those actions and their implications for the future of the race.

Oscar had had to harden his resolve tonight to kill the two girls. He had no doubt at all that what he had done was right, but there was something in him that resisted doing violence to a woman of his race—even when she clearly deserved it. It had been easier in the supermarket parking lots. All of those women were obviously of the lowest type—worthless White sluts who had married Blacks because they had no better prospects among men of their own race. But the girls tonight had been moderately attractive, even classy. Too bad.

As for the mulatto, there definitely had been more satisfaction for Oscar in killing him than the other Blacks. Partly it was because this one had publicly declared himself an enemy of the White race by his actions against the Whites of South Africa, and partly it was because he was such an arrogant, swaggering, uppity nigger. Maybe, too, it was because the girls with him might have amounted to something under different circumstances. In any event, Oscar suspected that his increased satisfaction soon would be matched by increased anguish in the ranks of the enemy.

His suspicion was confirmed later that evening. He and Adelaide were sitting up in bed to watch the 11 o'clock news together, as they often did. Tonight the presentation was ragged and disorganized, the obvious result of the news team having gotten the tape of the day's big story too late to edit it. Without any preliminaries the newscaster began, "It looks like the race killer has struck again!"

Oscar watched with fascination as the camera scanned the scene of his activity a mere three hours ago, now swarming with uniformed policemen, FBI agents, newsmen, and curious bystanders. FBI agents already had arrested a suspect and were questioning him, according to the newscaster. That brought an involuntary smile to Oscar's lips.

The real focus of the news was on the mulatto Oscar had killed, Tyrone Jones. There was only a cursory mention of the two White women, and then a long eulogy on Jones and his role in "the struggle for freedom and equality in South Africa." Senator Horowitz gave a brief interview, mentioning that he had been with Jones only a few minutes before the latter was shot, and that he had lost a "dear, dear friend." Horowitz went on to say that he intended to call for a Congressional investigation of the Jones shooting and the other killings of racially mixed couples. Then he leaned toward the camera with a twisted leer on his face: "Anyone who thinks that he can halt the progress we are making in race relations, in our efforts to break down the old barriers of hatred and prejudice separating the races, by these murders is terribly mistaken. We will put all of the resources of our government behind the endeavor to track down the sick killer or killers responsible for them. America will continue its march toward a fully integrated society, and no one will be permitted to stand in the way."

Then there was five seconds with the distraught parents of one of the women who had been shot. Adelaide shook her head in sympathy and murmured, "How terrible!"

"If she was with that Jones creature, she deserved to be shot," Oscar responded.

"Oh, Oscar! How can you say that? That's awful."

Oscar sighed and said nothing, but he thought to himself that he was going to have to begin talking with Adelaide about some things—soon.

V

O scar carefully laid aside the sheaf of clippings which he had assembled in his lap, stretched, yawned, leaned all the way back in his easy chair, and shut his eyes. It had been a busy week, and he needed a little time to think. He was almost grateful that Adelaide's mother was ill and Adelaide had flown back to Iowa for the weekend to be with her. He had spent all of this quiet Saturday morning reading news reports and editorial comment from more than a dozen magazines and newspapers he had picked up at the newsstand last night after dropping Adelaide off at the airport.

Much of the news and comment were about him—and related matters.

For the past ten days there had been hardly anything else in the news. Two days after the Jones hit—Wednesday of last week—the media reported the bombing of the home of a racially mixed couple in Buffalo and the machine-gunning from a passing car of a racially mixed group of people standing in line to get into a San Francisco discotheque noted for its mixed clientele. Seven persons had been killed and a dozen more wounded in the latter incident, and the police had arrested two White suspects. There were no leads in the Buffalo bombing.

On Thursday, almost buried in the continued media hullabaloo over the San Francisco shooting, accounts were given of the killing in Chicago of two White women—sisters—alleged to have been involved with Black men, and the severe beating of a racially mixed couple in their apartment in Philadelphia.

Then the dam burst. On Friday there were reports of 19 major attacks on racially mixed couples or groups around the country. For the first time there was the admission that there were a number of different activists at work, although in each case reference was made to "the Washington hate killer," and the incidents outside the Washington area were described as the work of "copycats." Arrests had been made in more than half the incidents.

Oscar shook his head with disbelief as he read the details. Most of those who were copying him appeared to be acting with incredible carelessness. It was as if they were all good ol' boys who had been sitting around with a beer in hand watching TV reports of one of his own exploits and had said to themselves, "Hey, neato! I think I'll do that too." And then they had gone out and done it, with only the most childishly inadequate preparation and planning. Weren't there any *serious* people left in America?

More encouraging were the skinheads, who had taken up Oscar's banner with real enthusiasm. There were many of them, they were highly visible, and they had no hesitation at all about wading into a racially mixed group with baseball bats, bicycle chains, and bricks. Whatever they did, of course, was wholly unplanned and more often than not was not lethal—although in one case a mixed couple had been knifed to death on a Cleveland street by several of them. On the whole, the race-mixers seemed to be more worried about encounters with roaming gangs of skinheads than with lone assassins.

The worry, in fact, had reached the point that mixed couples were openly expressing their fear of being seen in public. One news magazine reported that some White women in the Los Angeles area who formerly would have taken their mixed-race children shopping with them were now leaving them with neighbors instead. There was an interview with a Washington restaurant owner who estimated that the number of mixed couples at his tables had dropped off by more than eighty per cent since the attacks began being reported by the media.

The reaction by the System was vehement, vicious, and massive. Oscar was surprised. He had expected much media excitement and a major police effort, but he had never imagined there would be quite such an outpouring of rage and hatred. Some of the politicians, churchmen, educators, and others who had expressed themselves on TV had been almost incoherent with emotion. One Christian evangelist had been shaking uncontrollably—not with sorrow but with anger—when he denounced the attacks on racially mixed couples as an unholy attempt to thwart "God's plan for America." A rabbi with similar sentiments was literally frothing at the mouth. The president of Yale University, Baldwin Giaccomo, wept as he confessed his "shame that I am White . . . [and] have skin of the same color as the sick, demented creatures" who were carrying out the racial attacks.

As he watched that last performance Oscar had idly wondered how the good scholar would respond if it were suggested to him that some of the attacks might be the work of Black separatists—Farrakhan's Muslims, say—who had the same reasons for being opposed to miscegenation that racially conscious Whites had.

At the same time Oscar had realized that reason played no part in what he was witnessing. In some sense of the word all of these spokesmen were motivated by religious sentiment, even though a few of them might declare themselves as agnostics or atheists. They were motivated by a religious conviction that a racially mixed America was *better* than a White America, that a mulatto child was *better* than a White child, that a White woman who chose a Black mate was *better* than one who chose a White. They would deny it if the question were put to them starkly, Oscar knew; they would weasel and waffle and beat around the bush with platitudes about "human dignity" and "equality" and so on, but it was perfectly clear what they really believed.

Somehow Oscar had known all along that that was the way things were. He thought again of the hatred he had seen on the face of the young woman demonstrator in front of the South African Embassy and of the approval for that hatred on the face of the priest beside her. And yet he was still surprised. He knew that America had become thoroughly decadent, that decadence had grown deep roots, and that many segments of the population obtained their sustenance from those roots and would fight any attempt to pull them up. But this reaction to his attacks on miscegenation went far beyond the defense of vested interests. Oscar shook his head in wonder. There clearly was an unbridgeable gulf—not just in interests, but in understanding, in spirit—between himself and these people.

The printed commentary was more coherent than the televised statements but just as vicious. There were editorial calls for new Federal legislation imposing an automatic death penalty on anyone convicted of a racially motivated assault—and one of the most impassioned of these was from an editor who had for years been noted as an opponent of capital punishment.

The director of the American Civil Liberties Union argued in a lengthy letter to the editor of the *New York Times* that the ordinary civil rights of a criminal suspect should be suspended in the case of a White accused of attacking a non-White for racial reasons. A third writer—a Massachusetts legislator—proposed that, because of the difficulty in proving motivation, whenever a suspect was White and his victim non-White, the burden of proof be shifted to the defendant; he must prove that his actions had *not* been racially motivated in order to avoid the special penalties provided for "hate crimes."

The prize for malice, however, was taken by one of the *Washington Post*'s regular columnists, David Jacobs. He had asserted in his column last Friday that it was clear from the pattern of killings in the Washington area and from the attacks on racially mixed couples elsewhere that the attackers were sexually frustrated White males who resented the greater sexual attraction which Black males had for White women. He provided a historical backdrop by attributing the same motive of White sexual inadequacy to the lynchings of Blacks earlier in the century. Jacobs then went on to generalize, saying that *all* White racism had its roots in sexual envy. White racism would continue to be the greatest evil confronting the world until there was no longer a White race, he concluded, and the best thing for the government to do was to hasten that day by encouraging even more racial intermarriage. A tax break for mixed couples would be a good step in that direction, he opined.

That column had infuriated Oscar when he first read it eight days ago. Rereading it today he could only wonder about people like Jacobs. What motivated them? Jacobs seemed to be in a different class from Yale's guilt-stricken president or the outraged ministers and politicians. The words of his column radiated pure, cold hate. To him the White race was like a strain of especially dangerous spirochetes for which an antibiotic needed to be found.

At least, Oscar thought with considerable satisfaction, Jacobs would be writing no more columns for the *Post*. He had resolved to see to that himself last week, as soon as he had read Jacobs' column. And he had carried out his resolve within a few hours.

Unfortunately for Jacobs, his column had not been the only thing in last Friday's paper with his name on it. The "Style" section of the *Post* had reported a "publication party" to celebrate the appearance of a new book by another writer for the newspaper. The party, the "Style" article noted, was hosted by the author's "colleague David Jacobs in his fashionable Jones Court condo." The article had caught Oscar's eye only because he spotted the ugly leer of Congressman Horowitz in a photograph of some of the guests at Jacobs' party.

A quick call to the *Washington Post* had elicited the information that Jacobs normally didn't arrive at his office until 2:00 PM. A check of a Washington street map showed Jones Court as a one-block-long cul de sac. As it turned out there was only one building on the street that was a reasonable candidate for housing fashionable condominiums, and when Oscar drove into the unattended basement parking area just after noon he quickly spotted an automobile with a *Washington Post* staff sticker on the windshield.

When Jacobs came down to get into his car half an hour later, he never knew what hit him.

Thinking back over his killing of Jacobs, Oscar could hardly believe how easy it had been. There hadn't even been the nervousness and perspiration which preceded each of his earlier operations. He had done the whole thing as calmly—one might even say as casually—as if he had been delivering a pizza instead of carrying out a daylight assassination. Part of that was undoubtedly due to an unusual concatenation of lucky circumstances: spotting the clue to Jacobs' address immediately after reading his column, the writer's late work schedule, the unattended garage, the staff sticker visible on the windshield, Jacobs' prompt and convenient appearance at a time when there were no witnesses . . . .

The swiftness with which the job had been finished gave Oscar a tingle of pride. He smiled to think how that swiftness of retribution must have unnerved Jacobs' collaborators. But Oscar's pride was tempered by concern: he must guard against overconfidence and carelessness. He had never before been reckless enough to go after a target in broad daylight.

Another little worry that nagged at Oscar as he sorted out the events of the past few weeks in his mind was a feeling of aimlessness. Where was he headed? What sort of ultimate outcome of his actions was he seeking? Was his activity to remain a sort of therapeutic hobby? Or now that he had achieved his initial aim of provoking a massive response to his attacks on mixed couples and had stimulated a certain amount of imitative activity around the country, perhaps he should quit while the quitting was good and marry Adelaide.

He sighed at the prospect. He knew that he couldn't quit. He would fall back into the same malaise that had gripped him before. He was not the sort who could stand aside and watch the destruction of his race and his civilization like an uninvolved spectator. He *had* to act. Would it be sufficient, he wondered, to choose an occasional target—a David Jacobs, a Tyrone Jones, perhaps a Stephen Horowitz? Would that be enough to satisfy his conscience and still allow him to lead a more or less normal life with Adelaide?

He wasn't at all convinced that it would. At the same time he was not especially inclined to continue shooting an interracial couple every three or four days. That hardly seemed worth the risk now. If he were going to continue taking chances, he was inclined to raise the stakes, to go after bigger game. But whom? And why? What was to be the overall plan?

Oscar had no answer. He sighed again and shifted in his chair. He glanced idly at the stack of newspapers and magazines on the table beside him, and his eye fell again on the picture in last Friday's *Washington Post* of the guests at Jacobs' party. He picked up the paper and stared hard at the face of Congressman Stephen Horowitz for a full minute. What ugliness! What utter malice! A faint, grim ghost of a smile slowly came to his lips, and he muttered to himself, "Mine not to reason why; mine but to do and die."

He laid the newspaper aside. He had made up his mind about one thing, at least.

VI

O scar might not be able to cure his aimlessness quite yet, but he was determined not to let carelessness become a problem. He intended to kill Congressman Horowitz—very carefully. He was pacing back and forth now, thinking hard. He slammed a fist into an open hand, increasingly excited as he turned over various possibilities in his mind and made his plans.

The telephone rang. It was Adelaide.

"Hello, love. My mom is pretty sick, and things here are a mess. I think I'd better stay through Tuesday, at least. Do you mind?"

"Sure, I mind, baby. But do whatever you think you should."

Adelaide asked Oscar to call her office Monday morning and say that she had the flu and was too sick to come to the telephone.

"How'll you explain your usual gorgeous, exuberant, bouncing self at the office on Wednesday? If you're just over the flu, you should look pale, tired, and listless."

"I'm counting on you to produce the desired effect by screwing me half to death Tuesday night, lover," she laughed teasingly.

"Hey, sweetheart, you know that I'll do my very best for you. But you thrive on it! The more often we make love at night, the better you look the next morning, and the paler *I* am. Total abstinence is the only way to make *you* look pale."

Adelaide's call added a new element to Oscar's planning. He didn't want to rush the Horowitz project, but it *would* be nice if he could get it done before she returned. It was becoming increasingly difficult to do his night work when she was in town, without arousing her curiosity.

Horowitz, he knew, was a night owl. Oscar had noticed his picture in the "Style" section more than once during the past year, and he had spotted the legislator on an earlier occasion in the same Capitol Hill restaurant from which he had tailed Jones. That had been the first time he had taken Adelaide out to dinner, when he wanted to impress her. But he didn't think it would be a good idea to start eating there regularly. There was no telling how long it would be before Horowitz showed up again. Besides, it was the sort of place where everyone looked around to see who was at the other tables. Oscar had felt conspicuous there alone the last time, even sitting behind a plant. He needed some way to find out in advance where Horowitz would be on a given night.

No sooner had Oscar formulated the question in his mind, than he had the answer. Carl Perkins was always inviting Oscar to come along with him to the cocktail parties that one or another of the big defense contractors and the Beltway consulting firms seemed to be throwing every other night for their government friends. "It'll give you a chance to meet some of our leaders in the Congress," Carl had joked with him, knowing Oscar's intense dislike of politicians. "There are always a dozen or so of 'em there."

The fact that Oscar was a non-drinker was only one of the reasons he had never accepted Carl's invitations. But now he remembered the latest of them, which had been offered when he had called Carl last Wednesday. General Dynamics had just won a new billion-dollar contract and would be celebrating—Monday, Oscar thought it was. "It'll be a big one," Carl had said. "Everybody'll be there." And Oscar knew that Congressman Stephen Horowitz, Democrat of New York and chairman of the House Armed Services Committee among other things, almost certainly would be there too.

Oscar called Carl at his home. When he had finished discussing the paperwork detail on his current contract, which was the pretext for his call, he said, "Well, I expect to have some preliminary results on the new antenna pattern by Monday afternoon. Maybe we can have a bite together Monday evening, and I'll show you what I have."

"Thanks, pal, but I can't. I've got to be at the General Dynamics bash Monday. Why don't you let me take you and Adelaide as my guests?"

"Where will that be?" Oscar responded tentatively, as if he were considering accepting the invitation.

"The mezzanine ballroom at the Shoreham. Starts at eight o'clock."

"Thanks anyway, Carl, but I guess I'd better not. You know I'm not one for parties."

"You ought to give Adelaide a break sometime and show her off in public. She's too pretty for you to keep all to yourself."

"She's not really a party person either. Besides she has a bad headache today and thinks she may be coming down with the flu."

"Oh, oh! Better tell her to stay away from the office until it's gone. I can't afford to have the flu now. I'll be too busy until we get the new appropriations bill safely through the House. I'm scheduled to spend most of next week testifying before the Armed Services Committee."

Oscar smiled. Carl didn't know it, but Oscar was going to try very hard to change his schedule for him.

After lunch he drove to the Shoreham Hotel to look over the layout. The prospects for making the hit outside didn't look good. The traffic situation around the hotel was very awkward. It would be too easy to get stuck trying to get away in a car. The whole sidewalk area in front was open, and there were floodlights everywhere. There would be no shadows to loiter in at night. Oscar counted six police patrol cars within 100 yards of the main entrance. Too many big shots and too much security at this hotel all the time. Anyway Horowitz, who was always accompanied by his chauffeur-bodyguard, would undoubtedly be driven right up to the front entrance and be picked up at the same spot. No chance there, except for a suicide attack.

Inside, things seemed a little more promising. The main entrance to the mezzanine ballroom was in a side corridor. Oscar slipped into the darkened room, which was not locked, flipped on the lights, and surveyed the exits. There were several service doors, but nothing marked "Ladies" or "Gentlemen." That meant that the guests would have to use the rest rooms at the far end of the side corridor.

What were the chances that Horowitz would have to pee during the evening? Oscar wondered. At least, there would be a lot of coming and going between the ballroom and the rest rooms during the evening, making it much easier to slip inside without an invitation. If Oscar could get into the ballroom, he probably could get as close to Horowitz as he wanted. But what then? Try to slip something into Horowitz' drink?

Oscar grimaced. That was fairy-tale stuff. Besides, he would be taking too big a chance by entering the ballroom; Carl or someone else he knew from the Pentagon might spot him, and he didn't want anyone to know about his presence there. If Horowitz were killed, there would undoubtedly be a thorough checkout by the police afterward of everyone who had attended the party.

He turned the lights off and strolled down to the men's rest room at the end of the corridor. It was palatial: the wash basins were set in wide, marble counters, and there was even a shoeshine stand. There was also a double row of metal lockers in an alcove of the rest room; perhaps the place doubled as a changing room for the male staff, and they kept their street clothes in the lockers. The space behind the lockers was barely lighted and conceivably could be used as a hiding place, but Oscar didn't like the idea. Any guest who came into the rest room might peep behind the lockers merely from idle curiosity.

There was also a door at the opposite end of the rest room from the entrance, probably a storage closet. Oscar tried the knob. It was locked. Locks were a hobby of Oscar's. He pulled a small plastic case from his jacket pocket, selected a tool from it, and had the door open in 15 seconds. It was a closet, a fairly large one, but it was empty, with dust lying thick on the shelves.

That was interesting! Because the closet wasn't being used, there was very little chance that a hotel staff member would open it before or during the party. Oscar stepped inside and closed the door. Through the ventilation louvres in the upper panel he could see about five feet of tile floor directly in front of the closet door. He tried bending the inside edge of a louvre to increase his field of view, but the metal was too stiff for his fingers.

He opened the door for a little light and spotted a coat hook screwed into the back wall of the closet: one of the heavy, old-fashioned, cast-steel types. He unscrewed it, then wedged the end of it between two louvres and applied his weight. He closed the door and peered out again. This time he had a clear view of most of the room, and the louvres on the outside of the door showed no trace of his handiwork. Before he left he tore a blank page from his pocket address book, folded it into a tight wad, and wedged it into the opening in the striker plate on the door jamb. He adjusted the position of the wad so that the door, though still locked, could be opened with a strong jerk.

Oscar paused again at the entrance to the ballroom and stuck his head in for another quick look around. He didn't like the idea of having to depend on Horowitz' using the rest room—and, furthermore, on his being alone in the rest room for at least a few seconds—but he liked the idea of showing his face at the party even less. Better, he thought, to wait for Horowitz in the rest room and risk missing him than to risk being seen. If Horowitz didn't show up, then he'd have to get him later somewhere else.

On his way down to the lobby, Oscar considered one other possibility: putting a bomb in the ballroom and killing everyone at the party. It was a small ballroom, about 50 feet square, and it had a suspended tile ceiling. He could slip back into the place this evening with a couple of suitcases full of dynamite and have the bomb in place in the ceiling, with a radio-controlled detonator, in five minutes. A stranger carrying a couple of suitcases into a hotel, at any time of the day, should elicit no curiosity.

He thought more about the bomb idea as he drove home, and he finally decided against it. For one thing he had no explosives on hand, and it might take more than two days to obtain some through normal channels. He didn't want to rush things. He also didn't like the idea of an indiscriminate massacre, which would probably kill Carl along with everyone else. It wouldn't be a bad idea to go ahead and lay in a stock of explosives for future needs, though. He made a mental note to look into that when he had time.

Monday Oscar did some shopping. He visited two theatrical supply stores and purchased a wig, a pair of non-refracting eyeglasses, a makeup kit, and an assortment of false facial hair pieces: goatees, moustaches, whiskers, long sideburns, and so on.

At home Oscar found that the wig quite convincingly changed him from a blond to a brunette. A little color from the makeup kit applied to his eyebrows completed the transformation. The false eyeglasses changed his appearance even more. Examining the disguise in the mirror, Oscar was satisfied with all but one thing: the scar on his left cheek remained as noticeable as ever, and it was exactly the sort of detail a witness would remember.

He pasted on a set of long sideburns and side-whiskers. They effectively covered the scar, but the effect was too startling, especially with his piercing gray eyes peering out of all of the dark hair. He peeled the whiskers off and began experimenting with some of the other materials in his makeup kit. He finally settled for a large paste-on wart and half a dozen fake pimples. They didn't hide the scar completely, but they broke it up enough so that a casual observer would see only a very bad complexion, rather than a scar.

He was pretty sure that any police sketch developed from witnesses' descriptions would be far enough from the truth to be harmless. On the other hand there was no way he could make himself truly unrecognizable to someone who knew him—at least, not on such short notice. The shape of his head, the size and placement of his ears, his stature and bearing were all characteristic; more than once friends had spotted him at a distance in a crowd with only a rear view. Too bad he wasn't one of those nondescript, inconspicuous little fellows that no one ever notices, he thought.

Oscar had selected his weapons the day before. One was a garrotte he had fashioned himself from a piece of high-tensile steel control cable, as strong as piano wire but more flexible, with wooden handles and a sliding lock which kept the loop constricted until a catch was released. He would use that if he caught Horowitz alone in the rest room. It would have the advantage of being completely silent.

His other weapon was a spring-loaded hypodermic syringe mounted inside the tube of a ballpoint pen. The outside of the pen was completely normal in appearance, but when the button on the end was depressed a thin hypodermic needle poked half an inch out of the other end, and a powerful spring ejected the contents of the syringe through the needle. Oscar had loaded the syringe with a milliliter of a concentrated solution of syncurine, a powerful and fast-acting muscle relaxant.

If one unobtrusively pushed the pen against a man's leg or buttocks or back in a crowded room and fired it, the victim would feel the prick of the needle and a stinging sensation from the drug, and he probably would utter an exclamation and turn around to see what had happened or slap at the point of injection as at a stinging insect, but he would lose control of his legs and fall helpless to the ground within ten seconds and be completely paralyzed within 30 seconds. Death would inevitably follow from asphyxiation. If the assassin remained cool and feigned innocence, witnesses probably would not even notice the pen in his hand.

Oscar would use the pen if he could not catch Horowitz alone but could get close to him.

The last thing Oscar did before leaving home was spray the fingers on both hands with a clear, fast-drying lacquer. The lacquer made his fingers feel stiff and dry, but it also effectively prevented him from leaving fingerprints on anything he touched. It would be good for a couple of hours. He also had used it before making his survey of the hotel on Saturday.

As he drove to the Shoreham he felt the familiar tenseness and cold perspiration, and he was glad; he had been worried by their absence in the moments before he shot Jacobs and was afraid that without them he would become reckless. Probably, he thought, the difference was that he had acted against Jacobs in the heat of anger, whereas all of his other actions—like this one—were much more deliberate.

By the time Oscar had reached the mezzanine level of the hotel, just after eight o'clock, the tenseness and nervousness had been replaced by the usual icy calm. A dozen or so people were standing in the corridor outside the ballroom entrance, some of them holding drinks. Oscar quickly noted that all of those with drinks had adhesive name tags stuck to their coat lapels. Two men standing at the door seemed to be monitors, and as he passed the open doorway he saw a registration table just inside, where invitations were being checked and name tags issued. No chance of getting inside now, but things might relax a bit later in the evening. Oscar continued down the corridor toward the rest room.

There were two men in the rest room when Oscar entered. He took a place at one of the urinals and waited for the men to leave so that he could enter the closet. Unfortunately for Oscar, however, there was a steady traffic into and out of the rest room. He stood at the same urinal for five minutes, and still there was no opportunity to enter the closet. Oscar was beginning to feel conspicuous. He left the urinal and entered a stall.

Under the stall door he could see enough of the floor to monitor the occupancy of most of the room. After another 20 minutes, however, he began to despair of ever being alone in the rest room, much less being alone with Horowitz. He could not avoid a dark suspicion that everyone at the cocktail party had spent the whole evening beforehand drinking beer.

Finally there were no feet in Oscar's field of view. He stood up and surveyed the room. A stall door at the far end of the row of stalls was closed, but otherwise the rest room was empty. He strode toward the closet and had his hand on the doorknob when the rest room door banged open behind him again. Damn! He turned around, preparing to resume his post in the stall.

The man walking toward the urinals looked straight at Oscar, and Oscar's heart paused for a fraction of a second. It was Congressman Stephen Horowitz. Oscar tried not to let his emotion show on his face as he and Horowitz passed one another. How much time would he have before someone else came into the room or the man in the end stall came out? Ten seconds? He would be lucky if he had five seconds. It was now or never.

Oscar spun silently on his heel as Horowitz reached the urinals and began fumbling with his fly. He pulled the garrotte from beneath his jacket, swung the loop down over Horowitz' head, and yanked the handles apart, all in a single, flowing sequence of motions.

As Horowitz' hands jerked defensively toward his throat, Oscar applied every ounce of strength he had to the handles. The strangling wire lifted the smaller man clear of the floor, and his feet beat wildly in the air. Without waiting for Horowitz to stop struggling, Oscar jerked savagely backward on the garrotte and heaved him into the nearest stall. Supporting the still thrashing Horowitz with one hand, Oscar latched the stall door just as the rest room door banged open once more. He jammed Horowitz down onto the toilet seat and then sat heavily on top of him. He hoped no one would notice two pairs of feet under the stall door.

Although it seemed much longer, it could not have been more than another ten seconds until Horowitz gave one last, convulsive shudder and then ceased his struggle for air and life. Oscar saw a pool of urine spreading out across the floor of the stall as the man's bladder emptied. Oscar kept his position for another two or three minutes, then felt for Horowitz' pulse. There was none. He reached behind the man's head and with some difficulty released the catch on the garrotte. The cable, which had cut deeply into the flesh of Horowitz' neck, was dripping blood, and Oscar hastily wiped it dry with a wad of toilet paper.

Sounds of running water were coming from the wash basins, but Oscar could see no feet in the vicinity of his stall. Trying to avoid Horowitz' urine, he slid under the partition into the adjoining stall, leaving Horowitz slumped back against the wall but still on the toilet seat. Before leaving his own stall Oscar flushed the toilet for effect, then walked toward the basins to wash his hands and check his wig.

While Oscar was standing before the mirror straightening his tie—and surreptitiously pushing the garrotte into a more secure position inside his jacket—two more men entered the rest room. One headed straight for the urinals, but the other surveyed the room as if looking for someone, then took a position against the wall opposite the stalls and folded his arms across his chest. Oscar had never seen the man before, but he knew with certainty that it was Horowitz' bodyguard.

While drying his hands Oscar noticed that the pool of urine from Horowitz' stall was spreading visibly onto the tiles beyond the door. As he left the rest room he heard the toilet finally flush in the other occupied stall. Things were about to become interesting.

Turning the corner at the end of the corridor and leaving the partygoers behind him, Oscar glanced quickly at his watch. He had been in the rest room 32 minutes altogether, the last five of them with Horowitz,

VII

"Oscar, I want you to meet Harry Keller. He'll help you with the new affirmative action contract compliance paperwork. He's our expert. He's also the only guy I know who's more of a racist than you are." Carl grinned as he introduced a large, heavy-set man with dark hair and huge, gnarled hands.

"You must be kidding," Oscar replied, holding his hand out to the newcomer in Carl's office anyway. "All of your people in the affirmative action section that I've had anything to do with so far are fairies and nigger lovers."

"Oscar!" Adelaide gasped. Oscar had dropped by Carl's office primarily to pick up Adelaide, whose car was being repaired, but had taken the opportunity to complain to Carl about a new batch of forms which had been sent to him by the Pentagon.

Harry laughed, and Carl said: "The day after he heard the news about Horowitz last week, Harry was passing out cigars in the office, while everyone else was at half mast."

"You too?" Oscar directed his question to Carl.

"For the sake of appearance, Oscar, for the sake of appearance. After all, the man was head of the House Armed Services Committee, and all of our paychecks were dependent on him."

"It was more than appearance for some people around here," Harry contradicted. "That little creep in my section, McGann, actually got moist eyes and sniffles during the eulogy for Horowitz that came over the public address system Tuesday. When the Secretary got to the place in his speech about how much Horowitz had done to promote racial equality in the armed forces, McGann actually started sobbing. Now there's a man who really *feels* for our colored brothers."

Oscar snapped his fingers in recognition: "McGann! That's the name of the man who sent me that really prissy letter last year when I didn't fill in all of the blanks on an affirmative action questionnaire."

"Sounds like him," Harry responded. "He likes to go through the answers to those questionnaires with a magnifying glass, trying to sniff out the faintest scent of a bad attitude toward the government's minority-coddling programs."

"The man's just trying to do his job and get ahead," Carl said. "He knows what it takes to get promoted around here, which is more than can be said for you.

"You know what this guy did?" Carl pointed a thumb at Harry and turned to Oscar. "The FBI was swarming all over the Pentagon last week, because there were so many of our guys at the party where Horowitz was killed. While other people were taking the investigation very seriously and trying their best to answer the FBI's questions, Harry was breaking everybody in the office up with his jokes about Blacks. Managed to get himself an official reprimand from his section chief."

Harry's rejoinder to this was, "Say, Oscar, do you know what the three happiest years of a nigger's life are?"

"Sorry, I guess I don't."

"Second grade."

Everyone laughed at that, even Adelaide. But then Carl lowered his voice and said, "For Christ's sake, keep your voice down when you crack your Black jokes in here, Harry. I don't want a reprimand in my personnel file too."

"Actually, it's too late for you now, Carl. I may as well confess. My *real* job here is to tell racial jokes and then turn in the names of everyone who laughs. After I make my final report the only White employees who'll be left around here will be McGann and myself."

Everyone laughed again.

Oscar and Adelaide ended up giving Harry Keller a ride home in response to his invitation to have dinner with him and his wife while he gave Oscar a crash course in dealing with the Pentagon's latest forms. Harry's wife Colleen was a pleasant, relaxed woman of about 40. She seemed not to mind the surprise dinner guests, even though she had just gotten home from work herself.

After dinner they sat drinking coffee and chatting. "How'd someone with your sentiments get involved in the affirmative action program?" Oscar asked Harry.

"Sentiments have nothing to do with it. In the Civil Service you just take what they give you—although the fact that I used to teach sociology at the community college—you know, NVCC—may have led them to select me for the affirmative action section. Sociology professors tend to have that kind of rep. Anyway, for a couple of years before I started working for the Department of Defense I spent all my time on the road, selling broadcast studio equipment and visiting customers, and Colleen and I were apart too much—although it was in that job that I first met her. She works for one of my customers in Washington. So I applied for a Civil Service position, and they stuck me in the contract compliance section at the Pentagon. I still moonlight for my old company, though, but now that work is all by telephone."

"Why'd you switch from teaching to selling?" Oscar asked.

"Teaching became too hard on my conscience. It just got to the point where I couldn't tell all the lies and hide all the truths that were demanded of me. You wouldn't believe the ideological straight-jacket everyone teaching social sciences has to wear these days. One word that might offend some hypersensitive minority member, and they'll heave you out on the road."

"From what Carl says, you may be back on the road again soon," Oscar replied. "My experience with those 'love thy nigger' types you're working with now is that they have very little tolerance for anyone who doesn't share their sick view of the world."

"Oh, Carl exaggerates. Actually, I manage to keep my mouth shut at the office most of the time. It's just that I was so pleased when that bastard Horowitz got what he deserved that I couldn't hold myself back."

"Well, I don't see how you manage to work at all in that environment. I can understand how someone like Carl puts up with it; he's the least sentimental guy I've known. But it must be very hard on you having to keep your feelings bottled up inside and not being able to do or say anything. People with feelings need to be able to express them."

"I agree with you completely, Oscar. And I do express myself. Just not at work—or, at least, not as much as I'd like. In addition to my job at the Pentagon and my moonlighting I work for the National League."

"The National League? I've heard something about them—a neo-Nazi group, I believe. Is that right?"

"Depends on what 'neo-Nazi' means. That's one of those labels like 'fascist' or 'liberal' that people stick on anything they're opposed to. The news media call us 'neo-Nazis,' and that's undoubt-edly where you heard the term. The implications of that to most people are uniforms, swastika banners, and lots of 'sieg heiling.' But that's not us at all. I've got nothing against uniforms and banners, but we don't use 'em."

"What sort of things do you do?"

"Anything and everything that will help our cause."

"Which is?"

Harry thought for a minute, then began slowly: "Our cause is a secure and progressive future for our race. We want a White world some day—a White world that is conscious of itself and its mission; a world governed by eugenic principles; a world in which the goal of families as well as governments is the upward breeding of our race; a cleaner, greener world, with fewer but better people, living closer to Nature; a world in which quality once again rules over quantity, in which people's lives have purpose, in which beauty and excellence and honor once again have meaning and value."

Before Oscar could respond Adelaide chimed in, "Harry, you sound just like my grandpa. He's the racist in our family. He thinks that the whole world went to hell after the Second World War—says that if he'd known then what he knows now, he'd have gone to Germany and volunteered for the *Waffen-SS* instead of fighting in Roosevelt's army."

"You should have spent more time listening to your grandpa, sweetheart," Oscar said. Then he added, "I like your cause, Harry. You said you do anything and everything to promote it. Can you give me some specifics?"

"Well, at this time most of our effort is educational rather than political. We're trying to raise people's consciousness on racial issues, and then to motivate and direct those whose consciousness we do have some effect on. So we publish a lot of materials with a racial message: books, magazines, video tapes. Most of our members are professionals who are able to participate in this effort in one way or another. For example, I translate a lot of German material into English for our publishing department, and I keep the equipment in our video studio working."

"Harry's too modest," Colleen interjected. "He *built* the video studio from scratch and supplied all of the equipment. Whenever anything is being taped he's the studio engineer, handling the lighting, the sound, the cameras, and everything else. Then he helps with the editing of the tapes."

Harry shrugged modestly. "It was a natural assignment for me. After I began selling studio equipment I had to learn something about how it works and how to fix it. When we decided we needed a studio I was able to get my hands on a lot of good, used equipment for the organization for almost nothing."

Changing the subject, he continued, "Now, Colleen here is a first-class expediter. She works as an assistant general manager for KZR-TV during the week, and on weekends she takes care of the office chores for the League's Northern Virginia unit: purchasing, bill paying, banking, contacting members for meetings, and all the rest."

"You said you translate German too. Are your parents from Germany?" Oscar asked. He was a little bothered by the neo-Nazi tag and was looking for a tie-in to images he had in his mind from hundreds of television movies he had seen as a teen-ager: men with cruel faces in black uniforms, the light glinting evilly from their monocles as they barked orders in guttural accents and their subordinates unleashed huge, vicious dogs on frightened Jews. It wasn't that he believed in the literal reality of those images, but they bothered him nevertheless. Oscar always had been repelled by cruelty, whether to men or animals.

Harry answered Oscar's question: "Yes and no. They were from what's called Czechoslovakia today. They were born in Pilsen—a family of instrument makers there for more than a century—and then they lived in Prague until the end of the Second World War. I was born there in 1945. My father and older sisters were lynched by some of Mr. Roosevelt's boosters among the Czech population, after quite a bit of rather horrible abuse I gather. My mother never could bring herself to tell me all the details, but it gave her nightmares until the end of her life. Anyway, she escaped with me to Germany, and then we came to this country when I was five."

"So you're Czech?"

"No, German. Can't you tell from my name? It's as German as yours."

Oscar blushed. He thought of his name as English—and it was. But it also was German, he knew. The only difference was that the English spelled it with a "y" and the Germans with a "j." It meant "hunter." He also knew that Keller was a German name, now that he thought about it. And he knew that a German born in Czechoslovakia was no more a Czech than a Jew born in Poland was a Pole or a Swede born in China was a Chinaman. The English and the Germans and the Swedes were all part of the same family, all Germanic, regardless of where they happened to be born, just as Jews were Jews and Chinamen were Chinamen, regardless of their birthplace or country of citizenship.

Those were all things he had figured out for himself years ago. Sometimes, though, if he were not careful, he slipped back into old habits of thought which had been instilled in his mind through years of indoctrination by the schools and the entertainment media. Now, his thinking jogged by Harry's remark, he realized that all of the nasty connotations of "neo-Nazi" applied to himself as much as they did to Harry. That realization made him uneasy, but at the same time it stimulated his interest in finding out more about Harry and Colleen and the National League.

He took a new tack: "You said your group wants a future for our race which is both secure and progressive. Do you see any contradiction between those two things?"

Harry laughed. "There's been a lot of argument on that point. It's clear that over the long haul—that is, over the millions and hundreds of millions of years—progress has been the result of struggle, of hardship, of adversity, of a brutal pruning and weeding of the stock by Nature's harsh selection; in other words, it's been the result of a lack of security. Those who are secure stagnate, and those who are insecure struggle and advance.

"On the other hand," he continued, "races do die out. Sometimes conditions become so insecure that the whole race perishes. Conditions are such now that our race is in danger of perishing, partly because we're being outbred by other races in the same ecological niche and partly because we're miscegenating ourselves to death. It's clear that we are in danger now of too much insecurity."

"But," Oscar responded, "we mustn't abandon the general principle just because it seems to be working against us now. If we can't cope with the present insecurity and other races can, shouldn't we conclude that the cause of progress will be better served by their survival than by ours?"

"Of course, not," Harry responded, a trace of impatience in his voice. "Progress comes when all the competitors in the game struggle for survival, and the most fit wins. Our race isn't struggling. It's lying down and dying. Our job is to wake it up. When it's *trying to survive*, it'll whip all the other races with its hands tied behind its back.

"To be sure, fitness is a more subtle concept than one might think at first. Part of fitness is having not only the ability but also the will to survive; more than that, it's having a will that's not susceptible to being tricked into going to sleep by a clever and deceptive competitor. That's the heart of the problem. We've been tricked. But now we're going to wake ourselves up again. That's the task of the League.

"The only real question about the compatibility between security and progress comes when one already has solved the problem of racial survival. The question then is how we avoid stagnation once we have a White world. There are lots of ways to answer that, and some of our theoreticians debate the issue among themselves.

"But that's really another subject altogether. Perhaps I could have stated things a little more clearly from the start by saying that we want first to assure the survival of our race by waking it up and reigniting its natural fighting spirit, and then we want to reorient its values and its way of looking at things so that it strives to continue bettering itself instead of relaxing once the competitive struggle among the races has been won. Part of the way we'll try to assure progress undoubtedly will be to change our conditions of life as well as our attitudes, so that we can't relax even if we want to. As I said, the theoreticians have a lot of different ideas about that."

Oscar was impressed by the clarity of Harry's thinking. The man might seem to be just a good ol' boy, with his coarse appearance and his joking manner, but he clearly had a good mind and had figured out several things that were still rather fuzzy to Oscar. He said, "I'm sorry, Harry. I guess I was playing the Devil's advocate when I asked that question. I really can't argue with anything you've said."

"So, you old neo-Nazi," Harry grinned, "now that you're out of the closet, why don't you come to one of our meetings and meet some other people you'll agree with?"

Oscar was intrigued by the prospect, but he was also cautious. Considering his recent activities, he really couldn't afford to be associated with any group that the government would have its eye on. He gave Harry a noncommittal answer: "Thanks for the invitation, but I'm not a joiner. Anyway, I'd like to think about some of the things you said tonight before I'm bombarded with any more new ideas. Your high-powered logic has put me a little on the defensive. One thing I still can't figure out is why the media people have stuck you with that 'neo-Nazi' label, just because you want to assure the survival of the race. After all, they're White too."

Harry and Colleen both started to speak at once. "They're certainly not White," Colleen blurted out first. "Virtually all of the media are controlled by Jews, and they call the tune for everyone else in the media. The elimination of our race is at the top of their agenda."

Seeing the puzzled look on Oscar's face, Harry took over: "First, Oscar, let me correct your impression that I'm a high-powered logician. The things I've told you tonight are things that all of us in the League have been thinking about for a long time. It's not that we're smarter than anyone else; it's just that we stay conscious of certain things we believe are very important and which most other folks don't think about much. If they did, they'd be able to argue about the issues just as well as we do. I regard one of the biggest benefits of my League membership as its effect on my consciousness: it keeps me pointed in the right direction and worrying about the things in life that really matter.

"Second, Colleen is absolutely right. The news and entertainment media are controlled solidly by Jews, and Jews aren't White. Some of them may look White, but no racially conscious Jew thinks of himself as White, and the Jews as a group are the most racially conscious people on the face of this earth, by a big margin. They call their enemies—and that includes anyone they can't control—'neo-Nazis' because they've invested a lot of effort into making that a label of opprobrium; they've invested it with a heavy load of emotion, of feeling, so that most people react negatively to the word without having a clear understanding of what it means."

Adelaide, who had been listening but not talking, broke her silence once more: "Now you're sounding exactly like my grandpa again. He spent hours telling me about the Jews, but I never did understand it all."

Oscar stood up. He didn't like the way the conversation was heading. His fight against race-mixing was one thing, but he didn't see any point in getting involved in anti-Semitism. He knew a lot of people didn't like Jews, but so far as he was concerned they were White, and he'd known one or two who didn't like Blacks any better than he did. He remembered one of his fellow graduate students back in Colorado, Dan Levine. He had never personally liked Levine, who gave him a creepy feeling, but the fellow certainly was Jewish, and he was always cracking jokes about Blacks, even more so than Harry. "Harry and Colleen, thanks for the dinner. Adelaide and I have to run. And thanks again for the invitation to attend one of your meetings, Harry. I'll think about it and give you a call later."

VIII

O scar really did intend to think about what Harry and Colleen had said, but as it turned out he became preoccupied by other matters the very next day, and it was more than two weeks before his thoughts returned to their conversation. What absorbed his interest meanwhile was the continuing furor over his anti-miscegenation campaign and the assassination of Horowitz. It had been nearly a month since he had killed a racially mixed couple—Tyrone Jones and his two girl friends—and the news media were still in a virtual frenzy.

He still could not understand the intensity and duration of this frenzy. Drug gangs killed as many people on the streets of half a dozen of America's larger cities every two or three days as he had killed in his whole campaign. Furthermore these drug-war victims were nearly all non-Whites and so were especially beloved of the media. Yet a recent drug shoot-out in Washington which had killed five Blacks and a Colombian mestizo didn't even make the front page of the next day's *Washington Post*, which was taken up almost entirely with a report of the shooting of another interracial couple in Chicago, a heavily policed public demonstration in Manhattan by interracial and homosexual couples demanding more police protection, and the latest statements from the FBI about their investigation of the Horowitz assassination. He suspected that a new plague could break out and carry away a million victims in a week, and the news media would not give it as much coverage as they were giving to his killing of Horowitz.

Part of it, he reasoned, was a special perversity on the part of people who went into journalism as a profession. Beyond the role of the media themselves in fanning the flames, however, there evidently were various special interests at work—interests which felt threatened or offended by Oscar's activities. There were, he was surprised to learn, a number of organized groups of racially mixed couples, even one consisting solely of White males with Filipina wives. As he read of the existence of that particular group he felt regret that he had not devoted any of his nighttime efforts to its members.

Then there were the queers, who, despite their general antipathy toward the heterosexual world, seemed to have an affection for race-mixers, even those of the "straight" variety. Feminist groups also seemed to be especially incensed over his attacks on mixed couples. He couldn't figure the connection there either. Was it that all spiritually sick people, no matter what their malady, felt that their interests coincided?

The churches, however, were easily the most vociferous of the boosters of the race-mixers. Right down the line, from the primitive charismatics of backwoods Fundamentalism to the blandest of Unitarians and the trendiest of Episcopalians, they roared out their approval of miscegenation and their solidarity with its practitioners. There were memorial vigils almost daily, for one or another of the couples he had shot, by groups of ministers and priests on the Capitol steps. If there were any Christian groups which were not marching in lockstep with the others, it was only one or two of the smaller Eastern Orthodox churches, whose congregations consisted mostly of aging refugees from eastern Europe.

Now the churches were formally joining hands with the race-mixing groups, the homosexuals, and the rest. There was a full-page announcement in the *Washington Post* of a mass march on the Capitol to demonstrate public support for a new package of legislation being debated by the Congress. The march, scheduled for the middle of the following month, was being organized by a new coalition of leaders from 30 or 40 groups. It was called the People's Committee Against Hate, and the announcement in the *Post* listed several dozen of its members. The list was replete with bishops, cardinals, rabbis, and right reverends.

The legislation they were backing had been prepared by Horowitz and would have been introduced to the House by him if Oscar's garrotte had not cut his legislative career short. Its key bill was called the Horowitz Bill in his honor. It would outlaw all organizations which restricted membership on the basis of race. It would ban all books, periodicals, and other printed matter which might "promote racial hatred," and it provided for the establishment of a Federal Publications Board to examine and rule on any publications against which complaints were lodged. It would make any person who uttered, in the presence of witnesses, any statement denigrating a member of another race or expressing hostility toward members of his own race who associated with other races, liable to ten years imprisonment.

The news media conducted opinion polls three or four times a week and excitedly reported a growing public sentiment in favor of passage of the Horowitz Bill and its corollary legislation. Nearly 60 per cent of the public were for it, according to the latest poll. Oscar could only shake his head in wonder at the ease with which the American people could be manipulated by the media. It seemed as if all the media had to do was convince the public that everyone else was in favor of something, and then the sheep would fall all over themselves trying to get on the bandwagon.

The People's Committee, Oscar noted, was headquartered in the Connecticut Avenue Congregational Church, just north of Georgetown in the District. Meetings were taking place there practically every day, with religious leaders, members of the Congress, Hollywood celebrities, and other public figures as guest speakers. The principal purpose of the meetings, so far as he could see, was to provide a continuing input to the media. All of the television news programs featured snippets from each meeting.

As Oscar turned over in his mind the idea of attacking the People's Committee, he reflected on the fact that his assassination of Horowitz had not slowed down the race-mixers and their friends at all. If anything it had given them more ammunition to use in their campaign to stampede the public into accepting the massive curtailment of civil liberties which was inherent in the Horowitz Bill. He was pretty sure that if he shot one or two of the most prominent leaders of the People's Committee or blew up their headquarters the news media would manage to turn that into another argument for passage of the bill.

Oscar realized that he was no strategist. Part of the problem was that there were too many variables involved in making the sort of decisions with which he was faced. He just didn't have the time or the sources of information necessary to analyze each situation and predict the probable outcome of a given action on his part. He needed a general staff for that. He also needed a guiding principle, a program, a clearly defined goal, so that his individual actions reinforced one another. As it was he was acting on the basis of instinct, gut feeling, impulse, or whatever one wanted to call it.

Well, too bad about that! He would just have to follow his conscience and continue flying by the seat of his pants for the time being. One thing that his conscience told him was that his efforts were better spent going after the promoters of racial mixing than its practitioners. He had had such a good feeling after killing Horowitz that he really had a hankering now to take out a Senator or a bishop or a university president. That fit in with his general reasoning that he ought to continue escalating the conflict and leave the lower-level work to his imitators.

The latter had been giving a rather disappointing performance lately. Their activity seemed to have peaked about two weeks ago, around the time of the Horowitz hit. Now the papers were reporting only four or five serious attacks per day on mixed couples for the whole country. Part of the falloff seemed to be due to the high rate of arrests initially; the police, under extreme pressure from the media, were throwing all of their resources into the investigation of attacks on interracial couples. Apparently the supply of wild men, who would get the idea into their heads that they ought to follow Oscar's example by killing a pair of race-mixers and then would run out and do it without further deliberation, was being used up. The activists still on the loose were being more careful. Someone in Chicago—or perhaps it was more than one person—seemed to be doing quite well, and there was a string of six unsolved double killings in the Seattle area with the same *modus operandi*, but there weren't many bright spots elsewhere.

Another reason—a more encouraging one—for the decline in the number of attacks apparently was that, the recent demonstration in Manhattan notwithstanding, the race-mixers were going back into the closet to a certain extent; there just weren't as many targets on the street as there had been. The media were frantically trying to counter this trend. Every checkout-stand tabloid featured front-page photographs of mixed-race celebrity couples, week after week: an aging Elizabeth Taylor with her latest Black boyfriend, or Black basketball star Cleon Brown surrounded by an admiring throng of blond coeds. The television networks dredged up all the films with a race-mixing theme they had in their collections and began running them. Every news program featured an interview with at least one mixed couple, and there were hardly any other types of guests to be seen on the TV interview shows. But a large percentage of the race-mixers quite obviously were frightened and would continue to try to maintain a low profile.

The Connecticut Avenue Congregational Church was a large complex of interconnected stone buildings behind an old-fashioned iron picket fence. Oscar drove past the front twice and took several photographs with his Polaroid camera. He noted the two uniformed policemen standing at the top of the stone steps leading to the front entrance to the main building and suspected that there would be more inside. Then he drove slowly down the alley behind the complex. The fence, about seven feet high, ran along that side of the property as well, but there was a lot of tall shrubbery just inside the fence, and it looked like it might not be difficult to get onto the grounds from the alley at night without being seen.

Back home Oscar studied his photographs of the complex. There were, he noted, steel bars over all of the lower-floor windows: an essential feature for any building in the District of Columbia these days. Almost certainly every window and door also was connected to an alarm system. He didn't know whether the People's Committee held its semi-public meetings in the main sanctuary or in a separate auditorium. In any case, only two buildings in the complex were large enough for the purpose, and he quickly decided that one of them almost certainly held only Sunday school classrooms. So it had to be the main building, a really massive structure. Was there any way to get a bomb into the building?

The service gate in the alley fence led into a parking area behind an annex building. The rear door bore a sign reading "Deliveries." If he pretended to be making a delivery of office supplies, almost certainly he would be able to get a bomb no further than the annex without arousing suspicion. The main building obviously had a full basement, as indicated both by a stair descending to a basement door in the rear and by window wells for basement windows along the sides of the building. Again, bars and a probable alarm system seemed to make entrance to the basement no easier than to the ground floor. Could he get to the roof and then come in through an unprotected roof entrance?

Oscar made another reconnaissance, this time at night. A meeting was in progress, and it was clear from the pattern of lighted and unlighted windows that it was being held in the sanctuary, on the ground floor. Three basement windows near the front of the building were lighted, but the rest were dark. There were floodlights at the eaves level around the building illuminating the sides more or less uniformly, and there was another light over the basement door well. There were, however, a few dense areas of shrubbery at the sides of the building, toward the back, and the general pattern of windows in the building suggested that there almost certainly was a basement window well behind one group of shrubs.

He drove a block beyond the church, parked on a side street, and walked back to the alley which ran behind the complex. At a point where the fence was deeply shadowed by tall shrubs, he hauled himself over and then made his way silently to another group of shrubs closer to the building. Crouched close to the ground he pushed his way into the shrubbery and, as he had suspected he would, found himself next to a basement window well. Slipping his arm between the security bars and feeling the window sash with his fingers, he noted that it was made of wood rather than metal.

He placed his flashlight against the window glass and briefly illuminated the basement room into which it opened. It was a finished room, with framed pictures on one wall, but there were large stacks of cartons on the floor and on steel shelving against the far wall. Apparently the room was being used for storage. It was quite a large room, about 25 feet from front to back and extending more than halfway across the width of the sanctuary. The far end of the room was probably directly beneath the pulpit. There were doors in three walls, but they were all closed.

Back at his car again he glanced at his watch and remembered ruefully that he and Adelaide had dinner plans. As he drove toward her apartment, he formulated his plan of attack on the church.

IX

"Baby, I believe you've got the best set of tits on the East Coast,"
Oscar said admiringly, as he watched Adelaide lean over the table to pour a cup of coffee for him, the candlelight accentuating the contrast between the curves and hollows of her naked body. Neither of them had bothered to put their clothes back on after they had made love.

"Oh, have you been taking a survey?"

Before Oscar could think of an appropriately witty response, Adelaide continued: "You must be doing *something* really fascinating with your evenings. If not a tit survey, then what? Do you realize that you've kept me waiting for you until after nine o'clock for the last three nights? You said we would be going out to eat this evening, and that even if your work held you up you would be here by eight at the latest. Here it is ten o'clock, and I'm fixing your supper again. I know you weren't at home, because I called there an hour before you got here."

"I'm really sorry, baby," Oscar replied contritely. "I've just had a lot of running around to do the last few days. I spent all day at the computer working on the new contract, and then there were several chores I had to take care of this evening."

"All right, honey. I didn't think that you had been with another woman, because you certainly were terminally horny when you got here. I just wish you could arrange your work schedule so that we could have more time together. I start feeling sorry for myself sitting here in my apartment alone, night after night. Why can't you do your chores while I'm at work? Knowing the Air Force as I do, I'm sure that no contract you have with them could keep you as busy as you seem to be sometime."

Oscar really ached to level with her. Instead he replied, "I'll try to do better, baby. I really will. How was your day?"

Adelaide talked to him from the kitchen while she continued preparing their meal. Oscar occasionally interjected a comment or an answer, but his mind was busy on the more serious matter of the whole relationship between the two of them. Was there any way he could share with her his feelings and concerns?

He remembered a debate he had had with some of the other fliers back in Vietnam. It was during a period when the news media were featuring plans and proposals for an increased role for women in the armed forces. The initial proponents were the feminists and their supporters on the left, whose position was that women differed from men only in the configuration of their genitalia and could do virtually anything men could do, including fly military aircraft in combat, and do it just as well. The only reason they weren't doing it already was the repressive effect of society's "sexism," which on the one hand erected barriers of custom and law against women and on the other hand stunted their potential by brainwashing them into accepting traditional female roles. If the laws were changed, and if little girls were raised just like little boys—given baseball bats and cap pistols instead of dolls—they would grow up just as capable as men of being Green Berets or combat pilots.

The other side of the issue was represented by those whose only argument was that "society isn't ready for women to go into combat yet." At least, they were the only ones on the other side of the issue who were admitted into the forum by the media, creating the impression that the opponents of a military combat role for women really had no ground to stand on. So it wasn't long before the trendier politicians and bureaucrats, even some of the nation's military leaders with political ambitions, also took up the banner of the feminists.

The general opinion among Oscar's fellow airmen was that the feminist position was insupportable. There were one or two exceptions, but they were shallow men of a contrary disposition who always could be counted on to champion any unnatural cause, the freakier the better. Oscar was sure that no man who had flown in combat really believed that a woman could be a good combat pilot, no matter how fast her reflexes, how fine her coordination, how keen her vision.

The feminists claimed that men had an advantage as fighters only because they had more muscle, and that the advantage vanished in those combat situations where muscle wasn't decisive: combat flying, for example. Oscar, on the other hand, realized that men weren't better fighters *because* they had more muscle, but that men had more muscle *because* it gave them an advantage in their natural role as fighters. In women, even though they might be the most excellent of athletes, the fighting hormones were missing—and more: the fighting instinct, the innate fighting micro-skills, finely honed over a million generations of primate evolution, during which the males were the hunters and fighters, and the females the nurturers.

The cleverly crooked way in which the news media had handled the issue reinforced Oscar's already well developed distrust of the journalistic profession. But the debate had interested him and had led him to think about the psychic differences between men and women and the deep roots of these differences in the evolutionary past of the race.

Adelaide was a bright girl, one of the brightest he had ever known, and that pleased him. She could knowledgeably discuss some aspects of his antenna design work with him; she had even suggested a better algorithm than he had been using for one series of radiation calculations. She also was witty and well read for her age; in talking with her he could use a historical simile to illustrate a point, and she could respond in kind. Her intelligence made her a better companion.

Nevertheless, her mind did not work in the same way his did, and he was aware of the differences, subtle and slight as they might seem to a less perceptive observer. For one thing, her mental world was smaller, her horizon closer. What was real to her was the here and now; the past and the future, like distant landscapes in the present, were of much less interest. She was a good, practical worker on limited projects, but the mapping of world-historical vistas and making plans to transform them would seem unreal to her.

For another thing, Adelaide was not a generalizer. Her focus was on the trees, not the forest. She saw people as individuals. He did too, of course—but he also saw them as members of larger categories: as representatives of their races, their social classes, their religions, their interest groups. To understand a man, one had to consider what he *was*, where his roots were, his vital interests, with whom he identified—not just his individual idiosyncrasies.

The popular wisdom was on her side, of course. Everyone was *supposed* to see others only as individuals. But he was quite sure that she was not simply conforming to an artificial norm. Adelaide was not an artificial girl; quite the opposite. She had little use for pretense or convention. She was completely unmoved by all of the swirling currents of political and social trendiness.

He remembered her reaction when two obviously "gay" men had swished into a restaurant once where they were eating, sat down at a table near theirs, and held hands as they perused the menu. Despite the vogue homosexuals were enjoying, she had displayed a natural revulsion for the spectacle. She laughed at Black or Jewish jokes, if they were really funny. When he had lectured her once on the subject of the difference in intelligence between Blacks and Whites, and more generally, the difference in the ways the minds of the two races worked, she had found his analysis convincing.

But when an interracial couple was assassinated, she saw two people murdered, not a blow against miscegenation. He was sure that her reaction was natural and feminine, not ideological. And he had noticed the same general pattern in other women as well. All of this did not mean that Adelaide could not be brought around to an acceptance—perhaps even an approval—of what he was doing, just that it might not be easy. He decided to begin the task.

"Sweetheart, suppose we didn't know each other, and one of the Blacks at the Pentagon asked you for a date—say, that Black captain who gives you the eye whenever he comes into Carl's office while you're there—how would you react?"

Adelaide answered as she placed the final dishes on the table and sat down: "Actually, the man propositioned me the first week I was there. And I told him very sweetly, 'Thanks, but I'll have to check with my doctor first to see if it's all right. I've tested positive for AIDS, and I don't know whether or not it's in the contagious stage yet.' I guess the word got around, because I haven't had another proposition from a Black in more than a year. The other White girls are pestered by them all the time."

"You never told me about that. I'm surprised that you were ready for him with such an effective turnoff."

"It's my standard response to randy Blacks. One of the first things I learned in college was that an answer like that is the only thing that'll work. They simply won't take a polite 'no' for an answer. It's got to be either, 'Buzz off, nigger,' or something like my AIDS answer. During my first year at Iowa State they were really a problem. I was completely unprepared for it. There had been no Blacks at all in my high school—none in the whole county where I grew up, for that matter. But there were lots of them, most from out of state, at the university. They made such a nuisance of themselves I felt like a bitch in heat. I didn't want to be rude, and I didn't want to be thought a racist. I also didn't want to date any of them. I just wasn't attracted to them. Besides, it was general knowledge that girls who did date them usually got raped if they didn't give in voluntarily. They called it 'date rape,' but it was still rape—very often gang rape. The university administration gave the girls no backup at all. They wouldn't even admit there was a problem. Fortunately, I had a roommate who knew the score, and she helped me cope."

"Weren't there any support groups for White girls on campus? What about the church groups?"

"Are you serious, Oscar? The church groups were the worst of all. They thought their mission was to save girls like me from racism, not from being raped. They were always organizing dances and other social functions, and their big concern at every function was to pair off the White females with Black males. White men who showed up were made to feel unwelcome. They were so obvious about it!

"The only organized groups on campus which made an issue of rape were the feminists, but they didn't say anything about the racial aspect, of course."

"Of course. But I'll bet the racial conditions on campus helped them with their recruiting."

"Probably did. A lot of women who had had bad experiences with men—especially with Black men—were full of anger that no one else sympathized with them or would help them, and so they turned to the feminists."

"How did you manage to avoid falling into their clutches and being converted into a man-hater?" Oscar asked only half seriously.

"I was tempted to join one of the feminist groups during the time when I felt most insecure, as a freshman, just for moral support. And I probably would have, except the feminists' agenda, even in the least militant groups, went way beyond providing moral support for women. Most of them weren't just angry about the way women were treated; they were angry that they were women, instead of men, although they would never admit that. They campaigned against rape, but when you got to know them you realized that what they were really angry about was having to be on the bottom. To put it crudely, they wanted to be the rapists instead of the rapees, the fuckers instead of the fuckees. And since I've always been happy to be on the bottom, as long as there was a good man on top, I couldn't empathize with them."

"I'm grateful for that, baby. It would have been a real loss to the race if you'd become a dyke."

"Well, at least a loss to you, I hope," she smiled. "I don't know that I'm doing the race much good."

"Hmm. True. We ought to do something about that. We need to think seriously about getting you pregnant. It's really a crime against Nature for someone with your genes not to have five or six kids."

"I'm open to suggestions."

"Looks like I've put myself on the spot again," Oscar smiled. Then he frowned. "You know, baby, I've got some loose ends that I have to take care of. With a schedule like I'm keeping now we couldn't really have much of a home life together. I hope that I can work some things out in the next couple of months which will let me go into the business of being a husband and father with a clear conscience."

"Honey, it's true that your work schedule is pretty aggravating to me sometimes. But couples all over the world raise families with worse problems."

"I appreciate your flexibility, baby. One of the reasons I love you is that you seem able to take into stride almost any sort of problem which comes up, without complaining. But I believe I really am near the point of being able to make some changes which will be good for both of us—and for our children. I need to concentrate my energies on these things for just a while longer."

Oscar could see the disappointment and pain in Adelaide's eyes, and his soul writhed. He did not want to lie to her, but that is what he was doing. For the truth was that he had no clear idea of what lay ahead for him. What could he hope to have resolved in a couple of months? If he kept escalating his war against the System, he would likely be dead or in prison in that time. On the other hand, it was hard to imagine how he could escalate the war beyond what he was planning to do to the People's Committee Against Hate. The only possibility seemed to be to find a way of continuing the war by legal—or, at least, less risky—means. But how? He had drawn a blank every time he had tried to think along those lines.

He didn't know what else to say to Adelaide. There was simply no point in telling her exactly what he was doing. Even if she were ideologically and emotionally prepared to accept that knowledge, there was nothing she could do to help; she would just be frightened and worried. Yet he felt that he must tell her *something*. He didn't want her to think he was stalling because he didn't want to marry her. And he desperately wanted her to understand his motives, to share his conviction that he had to fight the evil that was threatening the whole meaning of their existence.

He tried again, his voice serious and, at first, hesitant: "You know how I feel about a lot of the changes that are taking place in this country, sweetheart. I've mentioned most of them to you at one time or another: the growth in racial mixing, the flood of non-White immigrants pouring into the cities, the increasingly obvious crookedness and lack of responsibility of the politicians, the destructive bias of the news and entertainment media, the breakdown of the country's morale, the decay of discipline and of standards everywhere, the loss of any sense of racial or cultural identity on the part of the dwindling White majority.

"I guess most people have thicker skins than I have, and they don't let these things bother them. But they do bother me—a lot. They bother me so much that it's hard for me to take anything else very seriously. My work has become for me nothing more than a way of making money. I can't get excited about it when I see so many other things going on—more important things, terrible things—that call out for my intervention. It's hard to plan ahead, to think about a career, when the future looks like the sort of place I wouldn't want to live in—or have our kids live in.

"I want to fight it, baby. I feel that I have to fight it. Nothing else seems real or worthwhile to me except fighting it. Nothing else but you, that is. When I'm with you I can put everything else out of my mind for a few hours. I can think about you and me, here and now. I can see you, feel you, hear you, smell you. I can luxuriate in your beauty, your softness, your womanliness, your sexiness, your love. But when we talk about marriage and children, then I have to think about more than here and now. I have to figure out how I can fight and also be a responsible husband and father at the same time. That's my problem, sweetheart, and I'm trying to work it out."

There was silence for a long moment, as the two looked into one another's eyes. Then Adelaide spoke: "Honey, you're an unusual man. You're not like any other man I've ever known. I think that your attitude is quixotic. I don't like many of the things that are happening today myself. I don't like some of the directions the world is headed, and I'd change them if I could. But I can't, and you can't either. There's nothing we can do. Anyway, our responsibility is not to take care of the world, but to take care of ourselves as best we can. There's a lot of dirt out there, and we can't change that. But we can keep our own lives clean and make clean lives for our children. That's all we can do."

"Maybe not even that much, baby. Sure, I guess you and I can keep ourselves clean. But things are falling apart pretty fast out there, and I'm not at all certain that we'll be able to guarantee clean lives for our kids. They'll be growing up in a country in which their own race will be barely a majority—and a badly fractured and split majority at that, while the minorities at least know how to stick together and vote together.

"And I guess that if I were a cold-blooded gambler I wouldn't put any of my money on a bet that we can do anything to head off the catastrophe. But I'm still not quite as sure as you are that nothing can be done. Perhaps I am quixotic, but for me while there's life there's hope. And I have to try. I wish I could make you understand how I feel about the inevitability of doing whatever we can, regardless of the odds."

Oscar thought for a moment, then he continued: "I guess you're aware of the gang rapes of White girls by bands of young Blacks which have been going on around here. Usually the news media won't say much about it, but it's really on the rise. There was that rape of the jogger in Rock Creek Park last week, for example, in which more than 20 teen-aged Blacks grabbed the girl and spent nearly two hours raping her repeatedly, right on the jogging path. Then they cut her throat and left her to die. It wouldn't have made such a splash in the media if she hadn't been a senator's niece.

"Suppose you and I were walking through the park and had come on that scene while the raping was in progress. Suppose I were unarmed, and it was a good mile to the nearest telephone. Some men, I suppose, could tell themselves that there was nothing they could do, except start running for the telephone, in the hope that they could get the cops there in 20 or 30 minutes. But for me there would be no choice. If the girl were a member of my race I would have to charge right into those Black animals and do whatever was humanly possible to rescue her. If I ran away I would not be able to live with myself. I would feel dirty and dishonorable forever afterward.

"And that's sort of the way it is with me and the world. It's my world, my race's world, and it's being gang-raped. I'd feel dishonorable, I couldn't be at peace with myself, if I didn't do what I could—even though doing it might come between you and me."

Adelaide smiled. "I could not love thee, dear, so much, loved I not honor more," she quoted.

"Exactly, my lovely Lucasta, exactly," Oscar came back.

"Well, honey, I'm still sure you're quixotic and that there's absolutely nothing you can do to change the course of history. But I just want you to know"—and here Adelaide's voice became low and husky—"that if you decide to go to war against the whole world, I'll be your camp follower, if you'll have me. And if you charge unarmed straight into the gates of Hell, I'll be running along behind you as fast as I can, if I believe you still love me."

Tears glistened in Adelaide's eyes, and Oscar found that he had a lump in his throat so hard that he could not speak. All he could do for a moment was reach clumsily across the dinner table and grasp her hand. His motion knocked over one of the candlesticks, which sputtered out. Then he rose swiftly from his chair, crossed to Adelaide's side of the table while she herself stood up, and crushed her tightly in his arms. They stood there silent and motionless, a single column of shadowed, gleaming flesh illuminated by the flickering light of the remaining candle.

X

Two nights later Oscar was ready to move against the People's Committee. He had prepared his tools and supplies, and the weather was right: a steady rain that would keep people indoors and muffle any noise he might inadvertently make.

Furthermore, the group had given special billing to the meeting being held tonight. The governors of Massachusetts and Wisconsin would be there to present resolutions of their respective state legislatures urging the Congress to pass the Horowitz Bill. Cardinal O'Rourke and Rabbi Rosen of the National Judeo-Christian Interfaith Council would be principal speakers, along with a Barry Shapiro of something called the Anti-Defamation League of B'nai B'rith, who also was to be the master of ceremonies. Several Congressmen would be attending.

The media would be well represented, which was good. The more of those rotten sons of bitches he could blow to hell, the better. Unfortunately, however, there probably would be especially heavy police protection tonight. Oscar's only real concern was that there not be any policemen patrolling the alley behind the church.

He drove first down the side street just north of the church complex. As he approached the alley entrance, his heart sank: a police cruiser was parked in the alley, blocking access, its nose projecting onto the sidewalk. He drove on around the block. The other end of the alley was clear. Peering into this end of the alley through the rain, which now had become quite heavy, he could not see the cruiser at all. He found a parking space only about 50 feet beyond the alley, on the other side of the street: quite a piece of luck, considering the large attendance at the meeting in the church. Oscar had spotted no other vacant spaces nearby and had been afraid he would have to carry his heavy, bulky equipment several blocks.

Before he stepped out of the car, he checked the pockets of his trench coat; all of the smaller items he needed were in place. He then walked around to the passenger door, slipped a heavily padded rope around his neck and across his shoulders underneath his coat, and carefully eased two 90-pound cylinders of acetylene, one fastened to each end of the harness, out of the passenger area. When he stood up the two cylinders hung to his knees and were covered by his coat. They doubled his girth, however, and he could not stand even a casual inspection at less than 50 yards without arousing immediate suspicion. Worse, he could not walk in anything approaching a normal fashion. The best he could manage with the load was an extremely awkward waddle.

He was nearly pooped by the time he reached the right spot in the iron fence, more than 100 yards down the alley. Fortunately, the police cruiser was still far enough away so that he could make out its outline only when it was occasionally illuminated by the headlights of a passing car on the side street ahead. As long as the cops stayed inside their vehicle, they certainly would not be able to see him.

He slipped out of the harness and then pushed the cylinders one at a time through the fence. They were a tight fit, and one stuck halfway through. He had to use all his strength to pull the pickets apart enough to free it. Then he went over the top himself, somewhat more awkwardly than the first time, but without losing any of the contents of his pockets. He rested for a couple of minutes, squatting in the wet darkness of the shrubs, before looping the rope over his shoulders again and crawling the remaining 25 yards to the building.

Once he had pushed his way through the shrubs concealing the window well and was stretched out along the basement wall with his head and shoulders next to the window, he was able to relax. From here on it would be a piece of cake. If he weren't quite so wet and cold he would even enjoy it. First he pulled his battery-operated drill from his right pocket, and then the half-inch bit with the turned-down shank. He tightened the bit in the chuck, dropping the chuck key in the process and groping in the mud and blackness for nearly a minute before finding it again. The plastic coating on his fingers made them clumsy and hampered his sense of touch as well.

Drilling a hole through the wooden window sash took only a few seconds. Oscar next pushed the end of a half-inch plastic tube into the hole. The other end of the tube was connected to one of the acetylene cylinders, which in turn was connected to the other by a four-foot length of rubber hose. He opened the valves wide on both cylinders and tensed as the gas roared through the tube and into the basement. To him the sound seemed as loud as a freight train rushing by at high speed, but he told himself that it probably would be barely audible over the noise of the rain to someone in the alley—or inside the sanctuary above, where the meeting was in progress.

He had intended to stow his drill and set a time squib while the cylinders were emptying, but the force of the flow caused the plastic tube to writhe and twist so violently that he had to hold it to prevent its coming out of the sash. Only after about five minutes had the pressure in the cylinders dropped to the point where he could safely release the tube.

The atmosphere in the large basement room must be pretty close to 10 per cent acetylene by now, Oscar estimated. Anything over 2.5 per cent would explode. By the time the cylinders were completely empty, the acetylene content of the room should be as high as 12 percent, assuming the leakage under the doors into the rest of the basement wasn't excessive. He had noted during his first reconnaissance that the heating plant for the whole church complex was located in an annex; at least, that was the only building with a chimney. That eased his fear of a premature explosion due to gas leaking into a part of the basement where a furnace might be located. Still, he didn't want to hang around any longer than necessary, because as gas seeped into other parts of the basement a spark from any source might cause a detonation.

He pulled a squib from his pocket and prepared to set it for 30 minutes. It was a device he had built himself, but it was modeled on similar ignition devices he had seen in Vietnam. It was a metal tube six inches long and just under half an inch in diameter. When a protective cap was unscrewed from one end, a protruding socket-head screw became accessible. He had taped an Allen wrench to the squib beforehand, so that he wouldn't have to grope in his pocket for it. A ball detent made it easy to turn the screw the exact distance desired: five minutes for each "click." Zero "clicks" was for instantaneous ignition, but in practice that meant approximately 30 seconds. When one had set the position of the screw one jammed it forcefully against any hard surface to rupture a tiny ampoule of acid inside the tube and begin the countdown.

Oscar had just fumbled the wrench into the socket, relying entirely on his badly impaired sense of touch, when the light in the basement room suddenly came on. He froze in horror, anticipating the explosion. Almost immediately, however, he realized that if there were going to be an explosion from the turning on of the light it would have been instantaneous. Probably the light switch was one of the modern, silent ones, using a mercury contactor in a sealed glass tube. If it had been an older, mechanical switch, he probably would be dead now, the spark from the closing of the contacts having set off the explosive mixture in the room.

All of these thoughts raced through his head in a split second. Now he had to act just as quickly. Obviously, someone had opened the door to the room. Perhaps the odor of the acetylene had been detected upstairs, or perhaps it was the sound of the rushing gas. In any case, the alarm would now be sounded, and the church would be evacuated. Furthermore, with a door open he couldn't count on the concentration of gas in the room remaining at the explosive level for more than a minute or so.

Without further thought he dropped the Allen wrench and slammed the end of the squib against the stone wall. Then he yanked the acetylene tube from the sash and pushed the squib into the hole. It clattered on the basement floor as Oscar scrambled to his feet. No time now to retrieve his nearly empty acetylene cylinders. He left them in the shrubs and sprinted for the fence.

He was over the top and halfway back to his car when the ground shook under his feet. An instant later the shock wave traveling through the air hit with an immensely satisfying boom. It seemed to Oscar that it had been less than 30 seconds since he had activated the squib. Not until he reached his car did he turn and look back toward the church. The building was still standing, but it was nearly obscured by a huge pall of black smoke. No flames were to be seen, but dense, black smoke was pouring from the windows of the sanctuary—which meant that the blast must at least have blown a substantial hole in the floor.

As he drove home, wet but happy, the first emergency vehicles went screaming past him in the opposite direction. It wasn't until the next morning, however, that he was able to hear a fairly accurate news report on the effects of the blast. Not only the pulpit, but the entire speakers' platform behind it had been blown right through the roof of the church, he learned. All of the notables on the platform—two governors, three Congressmen, a Senator, a cardinal, two bishops, a prominent rabbi, a TV talk-show host, two leading Hollywood actors, a much-acclaimed feminist writer, the head of a homosexual rights organization, the president of the NAACP, the B'nai B'rith's Shapiro, and four others, unnamed—had perished. Parts of some of them were still being scraped off the rafters of the sanctuary. In addition there were 41 dead, most from smoke inhalation, among the audience and the media personnel. Oscar's empty acetylene cylinders had been found, and the bombing already was being denounced as "the hate crime of the century."

That label was a challenge to Oscar. What could he do next that would eclipse his snuffing of the People's Committee? He had time to consider the matter, because he came down with a cold that very day—due at least in part, he suspected, to his exposure and exertion in the downpour of the previous night.

It was a Saturday, and Adelaide came over early. When she saw his condition she insisted that he stay at home and spend most of the weekend in bed under her ministrations. He complied without objection, glad for the rest and finding that he enjoyed being fussed over and waited on by her. With her as a nurse, having a cold was almost a pleasure.

More than ever he wanted to order his life in a way that would allow him to give her security and happiness and to father her children. And more than ever he felt compelled to continue combatting the evil forces which were destroying the very basis for the future existence of her kind. He wrestled with his dilemma during most of the following week, mentally re-exploring every possible avenue of activity which might provide a resolution.

One of the thoughts that kept recurring to Oscar was that everything he had done so far was like hacking at the heads of a Hydra. He was unable to inflict a mortal wound, and the harder he hacked, the more formidable the beast became. The latest evidence of this was the demand by several members of the Congress that, in response to last week's bombing, the Horowitz Bill be rushed to a vote as soon as possible. There clearly was a much larger supply of people who needed killing than he could ever hope to kill by himself. If he did not soon find a vital organ to strike at, all of his efforts would end up being counterproductive.

But what was a vital organ? The Congress? Not really; it seemed more to be a mere instrument of the forces of decay rather than the guiding will. Besides, he could kill hundreds of politicians, and the institution of Congress would continue its destructive work. The same was true of the news media; no matter how many journalists he killed, the press and the television networks would stay on their same, deadly course.

If he could not destroy a vital organ, perhaps there was some way of controlling one. Newspapers could be bought and sold, even television networks. The trouble was that the amounts of money required were simply beyond reach; big-city newspapers exchanged hands for $100 million or more, networks for billions. He could successfully rob banks or operate a counterfeiting press for 50 years without accumulating enough capital to buy the *Washington Post*.

By Thursday afternoon he still had no answer. The following Monday was a holiday for Adelaide, and he had promised to take her skiing over the three-day weekend. They would be leaving for the ski area tomorrow afternoon, and Oscar would be busy tomorrow morning completing several errands. Tonight he *had* to crank out some more results for Carl. And this afternoon it was necessary to take the car to the garage for a wheel alignment and a tune-up. He did not get home again with the car until after seven o'clock.

XI

Oscar hung his coat in the hall closet and headed for the kitchen to pour himself a glass of orange juice before beginning the night's work. Halfway into the kitchen, he knew something was wrong an instant before he heard the voice.

"Freeze, Yeager! FBI! Raise your arms over your head and face the wall. Now step back one pace and lean forward with your hands against the wall."

Oscar felt numb. For a fraction of a second he considered going on the attack. The man behind him, sensing his thought instantly, snarled, "Try it and you're dead, Yeager."

The man expertly frisked him, removing the Smith and Wesson Airweight .38 special which Oscar always carried tucked into his waistband.

"All right, Yeager, you can turn around now—slowly. Sit in that chair. We're going to have a nice, long talk."

For the first time Oscar saw the man who had disarmed him. He was a sturdy-looking, gray-haired man in his mid-fifties, about four inches shorter than Oscar, with steely blue eyes. He was wearing a business suit, and he held a revolver pointed unwaveringly at Oscar. He *looked* like an FBI agent, but Oscar already could sense that something other than an ordinary arrest was taking place. Why was there only one agent? The FBI never operated like that. He was not left wondering for long.

"Well, Yeager, let's get right to the point. I know what you've been doing. I've known for the last two weeks, even before you smoked that Hebe Shapiro and his stooges in the church over on Connecticut Avenue. God, that was a good job!" The man chuckled approvingly, but his revolver remained pointed at Oscar's chest.

"You could have been arrested as soon as I had you identified from the prints you left in the john at the Shoreham when you killed Horowitz. The only reason that we're sitting here now is that I like your style, Yeager. And I have some work for you—some real man's work, instead of the kid stuff you've been wasting your time with."

"Are you telling me," Oscar asked, unable to conceal his incredulity, "that the FBI approves of whatever it is you're alleging I've done?"

"Hell, no, Yeager! If anybody else at the Bureau knew what I know, you'd be chained to the wall in one of our maximum-security cells in the basement of the Hoover Building right now. The point is, I didn't tell anyone else. I kept my information on you to myself.

It was pure luck that of all the potential evidence we picked up at the Shoreham I gave everything else to other agents to check out and kept for myself the one item which led somewhere—namely, the print of your right thumb on a page from your address book which you had wadded up and jammed in the lock on the rest-room closet where you waited for Horowitz. I ran it through our Fingerprint Section and came up with your name and Air Force identification number.

"At that point the only thing on my mind was a wild hunch that maybe, just maybe, you were the guy we were looking for—and that there was no need to share the glory in nabbing you with anyone else yet. So I made you my own special project, while everyone else was working on other leads, none of which led them anywhere.

"I slipped into your place one night when you were staying over at your cutie's apartment and had a look at your layout in the basement. That's when I knew. At that point I should have swooped down on you with one of our SWAT teams, cameramen from all three networks, and a prepared statement for the press. I would have gotten my salary raised three grades. Instead, I spent two weeks finding out everything there is to know about you: all the places you lived when you were growing up, what your teachers in high school thought about you, your record in the Air Force, your graduate studies in Colorado. I talked with two of the girls you dated there, told them it was for a security clearance. I know you better now than your mother does.

"And I stayed on your tail and watched you do the job on Shapiro's People's Committee Against Hate."

"Why?" Oscar asked.

"Well, that takes a little explanation." The older man leaned back in his chair for a moment. He still held his revolver in his hand, but he was resting it in his lap now instead of keeping it aimed directly at Oscar's chest. He sighed. "I've been with the Bureau for 33 years. I've been the deputy chief of our Anti-Terrorism Section for the last nine years. I worked my way up back during the days when I was proud to be an FBI agent. Did you know that my father was in the Bureau for 26 years before I became a special agent? We were in the Bureau together for seven years, until he retired. He died two years ago."

"I recognize you now," Oscar replied, his numbness gone. "I saw you on the CBS Evening News last year, when the FBI was rounding up all of those Ku Klux Klan people. You were the one in charge of the FBI task force. Your name is Ryan—William Ryan."

Ryan did not respond directly to Oscar. He paused to gather his thoughts, then began again, speaking with more emphasis: "I've watched the Bureau change from a first-class law-enforcement agency to a politicized, mongrelized, third-rate secret-police bureaucracy, with the level of morale and efficiency you'd expect to find in Panama or Nicaragua. In the last 15 years the Jews have taken over the place and ruined it. Not that you find them out on the street busting the Mafia or shooting it out with Colombian drug smugglers like the rest of us. No, they're too busy running the 'racial sensitivity' classes all the agents have to take. And heading our Affirmative Action office. And worming their way into the Counterespionage Section, so that they can make sure we don't catch too many more of their cousins from Israel swiping American military secrets.

"Things change slowly in the government. From day to day you don't notice much difference. But it mounts up. It used to be a rare thing for an agent to go bad. Hoover would drum a man out of the Bureau for trying to beat a parking ticket or writing a bad check. In the last two years we've had 19 agents convicted on various felony charges—everything from selling drugs and pimping to spying for the Soviet Union. Eight others managed to beat the charges against them, and four of those guys are still with the Bureau!"

"Yes, I read about several of those cases in the newspapers," Oscar commented drily.

"Hell, not a tenth of it gets in the papers!" Ryan exploded. "We're able to keep most of it covered up. You know what I saw just last week? I went down to our analytical lab to check on the results of a test on some material from a crime site. There was no one in the lab, but I heard some noise coming from the stock room. I opened the door and found one of our Black special agents screwing the White lab technician on a table! And you know what? There wasn't a damned thing I could do to either of them! I filed a report, of course, but these days something like that is regarded by the bureaucracy as in the same league with being reported for loitering at the water cooler."

Ryan paused again, studying Oscar's face for a minute before continuing. "What's happening in the Bureau is just a reflection of what's happening everywhere. When America started going bad, there was no way for the Bureau to escape the same fate. If I've got you figured right, you've had about the same reaction to the general decay, Yeager, as I've had to the decay of the Bureau. The difference is that you've done something about it, and I haven't. I've just had to take it, year after year, and let the pressure build up."

"So, there are still some decent men in the FBI!" Oscar exclaimed in surprise. "I thought you fellows had all joined the other side."

"Oh, we have, Yeager, indeed we have, and you'd better believe it! You just don't understand the secret-police mentality," Ryan chuckled. "Don't you ever get the idea into your head that you can confide in anybody at the FBI. There are lots of us over there, especially the old-timers, who have decent instincts, men who hate the same rottenness you do and would like to have their children grow up in the same kind of world you would want for your kids. But we work for whoever signs our paychecks, and we clobber anybody who raises his hand against the System we're part of. We may be secretly glad when you waste some race-mixer in a parking lot, but we'd fall all over ourselves to be the first to nail you for it. We're the Jews' mercenaries, and we earn our keep. Not only that, we take personal offense when some son of a bitch like you challenges us."

Oscar thought for a second, then responded, "In other words, you got more than 150 Klansmen convicted last year on charges of conspiring to violate the civil rights of Blacks, because that's the job you're paid to do, but you didn't really enjoy it as much as you pretended to when you were describing the investigation and the arrests on tele . . . ."

"Wrong!" Ryan interrupted. "You *still* don't understand the secret-police mentality. I enjoyed busting those turds more than just about anything I've done for the Bureau. I wasn't pretending at all when I described them as 'the scum of the earth.' I know what you're thinking, Yeager. You're thinking that those Klansmen's hearts were in the right places, that they were just doing in their own way what you were doing in yours. But they were bums, losers. They were stupid. And they made the mistake of thinking they were smarter than we were. They challenged us. They waved their pricks in our faces. And so we cut their balls off."

"All right. I guess I've challenged you too. So now what are you going to do about it, Ryan?"

"That depends on you, Yeager. If you're a reasonable man, who knows when somebody's got him by the balls and accepts the fact, then maybe we can work together. On the other hand, if you want to play hard-ass with me, I'll crucify you. I'll call in the media right now and let 'em show me on the late news tonight walking you out of here in handcuffs."

"I regard myself as a reasonable man. What sort of work do you have in mind?"

"That's the answer I wanted to hear," Ryan beamed. "Don't worry about the work. You'll love it. It'll just be more of the same sort of thing you've proved yourself so good at. Except from now on I'll be choosing your targets for you." He paused for a moment, and the twinkle faded from his eyes. When he continued his voice was hard and icy. "Before we get into the details I want to impress on you that I'm a careful man, Yeager—a very careful man. There's no way out of this for you, except to do exactly what I tell you. If you ever try to double-cross me, it won't be handcuffs for you—it'll be a cold slab. And don't even think about trying to get the drop on me. It won't solve your problem for you. No others in the Bureau know what I know about you now, but I've taken steps to ensure that if anything happens to me they soon will."

There was silence as Ryan paused again to gather his thoughts. Oscar's face remained expressionless, but his mind was busy. He doubted Ryan's last claim; the man didn't strike him as the kind to waste his time on a futile, post-mortem revenge. He wouldn't have been likely to leave any of his evidence lying around his Bureau office where others might find it prematurely, because that would spell problems for him as well as for Oscar. If he really had taken any steps, then he should have spelled them out for Oscar. Only by being credible could they serve as an effective deterrent.

Suppose Ryan had left a sealed envelope with his wife. What could there be in it that would hold up in court, if Oscar had just one day to clean up a few loose ends and dispose of some incriminating items, such as his ordnance? A single thumb print by itself wouldn't convict him. At the thought of that thumb print he kicked himself mentally. He had been so careful to avoid leaving prints every time he had carried out an action! And then he had left one during a reconnaissance! And he hadn't even used that rest-room closet for the action!

Focusing on Ryan again, Oscar decided that if the man would let down his guard for just a fraction of a second, he could jump him, dispose of the body, and take some hasty measures to protect himself from a subsequent investigation—if there ever were one. If nothing happened for a month or two, he could then resume his former activity.

That course of action appealed to him much more than letting himself be used as Ryan's private hit man. He tried not to let his new resolve show in a tensing of his muscles. Jumping Ryan would not be easy. He would need total surprise.

XII

66I think I'll let you take out Kaplan first," Ryan resumed reflectively, almost as if he were thinking aloud. "That's David Kaplan, the little Hebe who's the number-three man in my own section. The other kikes in the Bureau are priming him to be jumped over my head to become chief of the Anti-Terrorism Section when the present chief gets canned for not being able to catch you."

"Is that why you want to get rid of him?" Oscar asked, allowing himself a slight smile. "You want the job for yourself?"

"You misjudge me, Yeager. I don't want you to bump him off just because he's a career threat. What kind of a jerk do you think I am?" There was exasperation in the other man's voice. "He's a Jew, dammit! He's one of the Yids who're taking over the Bureau."

Oscar hesitated, his puzzlement showing in his face. "You've mentioned Jews two or three times. Just what is it you have against them?"

It was Ryan's turn to look puzzled. "What do you mean, what do I have against them? I hate them for the same reasons you do. Now let's cut the crap and get down to business. Pick up that pad from the desk—slowly and carefully. I'm going to give you a complete personal rundown on Kaplan—physical description, work schedule, daily itinerary, personal habits—and I want you to take notes."

Oscar held up his hand. "Now wait just a minute, Ryan. If I'm going to be killing people for you, first I'd like to have at least a general idea of your rationale. I'm one of those troublesome types who needs to know *why* before he carries out an assignment. In this case I really haven't the foggiest. I think you've assumed that I know some things I don't. For one thing, I've never been fond of Jews as a group, but I don't really hate them, and I don't understand your references to their taking over the FBI. Why would they want to do that?"

The puzzled expression on Ryan's face had changed to a look of utter amazement as Oscar spoke. He stared wide-eyed at Oscar. "Jesus Christ! I can't believe it! I do not believe what I'm hearing! You sound like some ignorant *goy* who learned everything he knows from watching TV. You sound like the typical American voter. But you can't be that stupid. You didn't knock off Congressman Horowitz just because he was such an ugly bastard. You didn't blow up that B'nai B'rith honcho, Shapiro, just because he had bad breath. You didn't waste that kike columnist at the *Washington Post*, Jacobs, just because his opinions were too liberal for you. You're not going to try to tell me that it's just a coincidence they all happened to be Jews. Come off it, Yeager!"

Forgetting for a moment his resolution to watch for the first possible opportunity to jump Ryan and letting his irritation show, Oscar leaned forward in his seat and stabbed a finger at Ryan. "As a matter of fact, it is just a coincidence. I didn't even know Jacobs was Jewish. I shot him simply because he was the most obnoxious writer on the race question at the *Post*. I wasn't really aiming at Shapiro when I bombed the People's Committee; he just happened to be one of the people on the platform when I blew the place up. And I didn't kill Horowitz because he was Jewish; I killed him because he was the leader of the race-mixing faction in the House."

"Right! Just like Senator Mandelbaum is the head of the race-mixing faction in the Senate. Perhaps you hadn't noticed that he just happens to be a Hebe too," Ryan snorted in derision.

"Well, what if he is? What does that prove? There are plenty of race-mixers who aren't Jewish," Oscar replied somewhat defensively.

"Omigod, I believe the man is serious," Ryan moaned, clapping his free hand to his head and rolling his eyes up. "I suppose you also didn't realize that Shapiro was pulling all of the strings in the People's Committee Against Hate from the beginning, that all of those preachers and actors and faggots on the Committee were just window dressing?"

Oscar didn't answer, but he tensed, ready to hurl himself at the other man. Before he could move, however, Ryan was staring straight at him again. And although Ryan's right hand was still resting casually on his leg, the muzzle of his pistol remained pointed steadily at Oscar's chest.

"Maybe I overestimated you, Yeager. Maybe you're not smart enough for what I have in mind: a good tactician, perhaps, but certainly no strategist," Ryan mused. "But then, a good tactician is all I really need. I'll be the strategist. You don't have to understand the reasons for what you do."

"Try me," Oscar shot back. "You tell me the significance of the fact that Jewish people are somewhat more heavily involved than members of other religious groups in the effort to ram miscegenation down America's throat. You explain to me what that has to do with Kaplan and a Jewish plot to take over the FBI. I'll listen. Maybe I'll even understand."

Ryan glanced at his watch and sighed. "Yeager, if you've managed to live 40 years and still believe that the Jews are only a religious group, there's no way I can make you see the light tonight. It would take a week just to get you started toward an understanding of the Jews. I assumed you already had figured them out, but I guess I was wrong." Ryan shook his head sadly.

For a moment the older man remained undecided, then he sighed again, leaned back in his chair, and began: "All right, Yeager, you've noticed that Jews are more heavily involved in efforts to encourage race-mixing than others are. Have you also noticed their involvement in the news and entertainment media?"

Oscar blushed, feeling a bit like a retarded pupil. "Well, of course. Everyone knows that there are a lot of Jewish people in the media. It's their forte."

"Yeah, it's their fort, all right. Fort with no 'e.' It's their fortress, their citadel, their strategic headquarters for their campaign of annihilation against our kind," Ryan replied bitingly. "I suppose you believe that the reason the Jews own everything in Hollywood and the other strongholds of the entertainment industry is that they just have a knack for show business. Is that it? And I suppose you believe that, as a religious group, they acquired that knack from attending synagogue services. Or maybe it comes from their kosher diet. Right?"

Oscar's blush became more intense. "Well, they've always been good businessmen too. Some families get a good start in certain businesses, and then their descendants become more entrenched with each generation, like the Krupps in armaments and the Vanderbilts in railroads," Oscar answered lamely.

"You're reaching, boy, you're reaching. It's natural enough for a son to step into his father's shoes in the family business. Nothing sinister in that. But when all the sons in a family head for *other* businesses—other businesses in the *same industry*, that is—owned by families quite different from their own, and start buying them out and taking them over, and helping their cousins do the same, then one should at least suspect that this particular family wants to control the industry in question. And when one sees other families which are related in some distinctive way to this one—all the same ethnic minority, say—doing the same thing in the same industry, one should be even more suspicious.

"The Jews aren't the only minority in this country which behaves more or less like that, of course. There are the Hindus and the motel business, for example—or Gypsies and the used-car business. But then, owning a motel, or even a chain of motels, doesn't give a person quite the same clout as owning a big Hollywood production company or the *New York Times*, does it?

"In fact, Yeager, just think about it: I know that you aren't active in any church, but I also know that your family was Lutheran. Now let's just imagine. Let's just forget about the real world for a minute

and suppose that all of the Lutherans in Europe—your own ancestors—were a really tightly knit, well organized minority, and that
the non-Lutheran majority despised them, hated their guts, based on
centuries of bad experiences with them. And suppose that until about
a hundred years ago there were only a handful of Lutherans in this
country—a few scouts or advance men, one might say—and that
these advance men then sent word back to the rest of the Lutheran
tribe in Europe that the pickings were good in the United States, that
the really rough work of fighting the Indians and taming the wilder-
ness was done, and that the time was ripe to move in and take over.

"And suppose three or four million of your relatives then came
pouring into the country over the course of 30 years or so, remaining
just as tightly knit as they had been in Europe, bearing the same
burning hatred for the rest of the human race, and utterly determined
to get the upper hand. The first thing they'd have to do, of course,
would be to get a toehold. So they'd take over whatever industries
were available—the pushcart trade, the rag business, pawn shops—
and move up from there into more lucrative endeavors, like the
garment industry, the fur business, chain stores, and wholesale trade.

"So eventually they've established themselves in this country,
salted away plenty of loot, learned the local folkways, blended into
the local scenery as well as they can, and are ready to go for the
jugular. How would they do it? How would *you* do it? By getting a
corner on the button-hook market? By aiming at a stranglehold on
the proctology profession?"

Oscar remained silent, and Ryan continued his monologue: "No,
you know the answer as well as I, Yeager. They'd start grabbing the
mass media. In Europe they exercised their control through money,
through banking. They worked from the top down, by making
themselves invaluable to the rulers as moneylenders. Here things
are different, more democratic. Here the person who controls public
opinion wields more real power than the banker. Of course, the
Lutherans wouldn't be shy about grabbing control of the mon-
eylending business here, either. But if their aim was not just to gain
wealth for themselves, but to dominate and then destroy the non-
Lutheran majority among whom they lived, more than anything else
they'd go for every medium of entertainment and information they
could get their acquisitive hands on. They'd go for Hollywood.
They'd go for Broadway. They'd go for radio. They'd go for the
newspapers and magazines and comic books and book publishers.
And, of course, when TV came along later they'd control that too."

"Well, I admit that Jewish people are as thick as fleas on a dog
in Hollywood, but . . . ."

Ryan cut him off explosively, "Kee-rist, Yeager! Cut out that 'Jewish people' crap before I gag."

"All right. So the Jews control Hollywood. And it's true that the sort of entertainment Hollywood produces these days seems almost calculated to promote racial mixing and other forms of degeneracy. But . . . ."

"There's no 'almost' about it, Yeager," Ryan interrupted him again.

"I don't see how you can be so sure about that. The Mafia distributes drugs, which certainly are destructive to our society. But I believe it's pretty clear that the Mafia's aim is simply to make money, not to destroy society. They're simply taking advantage of a vice which already existed. How do you know the Jews don't have the same sort of motivation?"

Before Ryan could respond Oscar continued, "Actually, I shouldn't let you bully me into saying *the* Jews. *Some* Jews take advantage of our society's vices in order to make money. Most Jews don't. My dentist, Dr. Steinberg, is a Jew, I believe. The newsstand where I buy magazines is operated by a Jew. One of the contract people I deal with in the Pentagon is Jewish—excuse me, a Jew— and so was one of my best professors at Colorado. I simply can't buy the theory that they're all part of some gigantic conspiracy to destroy our race. I think that you're making a lot of unjustified assumptions.

"Our race certainly is being destroyed. But it's we ourselves who are the destroyers. We've let ourselves become decadent. We've lost our sense of identity and purpose. We're wallowing in our own vices. We've left ourselves open to exploitation by everyone else on the planet.

"If you want to pin the blame on a more specific group, you can blame your own employers, the greedy, gutless, lying politicians and bureaucrats who run the rotten and irresponsible government for which you're working."

Ryan shrugged. "Yeager, I have to agree with a large part of what you've said. The American people *are* decadent. The politicians *are* crooked—and believe me, I've seen a lot more solid evidence of *that* than you can even imagine in your wildest fantasies. The government *is* rotten. We *have* brought a lot of our present grief down on ourselves.

"But I'm not one to make unjustified or unnecessary assumptions. In that regard I'm a true disciple of Occam. Nor did I get where I am in the Bureau by being a crackpot theorist. There is solid, irrefutable, unambiguous evidence for everything I've said about the Jews—and plenty of it, although one may have to dig a bit to find all of it.

"I see from the books in your bookcase that you've done a little reading in history. Perhaps I shouldn't be surprised that you failed to learn much about the Jews, though. You have to be able to read between the lines of most history books written in the last 50 years in order to follow the Jews' trail. It's a taboo subject. There are lots of older books with explicit information in them, but you'll only find most of those in the larger university libraries, certainly not in bookstores. If you're interested I'll give you a list of titles sometime. By the way, you didn't know that I have a master's degree in history from Georgetown University, did you? Really, I'm not just a dumb cop, Yeager."

Ryan paused for a second and then continued: "Of course, you're right when you say that your dentist and the Jew who runs your neighborhood newsstand aren't participants in a conspiracy to destroy us. I'm sure that most Jews in this country have their hands full just making the payments on their condos and putting their kids through dental school. They don't have time for much conspiring.

"But you're also wrong. It depends upon how you look at it. I'll give you an example. The United States fought a war against Germany a few years back. It was a bloody, hard-fought war. It was a deadly serious war. Americans were told that Germany was our enemy. Germans were told that America was their enemy. We killed millions of them, and they killed hundreds of thousands of us.

"Now you can easily convince me that there were lots of German dentists and newsstand operators and university professors who didn't hate Americans and who weren't conspiring against us. They were just ordinary Germans, whose hands were full earning a living and raising their families. Some of them may not even have agreed with the policies of their government. Is it fair to say that all these Germans were our enemies?"

Ryan paused for effect and then answered his own question: "Of course, it is. They were our enemies because they paid with their taxes for the bullets their soldiers used against us. Even if they weren't in the trenches and the tanks, they were keeping the home front going, in one way or another. They thought of themselves as members of the German nation, and we were at war with the German nation.

"Do you get the idea, Yeager? Your Jewish dentist pays his taxes too, with his contributions to the United Jewish Appeal. He may not be in the front lines with the fellows from B'nai B'rith, but you can bet that he does his part on the home front in lots of little ways. He votes for the politicians who vote for your taxes to be sent to Israel.

He writes letters with the right slant to the editor of the *Washington Post*. He's probably very civic minded, working with the PTA, where he can keep an eye on the teachers hired by the school board; serving on the county library board, where he can have some input into the types of books the library stocks; and acting as a patron of the local art museum or theater group, where he can ensure that we get a few carved African masks and tom-toms in the museum or some really freaky stage performances, with an affirmative action cast.

"Or maybe your dentist is one of those really rare Jews who doesn't pay a bit of attention to what the B'nai B'rith tells him and doesn't even buy Israel Bonds. He still thinks of himself as a member of the Jewish people, and the Jewish people—the Jewish nation, the Jewish race, whatever you want to call the damned thing—is at war with our people, make no mistake about it.

"I've been in the front lines of one little part of that war long enough to have a pretty good understanding of it. Actually, my understanding began even before I joined the Bureau. My dad used to tell us at the dinner table about his work during and right after the Second World War. He had been working mostly on internal subversion until the war began, then they put him in the counterespionage section. That's when *he* learned about the Jews.

"These days whenever people hear about espionage during the war they think of German agents landed by submarine with maps of defense installations, or Japs with secret radio transmitters, that sort of thing. Actually the counterespionage people in the Bureau spent only about ten per cent of their time during the war catching Nazi and Jap spies, because they had to spend 90 per cent of their time trying to keep the Jews from stealing every secret we had and passing it along to the Soviet Union. My dad could never get over the fact that we were fighting the war for the Jews in the first place, and they showed their gratitude by selling us out to the Reds.

"If you learned anything at all from those history books," Ryan waved toward the bookcase, "you know that Roosevelt had been doing everything he could in 1940 and 1941 to provoke the Germans into declaring war. He had the Bureau fingering German agents in this country to the British, who had been at war with the Germans since September 1939, of course, and then playing dumb when those agents were murdered. He had our Navy tracking German ships and reporting their positions to the British, so they could be sunk. He let his Jewish Treasury secretary, Morgenthau, seize German assets in this country. Finally he ordered our Navy to shoot at German ships on sight. Hitler, however, refused to be provoked. Roosevelt eventually had to get us into the war by the back door, by setting us up for the Japanese 'surprise' attack on Pearl Harbor.

"And all the time a cabal of Jewish 'advisors'—Morgenthau, Baruch, Frankfurter, Rosenman, Cohen—was telling him exactly what to do and when to do it. And in turn they were on the phone every day with the head Jews in New York, London, and Moscow. Hoover had taps on half the telephones in Washington, and he knew everything that was going on.

"After the Germans attacked the Soviet Union in June 1941, Jews in every one of our defense establishments began swiping secret documents and giving them to the Soviets. Hoover complained to Roosevelt about it, but FDR wouldn't let him arrest them. About all Hoover could do was quietly warn some of the top military people and the big industrialists doing defense work, so that they could move Jewish subordinates to less sensitive positions and tighten up security. After Pearl Harbor, of course, the Soviet Union was officially our 'ally.' But even though Roosevelt continued to protect the Jews, Hoover kept the Bureau on top of everything that was going on, collecting evidence and biding his time.

"Then when FDR died early in 1945, Hoover lowered the boom on the kikes. The Bureau rounded up hundreds of them who were involved in espionage work for the Soviets. That's when my dad saw how the Jews are organized, how they work together and back each other up. Terrific pressure was brought on Hoover to stop arresting Jews for espionage. He would have caved in if he hadn't spent years gathering the means to protect himself. He had confidential dossiers on most of the top politicians. One of them would get an angry call from Morgenthau or one of the other Jewish leaders, demanding that something be done to curb the FBI. The politician would in turn call Hoover, and Hoover would invite him to drop by the Bureau for a friendly chat. Then Hoover would show him a few choice items from his personal dossier. The politician would immediately forget all about trying to pressure Hoover into halting the investigation of Jewish spies.

"Eventually, though, Hoover was forced to compromise with the Jews. A few dozen of them who had been caught red-handed—most notably the Rosenbergs and their accomplices—were put on trial and convicted. The investigative files on hundreds of others were quietly closed. And from that time on the Jews were determined to capture the Bureau for themselves. As long as Hoover was alive, however, they couldn't do much. And he built a lot of internal roadblocks into the FBI bureaucracy to slow them down even after he died in 1972.

"But they are persistent bastards, and they are well on the way to completing their takeover of the Bureau. It won't make much difference who's appointed Director after that; they'll control the internal workings of the Bureau—what's left of it—and do whatever they please. I've fought them to the extent I've been able. But I have a family, and I'm not the martyr type. Everything I've done has been in the way of bureaucratic infighting. I've gone by the book.

"Fortunately, however, there is a provident God in heaven, and he has delivered you into my hands. You're going to do some of the things I've wanted to do but couldn't." Ryan glanced at his watch again. "Now start taking notes, Yeager. I haven't got all night."

XIII

The Kaplan job was not difficult. Armed with a detailed knowledge of the man's habits and weekly schedule, a description of his automobile, and a wealth of other personal data, Oscar quickly laid his plans.

Kaplan was addicted to pornography, Ryan had told him. He kept a stack of kinky photographs in his desk and regularly showed them around the office to the other agents, despite the fact that most of them did not share his obsession and looked at the photographs now and then only from a morbid curiosity to see what weird, new perversions the Jewish agent was drooling over at the time. Kaplan was so hung up on the stuff, Ryan had said in a tone of obvious disgust, that he stopped by a porno store just four blocks from the Hoover Building every Wednesday evening on his way home; the store normally received its shipments of new stock on Wednesdays.

The idea of using Kaplan's vice as a means for bringing about his downfall appealed to Oscar. The porno store itself did not seem auspicious as a site, however. It was a narrow stall in the middle of an extraordinarily busy block, with no obvious parking facility. Furthermore, the timing of Kaplan's after-work visits to the store would make it necessary for Oscar to do his work in daylight. Nevertheless, he decided to be present at the expected time of Kaplan's next appearance there.

Decked out in the same wig, fake glasses, and other paraphernalia he had used at the Shoreham and with a brand new silenced pistol—a duplicate of the one he had used on Jones and Jacobs, with the same silencer screwed onto the muzzle—in a shoulder holster under his coat, Oscar strolled into Hyman's Novelty Book and Photo Shop for a quick look around, half an hour before Kaplan was due to leave his office. He had had to park more than six blocks away. He couldn't understand why Kaplan favored this particular porno store. There were three others in the same block, all larger, better lighted, and with more stock. Perhaps the appeal of this place was that it seemed to have relatively little business, and so a customer concerned about not being seen in such an establishment might feel more secure, or perhaps it carried some line of filth that the others didn't. Perusing the shelves he saw a sampling of just about every kind of perversion one could imagine: sadism, bondage, homosexuality, bestiality, interracial sex, and various other practices that seemed so bizarre to him that it was hard to imagine anyone deriving sexual pleasure from them. About all that seemed to be missing was material dealing with straight sex between men and women of the same race.

The man behind the counter, a grossly overweight, dark, greasy-looking specimen with a cigar in his mouth, was eyeing Oscar closely. Oscar glanced at his watch, strolled out, and took up a post two doors down, where he could appear to be absorbed in a study of the book titles in a crowded display window, yet still keep an eye on the entrance to Hyman's place.

He spotted Kaplan nearly a block away as the latter emerged from his car, which he had just parked illegally in front of a fire hydrant. If Oscar were to hit the man when he returned to his car, there would be scores of witnesses.

He made a quick decision. He had been watching the sparse traffic in and out of Hyman's door, and he knew that there were no customers in the shop at the moment, nor was anyone else likely to enter in the next minute. So Oscar himself quickly re-entered the store, about 15 seconds ahead of Kaplan.

Even as he came through the door he had his pistol in his hand, and he fired two shots into the proprietor's forehead at a range of about four feet without breaking his stride. The latter toppled sideways off his stool into the dark, narrow space behind the counter. The noise of the body crashing to the floor was louder than that of the silenced pistol shots, but Oscar was certain that no one on the busy, noisy sidewalk would notice either sound.

He continued a dozen feet down the narrow shop's single aisle, then turned on his heel just beyond a wire display rack of paperback books, which sufficed to conceal his gun hand. Oscar's head was bent over the rack as if he were examining a book, but he was peering over the top of his glasses at Kaplan as the man entered the shop.

Kaplan glanced with curiosity at the unattended counter and halted for a moment before hesitantly walking further into the shop, toward Oscar. When he was eight feet away, Oscar raised his hand and shot the man six times in the chest and head, firing rapidly. Kaplan fell face down, and Oscar bent over the body and fired two more shots into the back of his head.

Oscar ejected the empty magazine from his pistol and slipped in a loaded one, then leaned over the counter and fired four more shots into the side of the proprietor's head before returning the weapon to its holster. Finally, he took two small plastic packets of white powder from his coat pocket, kneeled beside Kaplan's corpse, and pressed the man's dead fingers onto them several times before sliding the packets into a pocket of Kaplan's suit coat. As an afterthought he took Kaplan's wallet.

The cocaine—both the idea and the actual packets—had come from Ryan, who thought it would be better to muddy the water a bit by leaving a hint that Kaplan's killing may have been connected to casual drug dealing instead of to his regular line of work. There was an average of two drug-related murders a day in Washington, and so the hint should meet little resistance.

Oscar buttoned his coat and stepped out onto the sidewalk. As he turned the corner at the end of the block he glanced back briefly. No one was near the entrance to Hyman's store. Back at his car he noted that it had been less than an hour since he had left home. He still had one errand to do before meeting Adelaide, and he should be able to finish it without missing the 7:30 deadline he had promised her he would try to keep.

His next stop was the Library of Congress, where he had the amazing good luck to find a parking space only two blocks away. He had tried to obtain some of the books he wanted at the suburban libraries, but, as Ryan had indicated, they were not to be found there. Here he expected his search to be more productive.

He had spent the first four days after his encounter with Ryan just trying to become accustomed to his changed situation, turning over in his mind the various possibilities now open to him. It was something that needed getting used to. The skiing trip with Adelaide had helped him orient himself. He had spent several more hours talking with her about race and human quality, race and history, racial conditions in America, the racial prospects for the future, and his own need to act against the manifest evil of the genocide he saw taking place, all without getting into the specific details of what he had been doing.

At the same time he had been puzzling over a new element in the picture: the Jews. After hearing what Ryan had said about Jews, his first inclination was to dismiss the man's remarks as cranky anti-Semitism, just as he had dismissed Keller's views on the Jews earlier. He had seen enough of that sort of mindless bigotry, and he had no patience with it. Ryan, with his old-fashioned, Irish-Catholic conservatism, had probably imbibed his dislike of Jews from some paleolithic Jesuit teacher in parochial school who still taught that Jews were "Christ killers," in defiance of the new party line from the Vatican. And Keller was tied in with that neo-Nazi group, which explained his own theories about the Jews.

One thing that made it hard to put the issue out of his mind was that neither Ryan nor Keller fit his mental image of a religious bigot. Both men were obviously quite intelligent and well informed. Keller was a trained scholar, and even Ryan might be considered one; certainly the FBI official showed none of the religious narrow-mindedness and superstition Oscar had encountered among more primitive Christians, Protestant and Catholic. And Keller didn't even profess Christianity. Keller especially, with his laid-back, easygoing manner, just wasn't the uptight, neurotic "hater" Oscar expected an anti-Semite to be.

Beyond these considerations there was a certain plausibility to what both men had said, and that really bothered him. He was sure there was a "catch" somewhere—that the apparent sense their statements made would fall apart under closer scrutiny. So far, however, in going over their arguments in his mind and in referring to books in his own library, he had not been able to find the flaw. He had a list of a dozen or so reference books he wanted to consult in the Library of Congress in order to settle the issue.

It was during the long drive home from skiing Monday night, when Adelaide had gone to sleep with her head in his lap, that he had first been able to reflect on the reasons why Keller and Ryan's anti-Semitism troubled him. More than the negative stereotype of Jew-haters he had accepted uncritically from the mass media, there was the conflict with his own ideas on race and history, which had not come to him easily and were not easily to be abandoned.

He realized that in the past he had had a tendency to be one-dimensional in his thinking on the subject. The dimension was intelligence. In Oscar's scheme the races of man were ordered in a simple hierarchy of intelligence. Individuals differed, of course, but on the average one could with reasonable accuracy judge the intelligence of races by noting their historical accomplishments—or by observing the performance of a large enough sample of individuals in the present. By either standard Blacks were an inferior race, and interbreeding between Whites and Blacks could only pull the former down. Jews, on the other hand, were clearly as intelligent as any other Whites—perhaps more so, if one judged them by current performance rather than by historical accomplishment, which, he had to admit, was rather scanty, despite their own vainglorious boast of being the inventors of monotheism and a moral light to the nations down through the ages.

The more he examined his racial scheme, the more he saw its inadequacies. It really was too simple. There were too many facts it didn't account for. Orientals, for example, clearly were *different* from Whites, both physically and psychically, but was it accurate to say that they were *inferior*? Certainly not on the basis of intelligence, as measured by standard IQ tests. How, then, to fit them into his racial hierarchy?

Clearly, the reality of racial difference was multi-dimensional. Average intelligence was only one of many, many characteristics which differed from race to race. In fact, what he called "intelligence" undoubtedly was a composite characteristic, which ought to be resolved into a number of components; some races seemed smarter in one way, others in another way.

Blacks, for example, had a capacity for verbal and behavioral mimicry which often concealed a real inadequacy in cognitive intelligence. He had seen through this protective coloration in school, where he had observed a number of Blacks with remarkably well-developed social skills, who were able to move comfortably in White circles and gave the impression of being alert and capable. They talked like Whites and dressed like Whites; they had separated themselves from the bulk of their race and seemed more like Whites than Blacks, if one ignored the obvious physical differences.

When put to the test, however, not one of them could measure up to White intellectual standards. Most of them seemed to be aware of that fact themselves, and so steered clear of situations where they would be put to the test. They avoided the rigorous disciplines like the plague, concentrating themselves in the pablum curricula, and the very few who did take mathematics, engineering, or science courses performed with uniform mediocrity.

So if one were evaluating races on the basis of the kind of intelligence required to be a good actor or public performer, Blacks would have a much higher relative rating than if judged on the basis of their ability to deal with abstract concepts and solve problems. One had to be very careful in talking about "inferiority" and "superiority." The terms made sense only when referred to a specific, well defined characteristic. A race judged inferior on the basis of one characteristic might be superior on the basis of another.

That was all well and good. He needed to refine his views substantially. He had been too simplistic in the past. Instead of analyzing things carefully and dispassionately, he had reacted hotly to the obvious fraud being perpetrated by the news and entertainment media, which tried to persuade everyone that Blacks were "equal" to Whites in intelligence, creativity, originality, and enterprise: that their feelings, tendencies, and thought processes were exactly like those of Whites—or were exactly like those Whites would have if their circumstances were the same as those of the Blacks. And in reacting he had focused on the most easily refutable element in the fraud: namely, that Blacks had the same cognitive intelligence, on the average, as Whites.

So what were the implications of a more realistic, multidimensional view of racial differences? How should that affect the role of the Jews in his scheme of things? Both Keller and Ryan had disagreed with his assumption that Jews were racially White. A couple of the books he was seeking dealt with the racial history of the Jews. He wanted to absorb the facts first and then think about the implications.

And what if the Jews' origins in the Middle East and their subsequent history gave them a significantly different genetic heritage from Whites of European ancestry? Keller and Ryan had suggested that the Jews possessed a special sort of inborn malevolence, a genetically based hatred of the world, which expressed itself in an all-encompassing, though cleverly concealed, campaign against their White neighbors. To Oscar that seemed fantastic.

More specifically, Keller and Ryan had made some allegations about the Jewish control of the news and entertainment media and the way in which that control was used. If true, those allegations would go a long way toward supporting their whole case against the Jews. If false, Oscar could fairly easily dismiss the case. Several of the books he was seeking at the Library of Congress were concerned with the men who ran the mass media.

XIV

What Oscar had expected to be a brief, simple research project—the checking of a few dozen facts, perhaps the reading of a book or two—turned out to be neither brief nor simple. He had spent an average of six hours a day for the past ten days poring over the 300-plus pages of photocopies he had made Wednesday of the previous week at the Library of Congress and over a good two dozen books to which that material had led him, the latter obtained through interlibrary loan via the Arlington library. It was Saturday afternoon now, and he was worried. Not only had he failed to disprove Ryan and Keller's thesis about the Jews, but he had convinced himself that they were at least partly right.

That is, he had verified several of their claims about what Jews were doing now and had done in the past; he still was far from ready to accept their assertion that the Jews as a whole regularly conspired together and acted in concert or that their collective motivation was to destroy the White race, however. In fact, he had turned up a couple of instances where the Jews seemed clearly to be divided into groups at odds with each other. And there were long periods of history during which they were quite powerful in one country or another, but apparently made no effort to destroy their hosts there.

One topic he had concentrated on was the Jewish role in the mass media, both because it was a matter of crucial importance and because the evidence was fairly easy to gather. He now realized that it was not just Hollywood the Jews controlled, but virtually the entire entertainment industry. In each entertainment medium he had examined—films, radio and television broadcasting, mass-circulation magazines, mass-market paperback books—the Jewish presence was overwhelming, and it consisted of much more than a few Jewish executives at the top. The largest producer of television entertainment programs, for example, was MCA, Inc., and virtually every director and officer of the giant corporation was a Jew.

The same was true of the news industry: every medium, and virtually every organ of every medium, was under either direct or indirect Jewish control.

What really amazed Oscar was the extent and depth of the Jewish influence in the media. In news, for instance, the top three newspapers in the country, in terms of influence—the *New York Times*, the *Washington Post*, and the *Wall Street Journal*—were all owned outright by Jews. There were many small, independent newspapers owned by non-Jews, and a few large ones as well, but even in these he found a surprisingly high percentage of Jews in key editorial positions.

Furthermore, he was made aware of the fact that it was not the nickels and dimes from subscribers which paid the editors' salaries and made the publishers' profits—it was the revenue from advertisers. The biggest advertisers in every big-city newspaper Oscar examined were the chain stores and department stores, and the Jewish presence in these was heavy enough so that if the Jewish businessmen in any city were unhappy with the editorial policies of the local newspaper and withheld their advertising from it, it could not survive.

Everything was not immediately obvious, of course. He had had to do quite a bit of digging to come up with all the facts, repeatedly checking lists of directors against biographical reference works to determine the ethnicity of doubtful cases. As an example, in checking out the Hollywood film industry he thought at first he had found a substantial non-Jewish moviemaker in the Walt Disney Studios. Further investigation revealed that although the company's founder, Walt Disney, had been a Gentile, within a few years after the man's death his heirs had been bought out by Jews, and Walt Disney Studios was currently as Jewish as the rest of Hollywood. Likewise with some of the other entities in the world of the mass media: Gentile names would be prominently associated with them, but when one looked closer one found that they were subsidiaries of other outfits, with Jews at the helm.

What did it all mean? It was becoming clear to Oscar that the Jews, just through their control of the mass media, had the *potential* for being the nasty adversaries of the White race Ryan and Keller claimed they were. And were they not in fact *acting* as adversaries? Were not the mass media the most racially destructive force at work in the world today?

As far back as Vietnam he had recognized the newspaper and television news people as an especially treacherous pack of scoundrels, who had deliberately set out to prevent an American victory and had succeeded. At the time he had put this down to a pro-communist bias. But could it not just as well have been that what they wanted to prevent was a *White* victory, and that their bias was anti-White more than pro-communist?

The trouble with that was that the majority of the rank-and-file news people weren't Jews; they were Whites, and yet he remembered them as a perverse, lying, smirking gang of bastards, who could hardly conceal their glee at every American reverse and who made a point of grossly misrepresenting everything they reported. Did they behave like that because their Jewish bosses told them to?

Oscar didn't believe it. He was sufficiently familiar with human nature to recognize all of the little signs which told him that their behavior was voluntary.

The same could be said for many of the aspects of the disintegration of White society after the Vietnam war. The media enthusiastically promoted every form of degeneracy and sickness, but the White population certainly was putting up no resistance to them. Could one fairly blame racial mixing, permissiveness and the decline of standards of behavior and performance, feminism, liberalism, the explosion of homosexuality, modern anti-art, the replacement of traditional White music with rock and other non-White forms, the spread of drugs, and a thousand other ills on the mass media, just because the media provided a tolerant atmosphere for these things? Couldn't it be that everyone, the general public as well as the media people, including the Jews, was just going along for the same ride? If that were the case, then the most the Jews could be blamed for was a failure to use the power of their news and entertainment media to combat degenerative tendencies in the population: in other words, a sin of omission rather than one of commission.

He really needed to talk to someone, and so he gave Harry Keller a call and arranged to meet him Sunday afternoon.

Then he called Adelaide to tell her he had finished his work for the day and to make arrangements for dinner. "I know it's only four o'clock, baby, but why don't you come on over now? I've been beating my brains out with a crash study program, and now I need your presence badly."

"Uh-huh! What you mean is you need my body."

"Well, that too."

"Oscar, you've been promising for more than a week to help me find a new pair of skis. Why can't we do that now?"

There was a slightly plaintive note in her voice. And it was true: her present skis were a little too long for her, and she had trouble keeping them under control. Furthermore, the bindings weren't satisfactory. They were her first skis, and she really hadn't known what she was doing when she bought them. After approximately her twentieth fall during their skiing trip two weeks ago, he had told her he would buy new skis and bindings for her as soon as they returned home. He had already put her off twice since then, first because he was preparing for the Kaplan job, and then because he was absorbed in his research project.

"Okay, sweetheart, we will. We can make love after dinner. Bring your boots over, and we'll take care of it. I think the store is open until six."

Then Ryan called. He didn't identify himself, but the voice was unmistakable: "Meet me at the entrance to the Clarendon metro station in 20 minutes."

"Is that really necessary? I have another appointment now. Can we meet tomorrow morning instead?"

"Yeager, you'd better be at that metro station in 20 minutes." Then Ryan hung up.

Shit! He really had to figure out how to get Ryan off his back soon. It was a sticky situation. Looking at it from Ryan's point of view, if Oscar ever got caught by someone else—the local police, say—how could Ryan be sure Oscar wouldn't involve him in order to gain some advantage? Even now, Oscar probably could tell a pretty convincing story about why he killed Kaplan, how he knew so many personal details about his victim, and so on.

No, clearly Ryan couldn't afford to give him many more assignments. And for the same reason, Ryan couldn't afford to arrest him himself. In fact, if the FBI agent wanted to sleep easily at night, he couldn't even afford to let Oscar continue living much longer. Very soon Oscar was going to have to deal with Ryan, before Ryan dealt with him. Even the meeting Ryan was demanding for this afternoon might be intended for the latter purpose.

Oscar didn't think so, though. Ryan had been too cold and peremptory on the telephone. If the man's intention were to lure Oscar to his own execution, he would have been a little friendlier and more expansive, in order to lull Oscar's suspicions. He hoped his intuition was correct as, with a heavy heart, he called Adelaide again to postpone their shopping date a third time.

Just inside the entrance to the metro station he spotted Ryan. He squeezed his left arm against the reassuring hardness of the weapon in his shoulder holster as the other man gestured to him to follow and began walking down the stairs toward the train platform. They took up a position in the shadow of a column near the far end of the platform with their backs against the station wall, where they could talk without being overheard and without being conspicuous.

"Congratulations, Yeager. You did a first-class job on Kaplan—not only putting the coke in his pocket like I suggested, but hitting him inside that sleazy porno joint. The details are gossip all over the Bureau. I saw to that. The Yids who had been pushing that perverted little turd as Yahweh's gift to the Bureau are keeping pretty quiet now." Ryan grinned, genuinely pleased.

"Now, listen carefully. Your next target is a man named Daniel Feldman. He's 33 years old with black hair and dark brown eyes. His hair is in tight ringlets close to the skull, almost like nigger wool. Medium complexion, maybe slightly on the 'olive' side. Height five feet ten inches. Medium build, about 160 pounds. His nose isn't big, but it's definitely Jewish, if you know what I mean." Ryan paused, watching Oscar's face.

Oscar said nothing, and Ryan pulled a photograph from his pocket and held it where Oscar could see it: "Study the face. You can't have this photo, so remember the details. Notice his cocky little grin. The bastard is always grinning. It's his trademark. At first I thought it's because he's nervous, insecure. Another thing that might lead a person to believe that is that he's a little jerky in his movements, and he always talks fast, like he's wound up too tight.

"Now I think the grin is calculated; it's Feldman's way of keeping people off their guard. And let me warn you, Yeager, he's a lot more dangerous than any rattlesnake you'll ever see, so be careful. He's a cold-blooded killer, and if you make a false move you won't get a chance to make another move. He doesn't play by any rules at all. If he even *thinks* you might be after him, with no evidence at all, he'll blow your brains out in front of 50 witnesses and worry about justifying himself later."

"Whom does he work for? The Mafia?"

"No, he's one of us, believe it or not," Ryan replied with a trace of incredulity in his voice, as if he couldn't believe it himself. "He's one of our dirty tricks specialists. The Bureau does a lot of things it really shouldn't, things which aren't strictly legal—in fact, some things which are illegal as hell. Feldman learned his tricks in the Israeli Defense Forces. He's a dual citizen. More than half of our dirty tricks people are.

"Let me tell you just one of the things he did for us. When we rounded up all of those Klansmen last year and put them away on conspiracy charges, it wasn't as clean an operation as you might think. We first grabbed a couple of them, pressured them to squeal on three or four of their buddies, pressured some of those in turn to squeal on others, and so on until we had them all.

"Most of those Klan jerks are easy to pressure; generally the ones who talk toughest and have the biggest arsenal of weapons at home are the easiest. Just tell 'em how many years they're facing and then stick 'em in a holding cell with about 30 niggers for the night. By morning they're ready to testify against their own mothers.

"But some of the bastards are stubborn, and we have to use more pressure. One of the weak ones told us that a buddy had a case of hand grenades, but when we grabbed the buddy he wouldn't tell us where he had his grenades stashed. I was there in this guy's house with three other agents and Feldman. We had handcuffed his wife too, as an accomplice. That's standard procedure. We generally have to let the women go later, but it gives us more leverage in persuading a man to talk if we've arrested his woman.

"The guy's two kids were there too: a seven-year-old boy and a 14-year-old girl, a good-looking little thing. So when the guy refuses to talk, Feldman starts playing with the girl, talking dirty to her, pinching her tits, putting his hand on her ass. Pretty soon he has her crying and scared out of her wits, backed up against a wall. I and another agent were holding the guy, and a third agent was holding his wife. The guy was putting up a big ruckus, shouting and cursing us, but not offering to tell us where his grenades were.

"Without any warning Feldman suddenly takes out his pecker, grabs the girl by her hair, starts screaming at her, and forces her to her knees. Then, in front of the guy and his wife and little boy, he puts his gun to her head and makes the girl give him a blow job. The guy goes right out of his mind. Before Feldman even has his pecker in her mouth, he's telling us where he buried the grenades. But Feldman goes ahead and makes the girl finish. It really made me sick."

"You were there too, Ryan. What happened is your responsibility too."

"Yeah, that's why Feldman's gotta go. We've got others just as bad, but Feldman's the only one I've worked with directly. He's the only one who can say I ever broke the rules. He's the one threat they can use against me if I make an open move against the Jews in the Bureau."

"What the hell is a police agency like the FBI doing with maniacs like Feldman working for it in the first place?"

"Jesus, Yeager, you're a dumb bastard! Feldman's not a maniac. He's just a Jew. He never really loses his cool. What he did to that girl—everything he does—is calculated, cold-blooded meanness. Why do you think he didn't rape her or beat her up instead? Because then there'd be physical evidence. Then she could go to a doctor, and he'd back up her story. It might even get in the papers, and we'd be in a mess. As it was he didn't leave a mark on her. He used terror to make her do what he wanted, and that doesn't show the way a beating would. Who'd believe the girl or the guy or his wife? They're redneck White racists, the lowest of the low in the eyes of the media. The news people just laugh at them when they complain about some of our methods.

"Of course, I don't approve of Feldman's tactics. He goes too far. In most cases we could get the same results without being quite so brutal. Still, every police agency needs people who're willing to be rough and break the rules, otherwise we'd lose our grip on the situation. We've got to be tougher and meaner than the guys we're up against, or we won't be able to control them. The trouble today is that *our* people, the ones who'd like this to be a decent country, are too soft. The Whites we're recruiting into the Bureau from the universities now are mostly wimps. They grew up believing in flower power and equal rights for criminals. They're wimps with guns and badges, but still wimps.

"So we've got a lot of these dual-citizenship Jewboys from the IDF in the Bureau to do the dirty work. They really know how to be vicious. They all practiced on Palestinians before we hired them. Christ, you ought to hear some of the stories Feldman tells about how they interrogate Palestinians over in Israel. They use the same principle he used on the Klan guy—that is, they make the poor bastard watch while they beat up on his wife and kids—only a lot worse. Over there they don't have to worry about physical evidence. They can use brute force as well as terror. Raping Palestinians' wives and daughters is one of the mildest things they do. He told me how they castrated an eleven-year-old Palestinian kid to force a confession out of a suspected terrorist—cut the little boy's balls off with a pair of scissors while his father was watching.

"As I said, I don't approve of that sort of thing myself. If you keep doing a good job for me like you did on Kaplan, we'll be able to get all the kikes like Feldman out of the Bureau."

"I must say, Ryan, what you've told me about Feldman would make this particular assignment a real pleasure. But how much longer do you think this little partnership of ours can go on? You don't really think you're going to get me to kill every Jewish agent in the FBI, do you?"

"The partnership will last as long as I want it to last, Yeager—unless you develop suicidal tendencies before I'm through with you," was the icy reply.

"Ryan, you talk pretty tough, but, believe it or not, I'm not going to let you use me for your purposes indefinitely." Oscar's voice was calm but very firm. "You think you've got me by the balls. But I'm sure you understand that I've also got you by the balls now. You start squeezing, and I'll start squeezing.

"Or maybe you figure you can safely terminate me when you're done with me or when I start giving you trouble—killed while resisting arrest, eh? It might behoove you to take into consideration the fact that I don't find such a prospect agreeable, and I'm not the type to just sit and wait for it to happen. I might decide to terminate you first and take my chances on what'll happen after that.

"So listen to this, Ryan. For the last 17 days I've been the junior partner in our enterprise, but now I've decided to give myself a promotion to full partner. Either you explain to me just what your plans are, and then we both decide that it will be mutually beneficial for us to continue working together, or we dissolve the partnership here and now—with or without bloodshed. What do you think about that, partner?"

"Yeager, you are a pain in the ass. I don't owe you a goddamned thing. You owe me everything. I've saved your butt." Ryan had switched from a threatening tone to one of exasperation. "This isn't the time or place to talk about long-range plans. If you absolutely have to know the reasons behind the assignments I'm giving you, I'll tell you later, when we have more time to talk. Now, the best place for you to catch Feldman . . . ."

Oscar interrupted impatiently, "I guess you didn't understand what I just told you, Ryan. Good-bye." Oscar started to walk away.

Ryan's right hand shot out toward Oscar's left arm. Oscar intercepted the other man's hand with his own left hand, and they locked grips. At the same time Oscar spun away from Ryan on his left heel, keeping his right hand out of reach as it went for his pistol, which he kept concealed beneath his coat while aiming at Ryan's chest.

"You son of a bitch!" This time there was barely controlled fury in Ryan's voice.

"Easy, boy!" Oscar came back. "I've got the drop on you now. Remember, I said it could be either with or without bloodshed. Push me just a little more, and I'll kill you right here."

For nearly a minute the two men remained motionless and tensed for action. Then the fury slowly drained from Ryan's eyes, and he relaxed his grip on Oscar's hand. "All right, Yeager," he sighed, "we'll talk."

"Fine. I'm going to turn your hand loose now so no one else on the platform will get the wrong idea about us, but I'm going to keep you covered. Don't get an urge to scratch any itches inside your coat."

Ryan cleared his throat. "The situation is this: my boss—that's Vic Rizzo, chief of the Anti-Terrorism Section—has been given an ultimatum. The Bureau is under terrific pressure to stop you, and now the Director has set a time limit for Vic. The Jews in the Bureau have been sniping at Vic and me for a long time, gradually undermining our positions, especially Vic's, with the aim of jumping Kaplan over me to section chief as soon as they could get rid of Vic. When you started snuffing interracial couples in January, they really turned up the heat on him—started leaking hints to the press that the reason you hadn't been caught is that he's incompetent.

"Now, of course, they've lost their candidate. And unless you do something really stupid, I can keep you from getting caught. In other words, in about a month I'm going to be chief of the Anti-Terrorism Section.

"That wouldn't be so important if Vic would take a stand against the Jews, but he won't. We've discussed the situation a hundred times. He's afraid of them. He knows they've been trying to get him out for years, but he won't fight back. I will—very discreetly, of course.

"In the past ten years the Anti-Terrorism Section has become one of the most important departments in the Bureau. In the future it'll be *the* most important, judging by the way American society is going. That's why the Jews were so hot to have Kaplan as its chief. The thing about it is that, with the exception of the Counter-Espionage Section, everything else the Bureau does is concerned with ordinary criminal activity: bank robberies, drugs, kidnapping, wire fraud, and the rest. The Anti-Terrorism Section, on the other hand, is concerned with *political* acts—the sort of thing you've been doing, the sort of thing those Klan assholes were talking about doing, the sort of thing the Puerto Rican nationalists have been doing off and on for 50 years. The FBI has been evolving toward a national political police force whose main job is not to solve crimes but to protect the System from those who want to overthrow it or change it by unconstitutional means. We're becoming an American version of the KGB.

"The country is unraveling, and our job is to hold it together—or, at least, to slow the process. With close to two million non-White immigrants pouring into the country each year—Hispanics, Haitians, Asians—with our central cities largely taken over by drug gangs, with Black wolf packs roaming out of control, with White kids learning about life in jungle-style schools where they're preyed on by non-Whites, with political corruption in Washington and in every statehouse and city hall growing by leaps and bounds, and with all the other crap that's going on now, the White majority that used to be the backbone of the country is breaking up, losing its grip. We've lost our sense of community, of solidarity. People don't care about the country any more; they're busy just taking care of themselves and their families. The country has become atomized into a million different factions, all yelling for what *they* want, and to hell with everybody else.

"Some people try to get what they want using their money and their political influence. That's okay. Others try to use violence or the threat of violence. That's not okay. That's terrorism. That's what we're paid to prevent.

"Used to be most of the terrorism was from the left: war protesters bombing banks and burning down ROTC buildings during the

1960s. After the Vietnam war it started coming more and more from the right: Whites against school busing, abortion clinic bombers, tax protesters. That's when the Jews decided it had to be stopped. They also were becoming more worried that the Arabs would carry the Palestinian struggle to this country.

"Anyway, the time is almost here when the government can't survive without an effective anti-terrorism force. There've been rumors in the Bureau for some time that the Anti-Terrorism Section eventually will be split off from the rest of the Bureau and will become the basis for a brand new Federal agency. We're going to be the new Praetorians. And I'm going to have something to say about the way those Praetorians are used. I'm going to make sure the right people are in the key positions everywhere in my section, so that there'll be no chance of the Jews taking it over. Feldman has to go, for the reason I've already mentioned. Then there are maybe three others we'll have to deal with in order for me to have a free hand. So don't worry about having to kill every Hebe in the Bureau."

"Well, Ryan, there still are a couple of things about your career plans that make me a little uneasy," Oscar replied. "First, you're basing everything on your assumption that there's really a Jewish conspiracy to take over the FBI and use it to the detriment of our race. Since we last met I've checked out a few things about the Jews, and they've certainly got their fingers in enough pies to make a reasonable man worry, but I'm still not convinced there's any conspiracy or even any malice behind their activities. Furthermore, I can't imagine the FBI being more hostile to our race under Jewish control than it is now. So it's difficult for me to see how my knocking off another four Jewish agents for you is going to further my own cause—to the extent I have a cause.

"And second, it seems to me that if I were in your shoes, the first thing I'd want to do after becoming head honcho in the Anti-Ter-rorism Section is put one Oscar Yeager out of action and take credit for it. I couldn't afford to have him continue raising hell and be blamed for not catching him. I'd be afraid of ending up like Rizzo. And I couldn't afford to take the chance that someone else would catch him first and find out what he knows. So I'd capture him single-handedly, then have to shoot him when he tried to escape. That would solve a couple of problems for me and at the same time prove to my superiors that they'd made the right move when they gave me Rizzo's job. What do you say to that, partner?"

"Jesus, Yeager, if you can't imagine the FBI being more of a threat to the survival of our race than it is now, you haven't got much imagination. Right now all the Bureau does is enforce civil rights laws you happen not to like. If the Jews take over they'll use the

Bureau to run everyone they consider a threat to their own plans right into the ground—and I mean *everyone*, those who obey the laws as well as those who don't. It'll be just the way it was in the Soviet Union in the 1920s and '30s, when Jewish secret police commissars like Jagoda and Yezhov had everyone murdered who had a book hostile to the Jews in his personal library, who was reported to have made an anti-Semitic remark, who even seemed too patriotic or too proud of his family or too honorable in his personal conduct.

"I mean, Christ, we get away with enough shady stuff now, but there are limits; we have to be careful that we don't get on the wrong side of the news media. If the Jews were running the Bureau there wouldn't be any limits, because they wouldn't have to worry about the media blowing the whistle on them. Creeps like Feldman wouldn't be restricted to redneck Kluxers; they could do anything they wanted to anybody's daughter."

"Hold it a second, Ryan. I hate to interrupt, but you just referred to Jagoda—Genrikh Jagoda, I believe his name was—the notorious Soviet secret police commissar. As I mentioned, I've been checking out a few things. I ran across an anti-Semitic tract that also said he was Jewish, but it gave no further information to back up that claim. It also claimed that most of the other Soviet commissars were Jews too. Do you really *know* that Jagoda was a Jew?"

"Sure. The man's real name was Herschel Yehuda. And about half of the commissars were Jews during the 1930s: that in a country where Jews made up about one per cent of the population. But stay away from the anti-Semitic tracts when you're trying to check out things like that. Most of those tracts are trash. The people who write them are notoriously careless with their facts. Go straight to the horse's mouth. The Jewish publications themselves back during that period used to brag about how their brethren in Russia were running the show. Every time one of them got a big promotion, it was reported in the Jewish papers and yearbooks. We've got all of that stuff on microfilm in the Bureau library, from the days when part of our job was to keep an eye on the Reds. You can also find it in the Library of Congress, if you know how to look for it.

"Anyway, Yeager, that's what you should be doing if you still believe that it's just a coincidence that the Jews have always managed to be right in the middle of every bit of anti-White and anti-Western nastiness from the days of the Roman Empire right down to their control of the news and entertainment media today. There's nothing I can say here this afternoon that'll convince you it's planned and it's malicious. You'll have to convince yourself by looking at the evidence, piece by piece, until you've seen so much of it that the preponderance overwhelms you."

Ryan paused for a second, then continued: "As for your second concern, look at it this way. You're *not* going to continue raising hell like a one-man terrorist army after I'm head of the Anti-Terrorism Section. You're right: I couldn't afford it. And you're too smart to waste your talents that way.

"Until now you've just been striking out blindly. Of course, Horowitz was a key player, and even a good strategist may have decided to take him out. But all of the others you've hit—with the exception of Kaplan—have been targets of opportunity. You've just been *reacting.* You haven't been planning. You've been doing what was easiest, taking out somebody who irked you at the moment, instead of doing what made the most sense in the context of a worthwhile objective.

"Now we can plan together. I have instant access to information you could never get by yourself: the information we need for effective planning. We've got *everything* about *everybody* in the Bureau's computers. We can not only pick the right targets together, but I can substantially improve your chances of getting the job done and getting away safely. You've got a nice little shop in your basement, but when it comes to special weapons and related gizmos, I can supply you with stuff you couldn't dream of making for yourself."

"Don't try to patronize me, Ryan. You're not likely to persuade me that when you're the head of the System's Praetorian Guard you're going to be helping me plan the best way to destabilize the System and then providing me with the logistical support to get the job done most efficiently."

"Can't you understand, Yeager? I'm not trying to con you. When I'm running the Anti-Terrorism Section I'll need you more than ever. In fact, I'll need you just as much as you'll need me. Like I told you a minute ago, no modern secret police force can fight terrorism successfully without using a little terrorism of its own.

"Remember when the Argentine Army was fighting the communist terrorists down there a few years ago? They never could have beaten them if they'd refused to take the gloves off and fight dirty. The same thing is true here today, which is why the Bureau uses people like Feldman. In the future I'll need to be able to resort to measures that even Feldman couldn't get away with. If I try to do it with Bureau people, I'll be taking too much of a chance. The Jews will be able to scream 'foul' whenever they want to. The media can turn against me, and I'll be put on trial the same way the Argentine generals were.

"That's why I need you—somebody I have no connection with. Somebody who can do things I can't be blamed for. Get the picture?"

Oscar didn't answer. He saw what Ryan had in mind, but he wondered whether the other man really believed that he would let himself be used as a dirty tricks specialist against poor, dumb slobs like those Klansmen, or against the people around the country who were imitating his own attacks on racially mixed couples. It was clear that the two men could help one another, but it was not at all clear that they had the same ultimate objective. He decided not to raise that issue now.

Ryan resumed: "I really don't need to catch you to stay in the good graces of the Director. Nobody else is really certain that one guy is responsible for all the things you've done, anyway. You've pulled off some spectacular stuff, but in terms of everything going on in the country you account for only a small fraction of the total incidents of terrorism. I can get all the glory I need just by continuing to round up the small fry. Besides, you're going to cut out that high-profile stuff now. I'll find somebody else we can blame for blowing up the People's Committee Against Hate, somebody who doesn't have a good alibi for that evening. That'll make the media happy.

"Now, to get back to Danny Feldman . . . ."

XV

"Harry, I've been absorbing facts about the Jews for the better part of two weeks: their role in founding and promoting the communist movement in the last century, their shenanigans to bring the United States into the First World War, their control of the news and entertainment media. The more I learn the more I realize I don't know. But I am learning. One thing that escapes me, however, is what it all means. I'm already convinced that the Jews are active and influential in national and world affairs far beyond their numbers. But is that something we really need to be concerned about? Does that really put us in a lot worse position than if some other group—the Baptists, say—had their power?"

Oscar had kept his appointment with Harry Keller. He also had kept his commitment to buy Adelaide a new pair of skis. After his meeting with Ryan the previous afternoon he had hurried directly to her apartment and hustled the surprised girl off to the ski store half an hour before it closed. Then he had taken her to a nice restaurant for dinner.

He wanted to make up for neglecting her during the past week, but he also was determined to spend every available minute in his continuing effort to learn about the Jews. For the latter purpose he had slipped out of bed at six o'clock this morning without waking her, fixed himself a pot of coffee, and studied his library materials for more than three hours, until she arose and prepared breakfast for them. He had even squeezed in another hour and a half of study after breakfast, while she, careful not to disturb him, had done some badly needed cleaning of his quarters.

Now she was sitting with him in a corner booth of an ice cream store opposite Harry and Colleen Keller. The place was brightly lighted and crowded. It hardly seemed appropriate for a confidential discussion, but there were teenagers in several other booths, and the background chatter provided a reasonable degree of privacy for Oscar's party.

"Hell, Oscar, I'd be worried if the Baptists were running the country—and I'm sure you would too."

"Well, I guess that wasn't a good example. There'd probably be arrest warrants out for all of us for not being in church this morning." Oscar grinned.

"The point is that any man with his wits about him has to worry when any group but his own wields power which affects his life," Harry responded. "Every group which seeks power has an agenda.

That's true whether they're Baptists or bird watchers or Martians—
or Jews. And since the agenda of every sensible group is formed in
accord with the group's specific interests, the one which has the
power to implement its agenda has a considerable advantage over
those which don't. That's the way the world works, the way it's
always worked.

"Of course, we hear a lot of patter about 'pluralistic democracy.'
We're told that in this country we have a system designed to keep
any one group from grabbing power for itself. In other words, there
is no agenda—and if one looks at the way our government operates,
it's easy to believe that." He gave a wry smile. "But the fact is,
Nature abhors a vacuum in the realm of human affairs as much as
in the physical realm. A society without an agenda is incomplete.
Eventually some group will impose its own agenda on the society,
although it may choose to conceal that fact from persons outside the
group. It may even modify its agenda to avoid conflict with certain
other groups in the society: 'Don't challenge our rule, and we'll
throw the choicest crumbs to you.'

"In any case, the question of which group's agenda shall have
precedence is a vital one for every person in the society. The natural
tendency is for each group to strive to advance its own agenda. We
want our group—that is, the group of persons with the same interests, the same agenda, as ours—to prevail. We don't want some
other group to prevail. That's pretty basic, but you'd be surprised at
how many people either haven't figured it out or who'll disagree
with it. Among the latter are the Christians, who believe it's better
to be shat on than to shit on, and the lunatic-fringe pluralists, who're
opposed to any group prevailing, especially their own.

"To answer your question further, we have to make some assumptions about specific groups' agendas. I assume you'll agree
that, generally speaking, if our group isn't on top it does make a
difference to us which group is. In other words, we should be
concerned about the intentions relative to us of any other group
which exercises any power or influence over our lives. Right?"

"Granted," Oscar replied. "But I believe we should be careful not
to exaggerate the power wielded by any group. I really doubt it
would be correct to say that the Jews are running the country, no
matter how much influence they may have over certain things, like
the mass media."

"In a sense I agree, Oscar. Certainly no single group exercises
total, direct power over every institution in America. For that to be
true, all the members of the Congress, all the judges in the Federal
courts, the people in the White House, the Joint Chiefs of Staff, the
masters of the media, the big bankers, and everyone else whose

decisions make a substantial difference for the country would have
to belong to the same group and be pulling in the same direction.

"Instead there are a lot of different groups pulling in different
directions: the pluralistic ideal. We could spend the rest of the year
discussing the complexities of power in America: who has power
over what and how much. But despite the complexities, it still is true
that some groups manage to get their way most of the time in the
matters which are of greatest concern to us. I think that a reasonable
way to approach the question is to look specifically at the power
wielded by the Jews as a group and see what effects it has. We can
also look at the question of motivation. Since you've been studying
the subject recently, perhaps you already have some ideas about
Jewish power."

"What I have is a jumble of facts rather than any ideas," Oscar
responded. "I hoped our discussion might lead me to a few ideas
which would allow me to organize the facts and draw some conclusions from them. I know, for instance, that Jews have a great deal
of influence in the mass media, and the mass media in turn have a
decisive role in determining most people's opinions and attitudes
on political and social issues. But are the Jews in the media acting
in concert and deliberately pushing public opinion in certain directions in accord with their own group agenda, or are they acting
independently and just sniffing out the mood of the public and the
general drift of events and then, good businessmen that they are,
feeding the public what will sell best? And if it's the latter, why
should we think that any other group of astute businessmen would
act more responsibly?"

"All right, Oscar. That's as good a place as any to start. I believe
we should begin by talking about the Jews' agenda. That'll allow
you to understand the extent to which they work as a group, why
they're so heavily concentrated in the media, and what they intend
to do with their media control. I want to show you a couple of things
they've written in that regard. Why don't you and Adelaide come
home with us?"

"Sure, if it's no trouble for you." Oscar looked at Colleen.

"Not at all."

"Hey, don't I get to finish my ice cream?" Adelaide protested.

"Take your time," Harry responded. "Boy, I'm going to enjoy
this," he chuckled, rubbing his hands together. "It seems like every
other time I've tried to talk about the Jews to someone he's either
been a person who instinctively hates them and is willing to believe
anything bad about them without question, or he's been one of those
soulless bastards without a center, one of those . . . those," he
sputtered for a second, trying to think of the right words. "You know,

one of those Mr. Everyman types, who's never read a book that wasn't on the *New York Times* list of best sellers and never had an opinion that wasn't approved by all three TV networks. I'm sure you've met plenty of them yourself; there are a hundred million of 'em out there. They know that people who don't like Jews are frowned on by all of their favorite talk-show hosts, and so they are absolutely determined not to believe anything bad about Jews. It doesn't matter how much proof you show them. They're as impervious to reason as any woman. Uh, no offense intended, girls.

"But you, Oscar, if I'm any judge of character, are a man who is compelled by reason. No matter how much you want to cling to an idea, I can tear it away from you just by showing you facts which contradict it. And no matter how much you are afraid of an idea, no matter how strongly you resist it, I can force you to accept it, simply by reasoning with you. This is going to be fun. You're going to be my first real convert." Harry chuckled again.

"We'll see about that," Oscar laughed. "I may be susceptible to reason, but it takes me a while to get used to a new idea before I can accept it, reason or no. If I don't feel comfortable with an explanation for something, if my intuition doesn't tell me it's right, then reason may not be enough."

"Hmm, sounds like a feminine mentality to me," said Colleen, who had been miffed by her husband's insinuation that women were not creatures of reason.

"Nothing the matter with intuition, dear, whether it's masculine or feminine," Harry tried to placate her. "I've never objected to feminine intuition—or to anything else about women, for that matter. I like them just the way they are. But you must admit that women don't deal with reality in quite the same way that men do. That's not a disparagement of women. But it is unbecoming of a man not to think like a man should think, which means to believe the evidence before his eyes, instead of what he thinks he's *supposed* to believe. We're living in an age of rigid ideological conformity, in which men submissively accept 'approved' ideas instead of having the courage to think for themselves. Submissiveness doesn't become a man."

Oscar said nothing, but he marveled to himself that Harry's words came so close to mirroring his own thoughts on the subject— thoughts which were by no means common these days. Added to his immediate liking for the man was a growing feeling that perhaps in him he would find a worthy ally.

XVI

In Harry and Colleen's living room Harry opened a black-bound book which he had brought in from his study. A number of slips of paper were inserted between the pages. "I want to read to you a few paragraphs which should shed a little light on Jewish motivation in dealing with non-Jews. The author is a Jew who is very highly regarded by the world Jewish community. I might even call him an authority on Jewish matters. And believe me, on a subject as controversial as this, it's much better to go to the Jews themselves for your information, instead of to their enemies—whose objectivity, I regret to say, cannot always be depended on."

"Exactly what someone else recently warned me about," Oscar replied.

Harry raised his book and said, "Here our Jewish authority is addressing his brethren in Jerusalem," and he began reading: "'Strangers shall build up thy walls, and their kings shall minister unto thee . . . . Therefore, thy gates shall be open continually . . . that men may bring unto thee the wealth of the Gentiles and that their kings may be brought. For the nation and kingdom that will not serve thee shall perish; yea, those nations shall be utterly wasted. . . . And the sons of them that afflicted thee shall come bending unto thee, and all they that despised thee shall bow themselves down at the soles of thy feet . . . . Thou shalt also suck the milk of the Gentiles . . . . And strangers shall stand and feed your flocks, and aliens shall be your plowmen and your vinedressers. . . . Ye shall eat the riches of the Gentiles, and in their glory shall ye boast yourselves.'"

Harry closed the book and remarked, "I was skipping around a bit, but all of that's from just two pages in chapters 60 and 61 of Isaiah. Have you ever heard anything more suggestive of parasitism, of a fundamentally parasitic attitude toward the rest of the world?"

Oscar's stubborn rejoinder was: "Harry, the Old Testament is a big book. You can find almost anything in it you want. Certainly what you've just read suggests a parasitic attitude on the part of the Jews. But I can't see why those passages are more fundamental or significant for understanding Jewish motivation than a thousand other passages, not suggestive of a parasitic attitude, which you might have read instead."

"Ah, but parasitism *is* fundamental to Judaism. The religion, if it's fit to be called that, is *based* on parasitism, on the exploitation of the Gentiles by the Jews. Throughout the Jewish scriptures one finds the attitude that the world owes the Jews a living, together with a seething resentment that the world hasn't done enough for them. Tell me, what is the most fundamental religious belief of the Jews? What is it that they consider distinctive about themselves?"

Oscar thought for a few seconds, then began hesitantly: "Well, I'm no expert in comparative religion, but I would say that it is their belief in their 'chosenness.'"

"Give the man a cigar!" Harry boomed out. "That's absolutely correct. Jews are, of course, a notoriously tribal people, more ethnocentric than any other racial or national group, including the Japanese. That is perhaps understandable, considering the great antiquity of their religion. It has its roots in their existence as a coalition of bands of predatory desert nomads, probably all related by blood ties. In recent millennia they have given their deity Yahweh, or Jehovah as the Christians call him, a universal aspect. But originally he was a strictly tribal god, a specifically Jewish god, the animistic spirit of a volcano in the Sinai Desert, a spirit which supposedly manifested itself to Moses as a burning bush on the slopes of the volcano during an eruption. Now, if you ever went to Sunday School in your childhood, perhaps you can tell me what happened after the burning bush spoke to Moses."

"Well, I believe that's when they made some sort of arrangement with Yahweh that resulted in their being 'chosen,'" Oscar replied.

"Right again! Boy, you're a real theologian, Oscar. Can you elaborate on this 'arrangement' you mentioned?"

"I'm sorry, I don't remember the details. They refer to it as 'the covenant,' I believe."

"Yes, the covenant. Actually, the word was used often in the Bible in its general sense of a deal or contract between various parties. But *the* covenant, the one that was engraved in stone and carried around in a special box, or 'ark,' is the bargain supposedly struck between Moses, on behalf of the whole tribe, and Yahweh in the Sinai. It is indisputably the basis of Judaism. It is the reason for the Jews thinking of themselves as 'the chosen people.' Devout Jews remind themselves of their bargain with their god in a number of ways. One way is by fastening a little box to the doorposts of their homes, with a scrap of parchment inside inscribed with a few details of the bargain, as set down in Moses' Deuteronomy. They call this device a *mezuzah*. Other little boxes with similar scraps of parchment are strapped to their heads and their arms during religious observances. They call those *tephillin*."

"I've heard of them," Oscar commented.

"Anyway, I think you'll agree with me that this bargain, this covenant, is fundamental. We should be able to tell something about the mentality of a people which has cherished its memory for 3,000 years by looking at its provisions, its details. Don't you think so?"

"Well, races generally create their religions in their own images," Oscar began cautiously. "In the case of a religion which is truly native—which came from the soul of a people instead of being imposed by a conqueror—I would think that a study of the religion would at least give some insights into the character of the people."

"I would think so too. Now listen to the details of old Yahweh's bargain with his chosen people. Actually, I'm going to have to skip around again, because the covenant is spread out a bit, interspersed with other odds and ends, and repeated in somewhat different words in several chapters of Deuteronomy."

Harry opened the book near the front and began reading again: "'These words which I command thee this day shall be in thine heart, and thou shalt teach them diligently unto thy children and shall talk of them when thou sittest in thine house and when thou walkest by the way and when thou liest down and when thou risest up. And thou shalt bind them for a sign upon thine hand, and they shall be as frontlets between thine eyes, and thou shalt write them upon the doorposts of thy house and upon thy gates.'"

He looked up and said, "Those are the orders to use *tephillin* and *mezuzoth*. Now listen to what the Jews get from Yahweh if they keep their side of the bargain." He resumed his reading: "'And it shall be, when the Lord thy god shall have brought thee into the land which he sware unto thy fathers, to Abraham, to Isaac, and to Jacob, to give thee great and goodly cities, *which thou buildedst not*, and houses full of all good things, *which thou filledst not*, and wells digged, *which thou diggedst not*, vineyards and olive trees, *which thou plantedst not . . . .*'"

He interrupted his reading again while he turned a few pages. "There are various things the Jews are required to do in order to get possession of all this loot from the Gentiles. Following the section I just read, the conditions are that they shall fear Yahweh, swear by his name, serve him, and not have anything to do with the gods of other peoples—'for the Lord thy god is a jealous god.'

"Ah, here we are. This is chapter 11. A lot of the same baloney I read from chapter six is repeated here, including the commandment to use *tephillin* and so on. Then comes the payoff."

He resumed his reading: "'For if ye shall diligently keep this commandment which I command you, to do it, to love the Lord your god, to walk in all his ways, and to cleave unto him, then will the Lord drive out all these nations from before you, and ye shall possess nations greater and mightier than yourselves. Every place whereon the sole of your foot shall tread shall be yours . . . . There shall no

man be able to stand before you; the Lord your god shall lay the fear
of you and the dread of you upon all the land that ye shall tread upon,
as he hath spoken unto you.'"

"Mind if I read that myself?" Oscar asked.

"Not at all. There's a lot of surplus verbiage in there, but the
passages I read—the ones that go to the heart of the Jews' covenant
with Yahweh—are marked in the margin. As you read just compare
what the Jews wanted from their god with what our own pagan
ancestors might have wanted in a similar situation. We might have
asked for courage on the battlefield, perhaps even for victory over
our enemies or for a plentiful harvest—but can you imagine us
begging specifically to be given the fruit of other peoples' labor,
without having to work for it ourselves?" Harry handed the Bible to
Oscar.

Oscar read silently for a few minutes while Adelaide chatted with
Colleen and Harry went into the kitchen for a pot of coffee and some
cups.

"I note," Oscar eventually commented, "that among the other
things the Jews are commanded to do in order to have those 'great
and goodly cities' delivered to them ready-made is the requirement
that they engage in genocide. In chapter seven it says, 'And thou
shalt *consume* all the peoples which the Lord thy god shall deliver
unto thee; thine eye shall not pity them.' Then a few chapters later
the commandment is repeated: 'Of the cities of these peoples which
the Lord thy god giveth thee for an inheritance thou shalt save alive
nothing that breatheth, but thou shalt utterly destroy them.' Then a
number of tribes are named which are to be exterminated down to
the last woman and child, apparently because they are unfortunate
enough to be the inhabitants of the cities coveted by Yahweh's
chosen people. I wonder if they find these exhortations to genocide
embarrassing today, in view of their eternal whining about what the
Germans did to them during the Second World War. Of course, this
stuff was supposedly written more than 3,000 years ago. I presume
they don't still take it seriously, and it would be unfair to hold it
against them."

Harry finished pouring a cup of coffee for Oscar and then
answered: "As a matter of fact, they take it very seriously. Jews are
the most religiously conservative of all peoples. They're just as
determined to stamp us out today as they were to stamp out the
Jebusites, the Amorites, and the Canaanites then. Remember, what
you are reading there is part of the covenant between the Jews and
their god. He promised the world to them, and we're in their way.
It is true, of course, that well over half of all Jews today regard
themselves as non-religious. But if you were to suggest publicly that

parts of their covenant with Jehovah are abhorrent to all fair-minded men and women and ought to be scrapped, you'd have the atheist Jews screaming just as loudly for your blood as the faithful synagogue-goers.

"If you'll think about it a minute, Oscar, you already know that's true. That's the sort of reaction you expect from Jews. If you so much as give one of them a crooked look, they're all wailing and screaming about 'anti-Semitism.' Where their own interests are concerned, they are utterly incapable of objectivity. So they not only see nothing incongruous in simultaneously demanding vengeance against Germans and cherishing their own genocidal covenant, but they have had the *chutzpah* to demand that the Christians change New Testament doctrine wherever it expresses hostility to Jews."

Harry took the Bible back from Oscar and flipped rapidly through the pages. "Here it is, in Matthew, chapter 27. Pilate, the Roman governor of Judea, is trying to deal with a mob of Jews who want Jesus to be killed for violating Jewish law. Pilate wants to turn Jesus loose, but the mob, which is being egged on by the Jewish rabbis and priests, demands his death. 'Pilate saith unto them, What shall I do unto Jesus which is called Christ? They all say, Let him be crucified. And he said, Why, what evil hath he done? But they cried out exceedingly, saying, Let him be crucified. So when Pilate saw that he prevailed nothing, but rather that a tumult was arising, he took water and washed his hands before the multitude, saying, I am innocent of the blood of this righteous man: see you to it. And all the people answered and said, His blood be on us and on our children.'

"That's pretty clear language, but a few years ago the Jews began complaining about it, because a small minority of the host population in this country and in Europe still took Christianity seriously— and they took at face value the Jews' acceptance of collective responsibility for Jesus' death. It resulted in anti-Semitism, the Jews said. So they demanded that the Christian churches change their teaching on that subject. And the churches did it! Now they all say that Matthew was wrong, that it was really the entire human race which was responsible for Jesus' death, not just the poor, blameless, loveable Jews. But just imagine the screams of anguish you'd hear if some Christian theologian said that it's about time for the Jews to renounce some of the more intolerant and bloodthirsty statements of old Yahweh!"

Oscar laughed, "I'm sure you're right. That's one thing I have noticed about them: they always have something to complain about. Whenever there's a conflict, it's always *your* fault, never theirs. No matter how far backward you bend over for them, it's never enough.

They always want more, and they act as if you owe it to them. I think that 'gimme' attitude of theirs, that eternal pushiness, is what has made most people dislike them.

"But just because they're easy to hate doesn't mean that they're parasites. They're hard workers, they're smart and creative, and it seems to me that they contribute at least enough to our civilization to make up for the damage they do with the media."

"Oscar, think about what you're saying. You have a narrow mental image of a parasite as a fat Negress surrounded by a swarm of illegitimate picaninnies, all on welfare. But that's almost a benign type of parasite, akin perhaps to a tapeworm. In Nature there are also other types of parasites, not so benign: types which might reasonably be compared with the rabies-carrying vampire bat. Parasites don't have to be mindless and passive, like a tapeworm or a welfare mammy. They may also be quite clever and aggressive, perhaps enough so to exist by their own efforts. But if their innate inclination is to 'suck the milk of the Gentiles'—if they even sanctify that ambition and hold it up as the basis of their spiritual existence, of their covenant with their tribal deity—and if they have a record spanning thousands of years, during which they have infiltrated and destroyed one society after another while living as a privileged minority among their potential victims, then it is accurate to describe them as parasites.

"No one who knows them will deny that Jews will work hard when there is the prospect of gain—harder, in fact, than many of the Gentiles who complain about them—or that they're clever. If you make a balance sheet of their contributions and their depredations, though—and do it carefully—I believe you'll change your mind as to their being an asset to our civilization. One of the things that makes that task tricky is that they control so many of the data that go into the balance sheet—and they are not bashful about blowing their own horns.

"Their boasting, in fact, is really outrageous. They never tire of reminding us that they are the creators of the West's religion and of a greatly disproportionate share of its literature, art, music, and science. They have so often repeated their claim that the four greatest thinkers and innovators of the last 2,000 years have been Jesus, Marx, Freud, and Einstein—all Jews—that they have most Gentiles, even those who should know better, believing it. I'm sure that you've heard that particular boast yourself a hundred times. Have you simply accepted it at face value, or have you questioned it?"

Oscar blushed and stammered, "Well, to tell the truth, I . . . ."

Harry cut him off and continued the monologue: "It's the same with nearly everyone. The fact that the Jews have been able to get away with such preposterous humbug virtually unchallenged is a tribute to their colossal ability to deceive. Just think about it. There is no doubt that Jesus was a religious reformer of exceptional ability and charisma, if we judge him by the supposed record of his life and teachings in the New Testament, but the religion founded by his followers certainly wasn't a Western religion. It gained a foothold among the slaves and other alien elements of the demimonde in the decaying Roman Empire, and then it was imposed on our Saxon ancestors by fire and sword. What it became during the thousand years since then certainly was colored by our own racial character, making it at times in the past rather different from the subversive creed used by Saul of Tarsus and his successors to undermine the power of Rome.

"During the last 50 years or so, however, its subversive, anti-Western tendencies have come to the fore again, and today it ranks right up there with the mass media and the Federal government as one of the principal agents of racial destruction. It is a religion of equality, of weakness, of regression and decay, of surrender and submission, of oblivion. If our race survives the next century it will only be because we have gotten the monkey of Christianity off our backs and have found our way to a genuinely Western spirituality again. The Jews may claim Jesus as one of their own if they wish, but in the long run I hardly believe that we will consider ourselves in their debt because of it.

"As for Marx, including him in their famous foursome is really a bit of impudence on their part. There's absolutely no doubt about his Jewishness; he came from a family of rabbis. And there's no doubt that he has had an effect on the Western world: his followers have murdered more of our people than anyone else in history—30 million in Russia alone. Worse, they've usually been selective in their murder, deliberately killing off the best elements of our race, because those have been the elements most resistant to Marx's nutty theories. Are we supposed to be grateful to the Jews for that?

"Marx's doctrine is as anti-Western as Jesus.' It too was designed to appeal to the dregs of Western society, the worst elements among us, and to pull down the best and the strongest to their level. To the Jews he may be a great man, but as a system builder, a political theoretician, he was a zero. Communism has been a bust wherever it has been tried among White people. It simply isn't workable, and it shows up its designer as a windy fraud.

"Freud, fortunately, hasn't had a chance to do us as much damage as Jesus and Marx, but that's not from lack of trying. Some of the bizarre notions of human motivation he foisted onto the Gentile world are still being promoted by his disciples. Imagine how many millions of dollars neurotic women have paid out to Freudian quacks posing as physicians or therapists!

"Can you see the common element in the effect all three Jews have had on our race? They were illusion builders. In each case the Jew involved concocted an illusion, and then his fellow Jews marketed the illusion to our people. In each case disaster followed. There was a lot more talent involved in the marketing than in any of the illusions themselves. The illusions would have simply faded away if a crew of talented hucksters hadn't taken them in charge and successfully peddled them.

"In the case of Christianity the head huckster was Saul of Tarsus, alias Paul; he was the one who infected the Roman underworld with it. In the case of Marxism, Bronstein, alias Trotsky, came to New York and recruited a gang of his fellow Jews to go back to Russia with him and help spread the virus. They were lucky enough to have the assistance of Lenin, a truly gifted part-Jew, who was an organizer and strategist as well as a huckster.

"And I don't have to tell you that the vast majority of the men who marketed Freud's hokum, just like the majority of those who still peddle it today, were Jews. In each case the Jews saw a weakness in the Gentile world which they could exploit; in each case they took an illusion concocted by a Jew and used it as a crowbar to pry an opening for themselves at the point of weakness."

Oscar interrupted: "And what about Einstein? Was he just a huckster too?" A trace of sarcasm might have been detectable in his voice.

"No, but many of those who promoted his image as the greatest genius of all times were. Einstein was a gifted scientist. Even if his name had been Smith or Jones, he would be greatly respected by other scientists today, although his name wouldn't be a household word. But because he was a Jew, when he began making his mark in the scientific world his fellow Jews cranked up their promotional machinery. And that's really the only reason why it makes a certain kind of sense to group Einstein with the other three: what they all had in common was a crew of Jewish hucksters persuading the Gentile world that there was more to their man than met the eye.

"I'm not a physicist, but one of our League members who is has told me that Einstein, although he deserves much credit, has been given a lot which rightfully belongs to others. For example, the mass media—even the high school and college undergraduate textbooks—credit him with being the sole creator of the theory of relativity, with being the man who taught the world that $E=mc^2$ and thus led us to nuclear energy. And that simply isn't true. Other physicists and mathematicians had been working with relativistic concepts before Einstein. The basic equations of relativity were derived by a Dutchman, Lorenz, and an Englishman, Fitzgerald, before Einstein got into the act. Even $E=mc^2$ isn't Einstein's equation; a German, Hasenoehrl, published this result in 1904 in connection with his theoretical calculations on the equivalence of energy and mass.

"Einstein took the work of these and other men as his base, and he added to it. He provided new explanations. For that he deserved credit. It's understandable that his fellow Jews would want to brag a bit about him, but they went way beyond that. The Jewish hucksters saw their opportunity to build another cult figure they could market to the Gentiles, and they did it. They exaggerated. They distorted. They promoted. And they crafted the whole illusion so cleverly that even the scientists—men who knew better—let themselves be carried along with the hoax. Men familiar with the work of Lorenz, Fitzgerald, Hasenoehrl, and other pioneers of relativity theory apparently thought it would be ill-mannered of them to speak out against the exaggeration of Einstein's role.

"Besides Einstein, of course, there have been other Jews who have made real contributions—although one must be cautious in accepting the claims made for many of them, just as in the case of Einstein. But one must try to balance against these positive figures an appallingly large number of Jewish culture wreckers and civilization destroyers. Just look at the wasteland which our art and music and literature have become since the Jews elbowed their way into it. They actually brag about their accomplishments in these areas too! They say, 'Look how many awards and prizes our Jewish writers have won.' Have you read any of the crap these Jewish Nobel laureates and Pulitzer Prize winners have churned out?"

"Um, I worked my way through Malamud's *The Fixer* in college. Competent writing, I suppose, but I found it a pretty forgettable book. Guess I could say about the same for Pasternak's *Doctor Zhivago*. Never could figure out what other people saw in those two. I also dipped into a couple of Norman Mailer's novels and got about halfway through *Portnoy's Complaint* by Roth. They were much worse than Malamud and Pasternak—real trash. They were worse than trash, in fact; they were sick. They were written by sick men, with a sick view of the world.

"At the time I was reading those things I didn't choose them because their authors were Jews; I chose them because they were being praised by the media—and by my professors and some of my peers—and designated as significant writing. After about my fifth or sixth Jewish novel, though, I found myself compelled to believe that there was just a *flavor* about Jewish writing that didn't agree with me.

"The thing about it was," Oscar leaned forward and spoke with more intensity, his thoughts evidently stimulated by the topic, "I couldn't identify with any of the characters. There were episodes in Jewish novels that were mildly amusing or even interesting. Often the style was good, though by no means always. But nothing in any of them really *moved* me. And I always left the ones I managed to finish with a feeling of mild depression.

"And it's not that I'm illiterate or unresponsive to good literature. I'm not ashamed to say that I've wept when reading Shakespeare. And what I read of his 20 years ago is still alive in my mind. I can quote great gobs of *Julius Caesar* and half a dozen other Shakespeare plays from memory. Hell, the same thing is true of *The Iliad*." Oscar laughed. "I guess it's not fair to expect other writers to come up to the standards set by Homer and Shakespeare. But there are plenty of less illustrious authors who've moved me too."

"Ever read any Jewish poetry?"

"Unfortunately, yes, a little. Did I just say that Mailer and Roth were sick? God, I don't know what word I can use to describe the Jewish poets I've sampled. I need something stronger than 'sick.' When I was an undergraduate Allen Ginsberg was required reading. I don't know how the professor was able to say with a straight face that the garbage Ginsberg wrote was poetry. There were a couple of others whose names I can't remember: some Holocaust verse, some really nutty stuff, all of it trivial. Considering how many Jewish novelists I've run across, I'm surprised there weren't more Jewish poets."

"Poetry doesn't pay very well."

"If you're trying to make the point that Jewish writing is alien and inconsequential stuff for the most part, I'll agree with you. But there's also a great deal of garbage being written by Gentiles, some really awful drivel which is praised by the *New York Times* book reviewers right along with the Jewish drivel. So I can't go along with you if you want to blame the decline of English literature on Jews."

"But that's exactly what I intend to do. Look at the pattern, Oscar. It's not just literature; it's our whole culture. In the 19th century our people created some of the greatest music ever composed: Beethoven and Wagner and Tchaikovsky and Schubert, Brahms and Chopin and Dvorak and Bizet and Liszt and Schumann and dozens of others. The 19th century was also a great century for literature and poetry—and for painting. Why did it all come to a screeching halt in the 20th century?"

"Did it? Seems to me there's been some good music written since 1900. What about Sibelius? And there've been some really good writers too. Steinbeck is one. Shaw is another. I'm sure I could think of half a dozen other serious writers of this century who did excellent work if I concentrated for a minute or so."

"You should have mentioned Richard Strauss," Adelaide chimed in. "He's a little too modern for me on the whole, but some of his music is quite good."

"Okay, okay. So I exaggerated a little," Harry resumed. "The fact remains, Sibelius and Shaw and Steinbeck and Strauss notwithstanding, that there has been a drastic decline in the level of artistic creativity in this century. Do you really dispute that?"

"I guess I'll agree with you so far as poetry is concerned," Oscar came back, trying to be conciliatory. "Some of Eliot's poetry is all right, and one or two things Pound wrote, but I have noticed that not much poetry with even the slightest appeal to me has been published in the last 60 years or so, and that's an enormous contrast with the English poetry of the 19th century, much of which I'm rather passionate about. I might agree with you on art too. There were some fine sculptors in Germany before the war—Breker, in particular— but most of the painting and sculpture being done these days are pure crap. Of course, that's strictly subjective. And I'd have to think about prose literature and music for a while before I could say whether or not I agree with you on those."

"For Christ's sake, Oscar, you shouldn't have to think about it. The music of the 19th century is represented by Beethoven and Wagner, by giants. Sibelius and Strauss may have been fine composers, but they weren't giants. Furthermore, they don't represent 20th-century music; they are the rare exceptions, not the 20th-century norm; they are holdovers from the previous century. The literature of the 19th century is represented by Dostoevsky and Dickens. Who in this century comes close to them?"

"When I think about it, it seems to me that it's not so much that there've been no good 20th-century novelists," Oscar replied. "A couple more names occurred to me while you were talking. Hamsun's *Growth of the Soil* was up to the 19th-century standard. Maugham's *Of Human Bondage* was first class, and some of Conrad's stories weren't really bad, though one wouldn't call them 'great.' One book written after the Second World War which had a strong effect on me was Orwell's *1984*. And I'm sure there were a number of others. No, I think the problem is not so much a lack of good writing as it is that the good stuff is drowned in such a flood of garbage."

"You're a hard case, Oscar. I'm not denying that some good books have been written since the First World War—probably even a few since the Second World War—but the standards for literature are way down, just as they are for music, painting, and the other arts. It's not just that there's a flood of garbage; it's that the garbage is what's held up as the standard. It's the garbage that's winning the prizes; it's the garbage that young writers are attempting to emulate. Will you admit that?"

"Well, okay. I could quibble about the details, but I think that in a broad sense you're right: standards are down."

"Right. And why are they down?"

"If I had to name a single reason, I'd say that it's the increasing level of economic democracy. In the 19th century the standards were set by an elite. There were no radios, juke boxes, phonographs, or tape players. Composers wrote music to be played in concert halls. Joe Sixpack and his wife didn't go to concerts. The people who did go were more discriminating than the people who buy phonograph records and cassette tapes now.

"Books were bought by the same elite. The reviewers and the critics wrote for this elite, not for the masses. Today the standard of living for Joe Sixpack is way up. His work week is much shorter. He has time for more recreation. He buys newspapers. He listens to the radio. He may even read a book every now and then. His kids have cassette tape players. His buying power, as a class, is much greater than that of the culture-bearing elite. So music and books are aimed at him more than at the elite. How's that for an explanation?"

"You're partly right," Harry responded. That is, even if there were no other reason for the fall of standards, they probably would be down because of the larger amount of money and leisure time at the disposal of the least discriminating elements of society. But you're overestimating the effect of economic democracy, and there are other reasons for what's happened.

"Do you really think that the art on display in the museums today is so ugly just because Joe Sixpack is a slob? Is Joe's wife to blame for the weird stuff that's winning prizes for poetry these days? I'm certain that if you took a poll you'd find that Joe Sixpack and his wife would favor the sculpture of Breker to that of Picasso or Henry Moore. And neither Joe nor his wife buys enough Jewish novels to make a difference to the publishers.

"No, the standards haven't just slipped along with the average intellectual level of the culture consumers; they've been deliberately pulled down."

"Harry's right, in a way," Adelaide entered the conversation again. "Today the elite—those who think of themselves as such—

would be more likely to favor the garbage than the masses would. But they think they're holding the standards up by doing so. It's the movement toward modernism, in which all the old values have been inverted. At least that's the case in literature and painting and sculpture. In music Oscar is probably more nearly right. The taste of the masses isn't for structured music, it's for rhythm. Primitive music, Black music, has had a big influence in determining what's played on the radio, because the radio audience is more primitive in its tastes than the concert audiences were."

Harry and Oscar both looked at her. "All right. There's another partial explanation," Harry said. "It's true that the people who buy art works and patronize museums today, along with those who run out to buy the hard-cover editions of every new piece of crap by Roth or Mailer as soon as it's published, are trendy featherbrains who've been educated way beyond their intellectual capacity. They're the new cultural elite. And they slavishly toe the modernist line laid down by the critics and the reviewers. An artist who has been given the critics' stamp of approval can unveil a steaming plate full of fresh cow turds at an exhibition, the critics will praise it to the sky as a major new work of art, and the members of the new elite will all be 'oohing' and 'ahing' and nodding their heads wisely and talking with each other about how much 'sensitivity' on the part of the artist is revealed by the way the turds are oozing off the edge of the plate.

"Joe Sixpack would just laugh. He doesn't have any cultural standards to uphold, so he doesn't pay any attention to the critics. But the new elite didn't decide all by itself that the trash being produced in the name of art today is art. The boobs who regard all representational art as 'fascist' didn't develop that opinion by themselves. They don't worship ugliness just because they're mentally ill. They worship it because their powers of discrimination really aren't all that much better than Joe's—and because the critics persuaded them that it's smart to worship it, that it's fashionable, that it shows how much cleverer they are than Joe and his wife.

"The modernist movement was created by the critics—which is to say, by the mass media. And that's just another way of saying that it was created by the Jews."

"Now, wait a minute," was Oscar's reply. "The Jews didn't invent the modernist movement. The tendency was there even in the last century. Some of the people involved were obviously sick or badly disturbed, and their art reflected their sickness. Others seemed more to be incompetents, who hadn't the talent or self-discipline to produce genuine art, so they ignored all the rules and produced whatever was easy for them. But for the most part the practitioners of modernism weren't Jews. Picasso wasn't a Jew. Henry Moore wasn't a Jew. A majority of the people today who're pouring out confused, meaningless pap and calling it 'poetry' or daubing a few splotches of paint here and there on a canvas and calling it 'art' are Gentiles."

"Hey, I didn't say that the practitioners of modernism were all Jews—although there are a lot more of them involved in it than their percentage of the general population would warrant. Sure, the tendency was always present. There have always been a certain number of lazy and incompetent people—and emotionally disturbed people—in every profession. In the past people with good taste simply ignored them. What's happened in this century is that the Jews have gained control of our mass media. That's happened concurrently with the growth in importance of the mass media resulting from economic democracy. Prior to this century there were no Jewish critics or reviewers to speak of. Now a majority of them are Jews. The ones who aren't follow the Jewish line, because they're employed by Jews.

"Not only that, the cultural market is controlled by Jews in other ways. You can write any sort of novel or any sort of poetry you want these days. You can even get it published—if you're willing to pay the publication expenses yourself. But if you want somebody else to publish it for you—a major publisher, with access to the chain bookstores—then you'd better tailor your literary creativity to suit what the publishers want. The same thing is true of the graphic and plastic arts. If the gallery owners don't like it, nobody'll see your work, and you'll starve.

"The Jews have selected out the sick and undisciplined elements from the Gentile art world, elements always kept in check by natural forces before, and they have promoted and encouraged them. They have added their own practitioners to these elements. They have shut off the healthy elements from contact with the public to the extent they could. And they have done a pretty good job of persuading a superficially educated class of consumers of art and literature that all the old cultural standards ought to be stood on their heads: that ugliness should be praised and beauty laughed at, that chaos is admirable and order contemptible, that art which reflects the true inner life of their people is 'racist' and is not worthy of the respect shown to every piece of alien junk produced by niggers, gooks, or wogs."

"But why, dammit? What's in it for the Jews? Why should they try to stifle the culture of the people among whom they're living and promote degeneracy and chaos in their place? It doesn't make sense. It's just asking for trouble. They would be better off by promoting the best elements in our culture instead of the worst." Oscar's impatience was audible in his voice.

"Why? I'll tell you why." Harry reached for the Bible again, opened it at one of the slips of paper, and began reading: "'I will set the Egyptians against the Egyptians, and they shall fight, everyone against his brother and everyone against his neighbor, city against city and kingdom against kingdom. And the spirit of Egypt shall fail in the midst thereof, and I will destroy the counsel thereof, and they shall seek to the idols and to the charmers and to them that have familiar spirits and to the wizards.'"

Harry looked up and asked, "Does that remind you of anything going on today? That was Isaiah's formula for nation-wrecking 2,700 years ago, but it seems to me that it could just as well be applied to what they've been doing in this country for the last 50 years. In fact, if you look at the bigger picture, Isaiah's formula might very well describe the way in which the Jews have dealt with the White world—with us and Europe, including Russia—for more than a century."

"Well, it's certainly true that the people running the mass media have done a pretty thorough job of destroying the counsel of the American people," Oscar replied, "but I can't accept what you've just read as proof that it's been deliberate, and I don't see what it has to do with their bias toward modernism."

Harry came back: "Isaiah's words are a bit quaint, but there's more of a fit to the present situation than just the destruction of our ability to reason and figure out how to save ourselves as a people. 'Everyone against his brother and everyone against his neighbor': isn't that a good way of describing the social atomization that's taken place in White society, the breakdown of our sense of racial and community solidarity? And was there ever before such a proliferation of charmers and wizards selling their various brands of spiritual snake oil as in America today?

"As for modernism, what is it but the repudiation of our culture, the culture we have shared with all other White people throughout our history? What the Greeks wrote and what the Greeks sculpted 2,500 years ago appeals to us today for the same reasons it appealed to the Greeks then. We respond to beauty and order in the same way. The feelings expressed by Homer and Sophocles are our feelings. What Dostoevsky wrote spoke to Englishmen and Germans as well as to Russians, just as Dickens spoke to Russians and Germans, and Goethe spoke to Russians and Englishmen. A painting by Rembrandt or Turner or Friedrich said the same thing to all Europeans, just as did a symphony by Beethoven. We do not respond in the same way to Chinese music or Negro sculpture—or Jewish novels.

Our culture tied us together, made us aware of our common heritage—and of our differences from those who did not share that
heritage. And the Jew, the eternal outsider trying to work his way
in, could not tolerate that. He had to break us up, destroy our
solidarity, make us believe that we had no more in common with
each other than with the Negro or the Chinaman—or the Jew.
Modernism is the essential strategy of the parasite."

Oscar leapt to his feet and slammed a fist into his other hand,
visibly agitated. "You still haven't proved anything. You keep
reading suggestive passages from the Bible, passages which indicate
hostility and a parasitic attitude on the part of the Jews. But proofs
based on the Bible are only for fools. You can 'prove' anything you
want with the Bible. The only thing this discussion has done for me
is make me realize that I have to re-examine, rethink, re-explore
many things I previously had accepted as true. In some cases I
suspect I'll realize that I had let myself be deceived by Jews, by
media under their control or influence. But I'm certainly not going
to let myself be persuaded to accept a theory of global conspiracy
and parasitism by the Jews on the basis of a few things they wrote
thousands of years ago."

"Bravo, Oscar! If our talk really will lead you to rethink a few
things, then I will have been completely successful. And I believe
it will, because it is evident that you regard the matters we have been
discussing with the gravity they deserve. You take these things
seriously. Even the slightest suspicion that I may be correct disturbs
you deeply. That is as it should be. Too often I've wasted my time
arguing with men who regarded our debate as nothing but an
intellectual exercise, a challenging diversion. Many times they were
intelligent men, but they had no souls, no sense of responsibility.
Whether I was right or wrong about the Jews or other issues we
debated was not really important to them; it was not real. The only
thing that was real to them was their own comfort, their own safety,
their own welfare. They felt no responsibility to the world around
them, no responsibility to their own race even. They were merely
observers of life—spectators—not participants. But you, I believe,
are a participant. Convincing these other fellows of the truth ulti-
mately made no difference, because they remained nothing more
than spectators. But when I finally have helped you to convince
yourself of the truth, it will make a difference. You'll do something
about it."

Oscar relaxed slightly and forced a smile. "I appreciate your
expression of confidence in me. Really, I have learned some things
today, and you've started me thinking about other things that I intend
to continue thinking about. Even the things you showed me in the

Bible provide food for thought. They had always been in front of my nose, but I had never looked at them—or at least I had never seen them in the light you cast on them for me. How did you learn so much about Moses and Isaiah? You don't impress me as the Bible-student type."

Harry laughed. "Well, thanks for that. Actually, one of our League members, Saul Rogers, used to be a Bible student, and he convinced me that the book is a gold mine of information about the Jews, regardless of how long ago it was written and whether or not most of them still believe it. If you and Adelaide can come over again next Sunday I'll introduce you to Saul.

"But please don't leave here today with the notion that I base my convictions about the Jews' role in world affairs on the Bible. As you said, it is only suggestive. It doesn't prove anything. But what you needed was a few suggestions, I thought. Proof is harder to come by. There's no single thing which really proves what the Jews are and what they're up to. *The Protocols of the Learned Elders of Zion* is the sort of thing one wishes one had as a compact, self-contained, all-encompassing proof. Unfortunately, that particular item probably isn't what it purports to be. It's just too neat to be genuine. The truth is generally not so tidy. I believe that on a subject as complex and difficult as that of the Jews, the truth can only gradually take shape in one's mind as one accumulates more and more evidence, from many sources. The Old Testament is one of those sources. Perhaps you're ready for a few more now.

"Let's see: you've been studying their role in the news and entertainment media, which is certainly essential. How about a little recent history—say, the Second World War?"

"Yes, that's something I'm interested in, and I intend to look into it soon."

"Good. I have some books you should take with you to get started. Come in here." Harry led the way into his study. He pulled a book from a shelf and handed it to Oscar. "If you appreciate Breker's art, this one'll get your blood boiling. It describes a few of the things our government did to 're-educate' the Germans after the war. One of those things was to send teams of GIs with sledge hammers around to smash up Breker's sculptures. Graphic works, paintings, they either burned or confiscated. Half the paintings in Germany's museums and other public buildings were looted by special 're-education' teams and locked away in government vaults. 'Nazi art' they called it. And I'm not talking about stuff with swastikas on it. They grabbed or destroyed all of the 20th-century art that didn't fit in with their modernist theme, everything that was healthy and natural, everything that reflected the German view of life. The whole program was run by Jews. Their names are all in here."

Harry selected another four books and gave them to Oscar. "These'll be a good introduction. You can spend six months just exploring the origins of the war, political factors influencing its conduct, and its aftermath that are never treated in the books that make it to the review section of the *New York Times*."

XVII

Oscar and Adelaide didn't visit Harry and Colleen again the next Sunday. In fact, it was nearly three weeks before they saw their new friends again. Meanwhile Oscar kept himself busy.

First and foremost was his study project. He continued his efforts to understand the Jews, reading the books that Harry had lent him and obtaining others from the library that references in Harry's led him to. At the same time, however, he began broadening the scope of his study, trying to answer for himself the more basic question of what had gone wrong in the Western world in the last hundred years or so to bring his race to its present sorry state. Was it an intrinsic flaw in Western civilization, was it the Jews, or was it a combination of things?

Oscar's intuition told him that, regardless of what he eventually decided was the role of the Jews, there had to be fundamental errors in the way his own people had been doing things. He needed to pin those things down and develop some ideas as to the changes that had to be made to put the race back on course again. It wasn't that he thought it would be anything he could accomplish by himself, but he had to have at least a direction for his activities. He had to know that what he was doing made sense in the framework of a larger plan. Ryan, after all, had been right. He had been reacting, doing the easy things, striking at any handy target which attracted his attention. He couldn't afford to keep that up, for several reasons. One was Adelaide. Another was Ryan. The most important was his own need to know that when he risked his life he was doing it for the right reason, not just to relieve frustration by striking out blindly at an enemy he had not even clearly identified. So he studied and he thought.

And he killed Danny Feldman for Ryan. He had more or less decided that he would carry out at least that assignment, and he was tentatively thinking of doing it within a couple of weeks, after he had worked out a detailed scenario. Then, on the Wednesday after his visit with the Kellers, Ryan called again. Again they met in the metro station.

"You've got to take out Feldman right away."

"I was planning to do that fairly soon. How about sometime toward the end of next week?"

"No. We've got to get him out of circulation within the next 48 hours. He can't be alive after 4:00 PM Friday."

"Dammit, Ryan, I have to figure the details of the job first. What's the rush?"

"The rush is that things are moving faster in the Bureau than I had thought they would. Rizzo is being canned next week, by Wednesday at the latest, and the new head of the section will be named. The Director intends to do it before the Senate Subcommittee on Security and Terrorism begins holding hearings next Thursday. This could be a prelude to what I told you about last week: a new anti-terrorism agency. I know that the Director has been discussing that possibility with Senator Herman, the chairman of the Judiciary Committee.

"The problem is that the word has been leaked to the Hebe caucus in the Bureau—undoubtedly by the committee's chief counsel, who's a Jew. Now they're scurrying around trying to head off my getting Rizzo's position. I know that all of them, including Feldman, are holding a pow-wow this weekend in a motel in Alexandria. We'll be listening to what's said at that meeting, but it's still essential to silence Feldman before then. If he's at that meeting, I know exactly what he'll say. He'll be giving them all the details about that Klan operation last year, and then they'll be figuring just how to use that against me. It's the only way they can possibly block me now."

"Instead of eavesdropping, why don't you just blow up the motel and solve your Jewish problem in the Bureau for good?"

"Are you crazy? We don't do that sort of thing. And I couldn't afford to have you do it either. Jesus, can you imagine the stink that would make—especially after Kaplan? They're already suspicious as hell about what happened to him. If all the rest of the Hebes in the Bureau suddenly got knocked off, every Jew in Congress, every Jewish organization in this country, and every Jew in the news media would be screaming his lungs out. I can't afford any more heat when Feldman goes—and there shouldn't be any, if you do the job right."

"So I've got 48 hours to figure this one out and then execute it. You expect a lot, Ryan."

"I have faith in you, Yeager. Now the thing about this Feldman job is it mustn't look like a hit. Understand? It's got to look like something else happened to him. I can help you with that to save you some time. When you leave here take the briefcase there on the floor beside me. In it you'll find one of our special gadgets. It's a dart pistol, which is effective up to a range of about 50 feet, although it's better to get in closer if you can. There are two darts with it. They're loaded with a very special drug: a powerful heart stimulant that'll cause his heart to literally tear itself apart. An autopsy will show the cause of death to be a heart attack. The drug itself is hydrolyzed to the point where it can't be detected in the victim's blood after 12 hours. All you've got to remember to do is get the dart out of him after he drops."

"It seems to me I've got one other little problem too. How do I keep him from shooting me before the drug does its thing?"

"The drug is very fast. His heart will be convulsing within 15 seconds of the time the dart hits him. He'll be in so much pain then he won't be able to do anything but roll around on the ground. His heart will have damaged itself irreparably within 30 seconds, and he'll be unconscious by that time. I'm sure you'll be able to stay out of harm's way for the first ten or 15 seconds."

"What does the FBI use gadgets like your dart gun for? Do you people really perform assassinations, like some of the paranoid leftists have been claiming for years?"

"Nah. We got this one from the Israelis. They use it against the leaders of Palestinian demonstrations in the Occupied Territories; they pop 'em right on the street without attracting attention or causing a commotion. They probably use it for assassinations in other countries too. It's rumored that they've knocked off former Nazi Party members all over the world with similar guns."

"Fascinating. The fact remains, I've got to hit Feldman either this evening or tomorrow evening. I can hardly walk into your headquarters and shoot him in his office while he's at work."

"Or tomorrow morning, before he gets to work—even Friday morning, but don't put if off any later than that. Good luck, Yeager. And remember, be careful! The bastard is dangerous." Ryan smiled and then turned on his heel and headed for the door of a subway train which had just stopped at the platform. Oscar picked up the briefcase.

After returning home he studied his scanty notes on Feldman. The man was 40 years old, married—to an Israeli woman—and had four children. He lived with his family in the Maryland suburb of Silver Spring. He was a moderate drinker and had regular habits, without any obvious quirks, as in the case of Kaplan. His only known weakness was gambling. He usually played poker with four other Jews on Thursday evenings, rotating the location from one home to another, and he and his wife made at least four trips a year to the casinos of Atlantic City or Las Vegas.

Oscar rubbed his head. In order to catch the man outside, it seemed that he would have to find a suitable location near the man's home and wait for him to leave for work in the morning or come home in the evening. That might be reasonable if he used his rifle; he might hope to find an unobtrusive place to park and pick the man off from a distance without even leaving his car. But that would cause serious problems for Ryan. How in hell was he going to get within 50 feet of an armed, trigger-happy killer like Feldman so he could use his dart gun, unless he could hide in some shrubbery beside the man's front door? He sighed. The first thing was to drive out to Silver Spring and look things over.

The Feldman residence was a large, new-looking house set more than a hundred feet back from the street behind half an acre of well-tended lawn. The graveled driveway curved around to the side of the house, where Oscar could just make out a garage door in the end wall as he drove past and then what appeared to be a tennis court beyond that. The Bureau evidently paid its minions well. A dozen large shade trees dotted the lawn, but there were no useful shrubs near either the front door or the garage door—just very low, ornamental plants. Besides, it was almost certain that the garage door had a radio-controlled opener, and that Feldman would enter and leave his car only inside the garage and would use an inside door between the garage and the rest of the house. Damn!

Then Oscar caught a glimpse of something from the corner of his eye which produced an instant spark of inspiration: a child's bicycle was leaning against one of the posts supporting the tennis net. That was the way to do it! He scouted out a good parking place some three blocks away and stopped his car there to look at his notes again. The Thursday-night poker games, according to Ryan's information, began at eight o'clock and lasted until about midnight. That meant that Feldman would be leaving home between 7:30 and 7:45 tomorrow evening—well after dark—unless the game were being held at his house this week. There was one chance in five of the latter being the case.

He wondered whether Ryan might know about that but decided almost immediately not to try to contact him; no point in upsetting him at this stage. The poker game would be his one chance of catching Feldman after dark, and there was nothing to be lost by trying it. If Feldman didn't go out tomorrow night, then Oscar would have to try again Friday morning when the man left for work—a much riskier enterprise. He drove past the house one more time to study the tree he had tentatively picked on the first pass: a big one, about halfway up the drive and 30 feet or so to the right of it. Now he had just one more thing to do before tomorrow night: steal a child's bicycle.

He found one on his way home: a bit dilapidated and rusty, with red fenders and balloon tires, about two-thirds the size of an adult bike. He spotted it leaning against a cinderblock wall at the end of a small shopping mall and pulled his car up beside it. Within half a minute he had it in the luggage compartment and was on his way again. He spent the rest of the afternoon studying, until Adelaide arrived for dinner at six.

When he parked in his preselected spot the next night, it was exactly seven o'clock. He took the bicycle from his trunk and rolled it along the sidewalk toward Feldman's house. As he neared his destination he became painfully aware that the sidewalks in the area were quite brightly illuminated by street lights, and he reproached himself for not having returned after dark the previous night in order to survey the lighting of the area and spot any potential problems. He actually had intended to do so, but Adelaide had been even more affectionate than usual, and after an unusually energetic and pleasurable series of romps with her he had fallen asleep and not awakened until she pulled the covers off him at 6:30 in the morning.

The sidewalk ended several hundred yards before he reached Feldman's driveway, and once there he noted that although the front and sides of the house itself were well lighted by floodlamps the nearest streetlight was more than 200 feet away, and the area around the tree he had picked was in deep shadow. "The Lord takes care of sinners," he muttered to himself with relief.

He had barely settled himself behind the tree when he heard the sound of the garage door opening; Feldman must be leaving earlier than he had estimated. He hastily placed the bicycle in the center of the drive about ten feet closer to the street than his tree and then darted back into its shadow. As he expected, Feldman's car braked sharply and halted directly opposite his tree. He heard the door opening, Feldman cursing, and then footsteps in the gravel. When he peered around the tree Feldman, spotlighted by his own headlights, was bending over to pick up the bicycle.

As the man straightened up, a dart struck him between his shoulder blades. He cursed loudly in Hebrew and whirled around, still holding the bicycle, but he was blinded by the glare of the headlights and could see nothing in Oscar's direction. He dropped the bicycle, drew a pistol, and ran back toward his car, still cursing. Oscar ducked back behind his tree and waited. Within a few seconds the cursing stopped, and Oscar heard a strangled scream, followed by unintelligible, animal-like noises.

Feldman was crumpled on the grass beside the open driver's door, his purpling face contorted. Oscar quickly located the dying man's pistol on the ground and lifted his body enough to slip it back into its holster. He plucked the shaft of the spent dart from the back of the man's coat, picked up the bicycle, and rolled it back toward his own car, whistling softly as he went. He should admit it to himself, he thought: he really enjoyed this sort of thing; furthermore, he wasn't at all bad at it.

On his way home he stopped at the shopping mall where he had found the bicycle and carefully leaned it against the wall again, just the way it had been the day before.

XVIII

Oscar was obliged to spend a portion of his time during the next few days preparing an interim report on his antenna design study for the Air Force. The design actually had been completed months before, but the immediate task was the extraction of a portion of the work from his calculations and their arrangement in a research report. The task was complicated by the need to obscure sufficiently the methods used so that the design work would seem more difficult than it actually had been. He intended to stretch this particular contract out just as long as he could, with appropriate cost overruns, of course. Fortunately, the Air Force was very accommodating in such matters.

The rest of his time was occupied by his principal study project. He had reached a stage in this where it helped him to clarify his ideas by discussing them with Adelaide, who was assisting him each evening with the preparation of the antenna report. He regarded their discussions as a way of raising her racial consciousness as well.

"Baby, it's certainly hard to get to the truth of this Jewish question," he said, putting down the book he had been reading and looking over at her. She was finishing the stapling of the five finished copies of the report. "I'm on my fourth book about the Bolshevik Revolution in Russia. It's quite clear that the Jews played a dominant role in it. In fact, the revolution never could have gotten off the ground without their participation. Its principal theorists, starting with Karl Marx, were Jews; it was financed by Jewish capitalists; and most of its officers and activists also belonged to the tribe. Without them Lenin would have been broke and practically alone. He would have had no operating funds and no lieutenants to carry out his schemes. What's not entirely clear is their motivation. Harry Keller would say that the revolution was simply a Jewish stratagem for gaining power for the Jews in Russia.

"On the other hand, everything the Jews themselves have written about it claims that the appeal communism had for them was based on their desire to promote social justice. Their hearts ached for the oppressed workers, and they felt a sense of moral outrage over the corruption and abuses of power in the czarist government. Some Jewish writers go so far as to say that the Jewish religion compelled them to take the side of the working class and to promote equality. In other words, their motivation was pure altruism.

"These Jewish claims of altruism are contradicted, however, by their actions. As soon as the Bolsheviks gained power they went on a rampage of murder and savagery worse than anything since the Mongol invasions 700 years earlier. They murdered not only the employers, the military officers and cadets, the civil servants, the aristocrats, and others who might have been remotely considered 'oppressors,' but millions of ordinary peasants and workers as well. And they can hardly resort to the excuse that the revolution got away from them, that other elements wrested control from the Jewish altruists and then betrayed the noble motives of the original Bolsheviks by instituting a reign of terror, because the record quite clearly shows that the Jews remained foremost among the terrorists and mass murderers after the revolution, just as they had been foremost in its instigation. The system of *gulag* slave-labor camps was organized by a Jew, and many of the most sadistic and murderous camp commissars were Jews. The same was true of the secret police. As late as 1941, two dozen years after the revolution, 41 per cent of the members of the Supreme Soviet were Jews. That statistic is in this U.S. government report prepared by the research staff of the Library of Congress," he said somewhat heatedly, as he waved a book with a greenish cover. "Can you imagine that? Nearly half the Supreme Soviet, and they're only one per cent of the population."

Adelaide looked at him attentively but did not speak, knowing that he hadn't finished yet. He continued: "By the late 1920s Stalin was the top man in the Soviet Union, but the Soviet government was very heavily Jewish. How can they evade responsibility for the crimes of the Soviet regime in the 1920s and 1930s? The funny thing is they don't even try. To read what they've written on the period before 1950, everything was rosy. It was only after Stalin turned on them and began weeding them from the bureaucracy that they had anything bad to say about the Soviet Union. Nowadays they're continually whining about how they're 'persecuted' over there, but when one looks at the facts it's clear that they're still better off than most other Soviet citizens. They still hold a disproportionate share of the soft jobs. What they mean by 'persecution' is that they don't get everything they want these days. They say they're denied the right to emigrate, but, hell, a lot more of them are allowed to emigrate each year than any other ethnic group.

"Everything written about the Soviet Union within the last 20 years by a Jew complains about just two things: the great purge of the Communist Party during the late 1930s, when thousands of Jewish bureaucrats were yanked out of their plush party offices and sent to the labor camps by Stalin, and the outcome of the so-called 'doctors' plot' in 1953, when Stalin supposedly was preparing to send an even bigger batch of them off to the *gulag* before he suddenly died. But of the millions of Ukrainians murdered in 1931, the thousands of Balts tortured to death in 1940, and the hundreds of thousands, of all nationalities, who were liquidated in 1945 there's not a word!

"I can't decide whether it's that they're deliberately trying to deceive their readers by pretending that these things didn't happen or whether they're simply assuming that these enormous atrocities aren't really worth mentioning because the victims weren't Jews—and besides, the less said about them the better, because Jews bore a lot of the responsibility for them. In the first case they have to be the biggest liars in history, and in the second case they have to be so arrogantly self-centered that it takes one's breath away to think about it. It's like, if I commit an offense against you it's all right, because you aren't one of God's chosen, but if you even think about committing an offense against me, it's genocide and blasphemy. But these aren't Jewish religious fanatics who write these books; they're Jewish academics, most of them atheists.

"When I started studying this subject I was determined not to accept the thesis that Harry Keller and another fellow I know have been trying to sell me: namely, that the whole communist movement was simply a Jewish power grab from the beginning. I thought I could see too many inconsistencies and contradictions. There was the Zionist movement, for one thing. If all the Jews were pushing communism as a way of getting the riches of the Gentiles into their hands, to use Isaiah's words, then why were so many of them in Russia involved in Zionism instead? Why weren't they all working together to push communism?

"One of the most interesting documents I've gotten from the Library of Congress is a copy of an article Winston Churchill wrote about the Jews for the London *Illustrated Sunday Herald* in 1920. Churchill, who certainly was in a position to know the facts, clearly labeled communism as a Jewish movement for world domination."

Oscar picked up a paper from the table beside his chair. "Here, listen to what he said. This is the issue of February 8, 1920, just a little over two years after they took over Russia." He searched for the place he wanted and then began reading: "'This movement among the Jews is not new. From the days of Spartacus-Weishaupt to those of Karl Marx and down to Trotsky in Russia, Bela Kun in Hungary, Rosa Luxembourg in Germany, and Emma Goldman in the United States, this world-wide conspiracy for the overthrow of civilization and for the reconstitution of society on the basis of arrested development, of envious malevolence, and impossible equality has been steadily growing.... There is no need to exaggerate the part played in the creation of Bolshevism and in the actual bringing about of the Russian Revolution by these international and for the most part atheistical Jews. It certainly is a very great one; it probably outweighs all others. With the notable exception of Lenin, the majority of the leading figures are Jews. Moreover the principal inspiration and driving power comes from the Jewish leaders.'

"Then he goes on to talk about Zionism as a sort of antidote to communism. The good Jews, he says, are Zionists, and the bad ones are communists. I wonder if he'd have said that if he'd known how the Zionist Jews would treat the Palestinians after they grabbed Palestine. The Israelis today, in fact, are behaving toward the Palestinians just about the way the Jewish Bolsheviks behaved toward the Ukrainians and Russians after the Russian Revolution.

"Anyway, although Churchill recognized communism as a Jewish movement, he was careful to say that only a portion of the world's Jews were involved in it. Well, that's reasonable; you wouldn't expect all the members of any race or ethnic group to have the same political and social ideas. But the puzzling thing about it is that I've run into lots of hints that the Zionist Jews and the communist Jews weren't really hostile to each other. For example, when the communists took over Russia, they destroyed thousands of Christian churches, but they didn't harm the synagogues. Churchill mentions this fact too. And then there were Jewish capitalists in this country giving millions of dollars to both the Jewish communists and to the Zionists. It all makes one suspect that the Jews were simply using a mixed strategy, some of them going for power via the Zionist route and some via the communist route.

"Maybe I'm wrong about that. But the most incriminating evidence of all is the way the news media and Jewish writers have dealt with communism. Like I said, prior to about 1950 it wasn't just Gentiles like Churchill who were acknowledging the Jewishness of communism. The Jews themselves were boasting about it—but they were claiming it was all altruism: a better break for the working class and so on. Not a word of the monstrous atrocities communists had committed. Then, when the so-called 'cold war' began and communism was no longer fashionable in the West, no more books were published in which Jews admitted their role in communism; instead they began whining that they were *victims* of communism—the principal victims, in fact, if one were to believe them. I guess it's just a fluke that the cold war began about the time that Stalin had broken the power of the Jewish faction in the Soviet government, and Russians were beginning to regain power in their own country."

He reflected for a moment on what he had just said, then continued: "On second thought, maybe it's not a fluke at all. Maybe the change of attitudes toward the Soviet Union in the West was engineered by the media here in response to the changing fortunes of the Jews in the Soviet Union. I'll have to do some more reading along that line. Anyway, it's only been in the last few years that the horrors of the Soviet regime have been given a full airing in the West. One could always find the facts about the extermination of the *kulaks* in the Ukraine or the slaughter of the Polish officer corps in the Katyn Forest in the libraries, in scholarly works and government reports, but never in anything that might affect public opinion. Now that's out in the open—but none of the mass-circulation materials about those things being published today mention the Jews' responsibility for them. The one exception, perhaps, is Solzhenitsyn's treatment of the *gulag* system, but I'm not sure how many people have really read that. And even there one has to read between the lines to get the message.

"You see, if they would show even a superficial appearance of frankness and contrition, then I wouldn't be so suspicious. If they would just come right out and say, 'Well, we thought communism would be good for the world. We thought it would help oppressed people. So we cooked it up and brought off the Russian Revolution with it. But then we did some terrible things, and we're really sorry for it. We never should have fooled around with communism.' If they would say something like that, then I could be a lot more sympathetic toward them. But not one of them has. Instead, everything they've written on the subject has been crooked: *everything*. First they admitted their role in communism but denied the atrocities. Now they admit the atrocities but deny their role.

"On this one subject I'm completely convinced. I've finally dug up enough evidence. And now I'm suspicious of the standard line being handed out on everything else involving them: the Second World War and the so-called 'Holocaust,' for example. But I'm beginning to despair of ever knowing the full truth about these things. It's taken me weeks of study just to reach a few solid conclusions about the Jewish role in communism. To do that I've had to dig through layer after layer of obfuscation and misdirection and contradiction. I've still got dozens of major questions in my mind about communism, Zionism, and the relations between them, and the signposts are pointing in six different directions. It's very frustrating. It's as if the issues have been deliberately muddied, so people like me would have a hard time getting at the truth."

"Hey, that reminds me of something I heard back in Iowa," Adelaide interrupted his monologue. "One of the graduate teaching assistants who taught my recitation section in freshman math was a Jew, David Schwarz. He was married, but he still tried to get me to date him. In fact, he was a real pest. Whenever he'd spot me in the student activity center he'd come over and start talking to me.

Somehow he found out my telephone number and used to call me in my apartment too. He was a compulsive talker. He especially liked to talk about politics and economics—pretty esoteric stuff, generally, like how the price of gold would go up whenever there seemed to be a good chance the Democrats would win an election.

"It was a little bit of a ticklish situation. I was afraid to offend him, and so I figured that as long as I could keep him at arm's length it was okay to let him talk. I even asked him questions sometimes. Once I asked him a question about the national debt. He gave me this 20-minute explanation that left me totally confused. Part of what he said seemed to contradict other parts. I told him, 'Gee, I'm confused. Why does it have to be so complicated?'

"He looked at me for a minute and then said very seriously, as if he were letting me in on some kind of secret, 'It has to be complicated, otherwise too many people would figure out what's going on with the economy.' He leaned over close to me and whispered, 'Keeping people confused can be the best defense. Whenever you want to reach some objective, you must split your forces and have some of them go for the opposite of what you want, so no one will be able to pin you down and put a label on you, and you'll be able to preempt any really effective opposition at the same time. And after you've reached your objective, explain what you've done with so many contradictions that no one will be certain just what it was you were really after in the first place.'

"I don't know what that little piece of wisdom had to do with the national debt. I think he was just trying to impress me with his sophistication—you know, Machiavellian and all that—and my confession that I was confused triggered some association in his mind with another subject, presumably political. Despite his wordiness, David really wasn't as bright as he wanted people to think. But he *was* weird; he thought the explanation for everything that happened was a conspiracy on the part of some special-interest group, and that things were never what they seemed to be. He must have picked up that little maxim about the value of confusion some place. I didn't ask him about it at the time, but it stuck in my mind, and what you just said recalled it."

XIX

It probably would snow during the day, Oscar guessed as he retrieved the newspaper from his front porch. The temperature was about 30 degrees, and the sky was heavily overcast. He stretched, yawned, and sniffed the air in the early-morning darkness. He had just gotten home after spending the night at Adelaide's apartment again. He felt that he needed at least another hour of sleep. Why did she have to leave for work so early?

It wasn't until he had removed the rubber band from the paper and dropped it on the dining-room table that the headline caught his eye. Then his drowsiness evaporated instantly. The big news on the front page of the *Washington Post* was the passage of the Horowitz Bill. He poured himself a cup of coffee and sat down to read the details.

On page four was a much smaller article announcing the enactment of legislation providing for the establishment of a new government agency to combat terrorism. How appropriate that the two pieces of legislation should come at the same time, Oscar thought. The stories in the *Post* treated them as completely independent developments, but he suspected that the legislative wire-pullers were very much aware of the connection. He made a mental note to ask Ryan about that the next time he saw him.

The *Post* indicated that it probably would be two months or longer before the provisions of the Horowitz Act could be fully implemented. The President, who had signed it immediately, already had appointed a panel of prominent religious leaders and representatives of minority groups to oversee the setting up of the bureaucratic apparatus for screening publications and designating those found offensive as "hate material."

There was an interview with the director of the American Civil Liberties Union, who noted that his group had "reservations" about the new law. Something definitely was needed to curb the hatemongers, he said, but he hoped that the Congress had not gone too far and that the law would be administered in a way that would not infringe on free speech or freedom of the press. Oscar snorted in derision when he read that. "Some guardian of our liberties!" he muttered.

The article about the new anti-terrorism agency was of greater interest to him, especially the final paragraph, which read: "The man chosen to head the new agency is William Ryan of the FBI, who had been promoted just last week to chief of the Bureau's Anti-Terrorism Section after serving for nine years as its deputy chief. Mr. Ryan has an excellent record with the Bureau. His most notable accomplishment came early last year, when he headed a task force which rounded up nearly 200 members of the Ku Klux Klan and other White-supremacy groups who were involved in a conspiracy to violate the civil rights of non-Whites. His appointment is expected to be confirmed by the Senate Judiciary Committee within the week."

Oscar moved from the kitchen to the living room, where he settled in his easy chair, leaned back, and closed his eyes. So things had worked out exactly the way Ryan had expected, he thought. He could not help but feel a little pride when he considered how essential his own efforts had been in achieving an outcome so portentous, but his pride was overshadowed by foreboding. He still had not resolved the problem of his relationship with Ryan, and now that problem had assumed a new urgency and importance.

His study program was continuing, but for the past week he had been turning over in his mind even larger questions than those associated with the Jews. He was by now quite convinced that the Jews' grip on the news and entertainment media had to be broken, regardless of whether he eventually came to agree fully with Ryan and Keller's assessment of their overall role in White society or not.

But how? What was the proper course of action? He needed a strategy now, and he was determined to find one before carrying out any more actions, either on his own initiative or at Ryan's behest.

One thing that was quite clear was that his solo actions could not accomplish much of lasting importance by themselves. They could not dispossess the Jews of their media control; they could not halt the decay of White society or Western civilization; they could not even stop miscegenation. If one was to have more than solo actions, then one needed an organization. Keller's group, the National League, was the only one he was aware of that seemed to be seriously addressing the social and racial ills that concerned him. But it was strictly an educational organization; Keller had stressed to him at their last meeting that it shunned all illegal activity and focused instead on publishing and distributing books, pamphlets, magazines, video tapes, and other educational materials. It seemed to Oscar that the Horowitz Act would very soon put the National League out of business, unless it changed its policy and began defying the law by going over to underground publishing.

For that matter, any organization which posed a serious threat to the people in power suffered from the same vulnerability: it could simply be outlawed. To get around that one had to be willing from the beginning to break the law, and one had to be able to do so with some degree of impunity. One needed, in other words, both organized activity *and* the sort of capability that Oscar had developed. The unique relationship he had with Ryan could certainly be helpful along those lines, he reflected.

He built a scenario in his mind: Keller's organization publishing materials like the 1920 newspaper article on the Jews by Churchill he had found so illuminating, using its channels of distribution to get its materials to the public and its organizational apparatus to recruit new writers and printers and activists from among those persons awakened by its publishing efforts—while he dealt with the problems raised by the Horowitz Act, relaying warnings of possible police actions from Ryan, liquidating informers, and performing other extraordinary chores necessary to the viability of an illegal, underground educational organization.

But more was needed—much more. No power as solidly entrenched as that which ruled America could be uprooted by any mob of outsiders howling at the gate. To have any hope of making real changes of sufficient magnitude to reverse the tide of decay, one had to have insiders as well, people with their hands on at least some of the levers of power.

He got up and began pacing the floor, his hands clasped behind him. What were the levers of power which might be accessible? There was the government itself, of course. Any organization which could get one or more of its members into the Congress would have both a national forum and a means for protecting itself, even if it were able to exert no significant influence on the legislative process. Then there was the executive branch, where Ryan's new agency might hold possibilities—at least as a listening post, perhaps even as a base for launching a *coup d'etat* some day, if Ryan's predictions that it eventually would become a real Praetorian Guard proved accurate. That certainly was a factor to consider in deciding the terms on which he would collaborate with Ryan in the future.

There were other levers too: the big labor unions, the established churches, some of the biggest banks and other capital-based institutions. But there was nothing, in the government or elsewhere, to rival the power of the mass media. He did not see how any group could hope to gain and hold a significant share of power if it were vigorously and solidly opposed by the mass media. On the other hand, if an organization or an individual had the backing of even a fraction of the media, it would have an enormous advantage in the quest for power. There had to be a way to break into the media, but Oscar hadn't the faintest idea what it might be. Keller had told him that the National League was developing its own media, which eventually would rival the ones controlled by the Jews, but that seemed to Oscar an unrealistically optimistic forecast. How long would such a development take? Thirty years, perhaps? Would there be anything left to salvage then?

Oscar's thoughts were interrupted by the telephone. He wondered who would be calling so early. Even as he picked up the handset, however, a flash of intuition told him who the caller was. The sound of the voice confirmed his intuition: "Good morning. We need to talk again. I called early so I'd be sure of catching you and so you'd be able to plan on spending about an hour with me, between ten and 11 tonight. The metro station is no longer a satisfactory spot, in view of my new prominence; some newsman might spot us. Meet me in the south parking lot at the Pentagon. I'll be parked in a black Ford sedan in the extreme southwest corner of the lot."

XX

O scar pulled into the south parking lot an hour before the appointed time and chose a parking slot a good hundred yards from the southwest corner, where he could wait inconspicuously in a row of other cars yet still have a clear view of both the designated corner and the most probable avenue of approach to it. Being farthest from the Pentagon, the corner and the area around it were vacant at this time of night, except for the trash which had piled up even more densely there than on the rest of the vast expanse of cracked and litter-strewn asphalt. A light drizzle had begun, and he had to keep his side window down in order to prevent the inside of the windshield from fogging.

He spotted Ryan's car driving down the outside lane of the lot at ten minutes before ten. He picked up the binoculars which had been beside him on the seat and focused on the moving vehicle as it passed between him and the pole-mounted floodlight at the edge of the asphalt. The car had only one occupant. Ryan drove past the corner and slowly made a full circuit of the lot. Evidently he failed to spot Oscar's car, because he returned to the southwest corner, turned off his lights and waited. He was being cautious too, it seemed.

Oscar had no way of knowing what was on Ryan's mind tonight, but the uncharacteristically friendly tone of the man's telephone call this morning had put him on his guard. He waited another five minutes, checked his pistol to make sure that it was free in its holster, then silently left his car and walked toward Ryan's, remaining concealed by other parked cars as long as possible. Ryan saw him coming when he was 50 feet away and leaned over to open the passenger door. Before Oscar entered the car he took a quick look into the space behind the front seat to make sure no one was hiding there.

Ryan's trained eye caught the movement. "What do you think, Yeager—that I invited you here to take you for a one-way ride?" He chuckled. "Actually, I'm quite pleased with you. If it weren't for your very professional work, the President's appointee to head the Committee for Public Security would undoubtedly be someone of the Hebrew persuasion, instead of yours truly."

"Was that just an unconscious slip on your part, Ryan, when you used the word 'committee' just now instead of 'agency'?"

"Jesus! Did I say that? I'm really going to have to watch myself. You know, I had nothing to do with the choice of the name, and I was amazed when they picked something which was so suggestive of the Soviets' Committee for State Security, better known by its Russian initials, KGB. It's been on my mind all day."

Ryan's fleeting frown disappeared, and his barely contained exhilaration returned. "The similarity in names is appropriate, believe me. I've been in conferences with the big shots in the Congress, with the Director of the Bureau, and with the President's staff all week. This new agency is going to be a doozy, and the big boys have been planning it for a long time. Did you know that I'm going to have what amounts to Cabinet rank? That won't be announced for another couple of months, but I'll still be present at all Cabinet meetings from now on, and I'll be reporting directly to the President himself. In other words, despite what the papers said today, my agency is going to be pulled out from under the jurisdiction of the Department of Justice altogether."

"So you really are going to be the commander of the Praetorian Guard?"

"It looks like that's what it amounts to, although no one will quite come out and say that. There's been pressure from several directions to move this way. When the Palestinians started picking off prominent Hebes and blowing up Zionist offices in the United States last year, the Jews wanted the Bureau to drop everything else and catch Palestinians. We grabbed a couple of them, but it wasn't enough for the Jews, and they were complaining at the highest levels that the Bureau was too cumbersome and inefficient to deal effectively with Arab terrorism in this country. They wanted to bring the Mossad in and give them free rein here. Everybody balked at that, but just by coincidence some of the President's people already had been working with a group in the Congress—the leading figure there being Senator Herman—to form a new agency to deal with civil disorder when the economy bottoms out next time.

"They've been holding unemployment under eight per cent with smoke and mirrors for the past two years. All the paper shuffling in the world won't let them get away with that much longer. They're figuring on an extended period of rising unemployment, starting this summer. It may last five years or longer—during which the rate may hit 15 per cent, perhaps even higher. That's the consequence of failing to control our borders and letting the Japs take away half our basic industry.

"They've got all sorts of long-range schemes worked out for stabilizing things at a lower average standard of living for Americans, but they're afraid of civil disorder before all of the dust settles."

"You mean food riots, like in Argentina and Brazil?"

"Worse than that, actually. They can control food riots by sending in the National Guard and using tear gas or shooting a few rioters.

What they're really afraid of is revolution: not just spontaneous riots, but planned disturbances by people who want to overturn the government. They want a single government agency which can serve both as a secret police force to keep tabs on subversive activity and as a counter-revolutionary strike force. They didn't want to give that job to the Bureau because, for one thing, they haven't been very happy with the Bureau's performance lately. They aren't worried if we let a few bank robbers or forgers slip through our fingers, but they're scared to death of political violence—which will be aimed at them. Your activity and the cry for government action it raised among the pro-minority forces speeded the whole planning process up and persuaded them that this was the time to make the announcement of a new agency, when they could count on media support for the move.

"Anyway, they figured that it was easier to start a new agency than to reorganize the Bureau. Besides, I'm going to have extraordinary freedom of action, and they don't want to give that much freedom to the Bureau, with its jurisdiction over ordinary criminal matters. What worries them about that, I believe, is that the Bureau would start tapping their phones, bugging their offices, and opening their mail, and then half of the government would end up in prison for being on the take." Ryan chuckled again. "So my agency will have the freedom to tap phones without court orders and to use thumbscrews on suspects, but our mission won't be to catch the white-collar crooks in the Congress or the Federal bureaucracy; it'll just be to keep the government from being overthrown."

"Are you happy with your mission?" Oscar asked.

"Yes, Yeager, I am. What this country needs is a little order and discipline, and I'll be pleased to have a hand in providing those things. The role of my agency will become quite large during the recession of the next few years, and it'll become even larger after that. The country's going to change permanently. Hell, it's already changed permanently. The government won't be able to exist without the Agency for Public Security to prop it up. Revolutionary action is going to be a permanent feature of American life from now on: from the Arabs, from the left, from the right, from the Blacks, from the Spics, from the Whites. The country has lost all its cohesion. It's only everybody's fat paycheck that's holding things together now. When that goes the shit will hit the fan, and things will never be the same again. The President and Senator Herman don't realize that—at least, not fully—but I do.

"There is, unfortunately, a Jew in the ointment, one might say, and that's the main thing I want to discuss with you. The Hebes moved heaven and earth to try to keep me from getting the appointment to the new agency. Senator Herman called me aside after a meeting this afternoon, and he said to me, 'What's your ethnic background, son?'" Ryan mimicked the hoarse, quavery voice of the elderly legislator.

"I told him Irish Catholic, and he said, 'Well, I thought so. But you know, I've had every Jew in the Senate—a good dozen of them—plus about sixteen delegations of rabbis and Jewish business-men come to me and tell me that you aren't the right man for this job. They must have thought your background was German Nazi. When I asked them what they had against you no one had anything definite to say, but they all had a candidate of their own.' Then the old coot leaned over and whispered in my ear, 'I just want you to know,' he said, 'that if the Jews are that strongly against you, then I'm for you, and I intend to see that your nomination is approved. And the President feels the same way.'

"He'll have his committee vote on it tomorrow and then send it to the whole Senate immediately, before the Jews can build up any more steam in their effort to block me. The man they want, now that they can't have Kaplan, is Sherman Davidson, the assistant attorney general who heads the Office of Special Investigations, the Star Chamber outfit that was set up to keep the 'Holocaust' baloney alive by hunting down alleged 'war criminals' left over from the Second World War. Jesus, that was fifty years ago! Can you believe those Hebes?"

"So, are you thinking about arranging a fatal heart attack for Davidson?"

"No, I don't think that'll be necessary. I believe everything will go all right tomorrow, and then we won't have to worry about him. But we will have a continuing problem with the Jews. I think they're the only ones in our government besides me who understand the significance of the new agency and realize how much power it'll wield in the future.

"I'm telling you all these things in your role as my partner, Yeager, so you'll be able to understand the big picture. I don't know when I'll need you for another special operation, but I'm sure it'll be pretty soon. One thing about the kikes is that they never give up. What I suspect our next major operation will be is a move against the Mossad. Their agents are scattered through our government. The Bureau has most of them spotted, but we were never allowed to move against them. They're protected at the highest levels. I won't be allowed to take them out either—at least, not directly, as the situation stands now. Even Senator Herman would turn against me if I started liquidating Mossad agents, because the Yids would mobilize their Fundamentalist Christian stooges, who make up half of his constituency, to start wailing about 'poor, defenseless, little Israel,' and the controlled media would be screaming for my hide. But the Mossad is a terrorist organization, and I don't intend to let it operate on my turf.

"Besides, since the Jews didn't get their way with Kaplan or Davidson, they'll probably try to use the Mossad to make trouble for me and discredit me. In any event, I'll eventually have to get rid of the Mossad's agents in this country—all of them. I'm inclined to do it sooner instead of later, before they have time to make their first move against me. And you're going to have to help me. I think you'll find them an interesting challenge."

Ryan turned and reached for a bulky package on the rear seat. "I've assembled an information packet for you. Some of the stuff in here—general background descriptions of a number of Israel's clandestine operations—has been declassified, but most of it is top secret. It's got everything from the Bureau's files on the Mossad, including names, addresses, photographs, and other information on all the agents in this country we know about. It'll be my ass if you're caught with this stuff, so keep it in a safe place. But study it, especially the personnel information. Memorize the names and addresses and faces.

"The only reason I'm giving you this material now, is that we're really going to have to be much more careful in the future. We can't afford any more meetings. I wouldn't be surprised if the Mossad tries to put a permanent tail on me, but I don't think they've had time to get set up for that yet. I know they'll be trying to intercept all my telephone calls, and so that's the first thing I've taken care of. I've set up an absolutely secure phone in my home. The telephone company hasn't even the faintest idea it exists. The line runs from my study through the sewer tunnel to . . . well, the details aren't important. Here's the number." He handed Oscar a small slip of paper. "Don't call me unless it's really important, and try to keep your calls between 5:30 and 6:00 AM or 11:00 and 11:30 PM. When I have other documentary material or any special gadgets for you I'll leave them at a secure drop and give you a call to pick them up.

"And, Yeager—no more of your Lone Ranger stuff, understand? There are to be absolutely no independent operations of your own which I haven't authorized: no snuffing mixed couples, no shooting pesky reporters, no assassinating Congressional leaders, no blowing up churches. Got it?"

Oscar was irritated by Ryan's tone, and he felt a strong urge to tell the other man to mind his own business. A split second of reflection steered him away from such an inappropriate choice of words, however, and instead he said: "I'd been thinking about

changing my activity anyway, to something more along the educational line."

"What do you mean by that?" Ryan asked, the suspicion heavy
in his voice.

"I've done a lot of studying since you started me thinking about
the Jews. I haven't accepted all of your claims, but I have found
some really startling evidence of several things, such as the Jewish
role in launching and spreading communism in the first half of this
century, and the very heavy Jewish influence in the news and
entertainment media. Some items I've gotten from the Library of
Congress could easily be made up into pamphlets or even leaflets
for mass distribution. I believe they'll really open some eyes and
will help to counter the Jewish media control."

There was silence for a few seconds, while Ryan stared incredu-
lously at Oscar. Then the older man burst into laughter. When he
regained control of himself he shook his head and said, still chuck-
ling, "Yeager, for a fellow who's so good at figuring out how to
snuff bad guys, you sure are a flop at figuring out how to educate
people."

Oscar blushed deeply, confused and angered by Ryan's failure
to grasp his intentions. "Well, I didn't mean that the materials I had
in mind would completely *educate* the public about the origins of
communism or the reasons for the bias of the media. I still have a
lot left to learn myself about those things. But certainly they'll start
people thinking. One of the things I found is a 1920 article in a major
British newspaper by Winston Churchill . . . ."

He was interrupted by another outburst from Ryan: "Start the
people thinking! Are you serious, man? Do you really believe that
those people out there are capable of *thought*? Do you think that
they *care* who's responsible for the murders of all those poor
bastards in Russia? Do you honestly believe that they would change
anything they're doing, if you could somehow pound into their
heads the truth about what the Jews have been doing to them in this
country?"

"Well, I . . . I'm not sure what you're trying to say, Ryan." Oscar
felt his anger rising again. "I certainly had *my* eyes opened by the
evidence I found. I know that the public often doesn't seem very
bright, but there must be lots of others out there like me who will be
challenged to find out more when they're presented with facts like
those in the Churchill article. And I intend to make it easy for them,
with references to books where they can learn more. All they have
to do is go to the library . . . ."

Oscar was interrupted for a third time by Ryan's laughter, which
came in peals this time and left Ryan gasping for air, with tears

rolling down his cheeks. "Go to the library! How many of the voters in this country do you think have *ever seen* the inside of a library since they left school? It's less than three per cent, according to the American Library Association, and nearly all of those use the library only as a source of cheap romances. Americans simply don't read serious books.

"But that's not even the worst of it. Listen, you could get around the library problem by leaving off the references and just packing the facts into a pamphlet. A couple of dozen pages should suffice to present the facts about the control of the mass media. You could stand on a street corner with a stack of such pamphlets and a pocketful of money, offering all comers 20 bucks to sit down and read a pamphlet right there on the spot. You'd get a lot of takers, but it wouldn't make an iota of difference. It's like I just told you: *they don't care.* They don't give a shit. They're not interested in ideas. They're not interested in truth. They couldn't recognize a fact if it ran up and bit 'em on the ass. Furthermore, they wouldn't even absorb the information and pass it on to someone else in casual conversation, because they've been programmed not to absorb that sort of thing.

"You said there must be lots of others like you out there, but there aren't. You're unique. You don't like the race mixing that's going on in this country, so you did something about it. You started blowing away mixed couples. You strangled the biggest promoter of race mixing in the Congress. You blew a committee of race-mixing celebrities to smithereens. There are millions of other people out there who don't like race mixing either. The last Gallup poll I saw said 27 per cent of White Americans disapprove of marriages between Whites and Blacks, and I personally think that the actual percentage is a good bit higher than that. But what have any of those folks done about it? Nothing. Not a damned thing. Not even the ones who really get steamed when they see a White woman with a nigger. They've got no balls. They've got no imagination. They're constitutionally incapable of doing anything original.

"Do you really believe this country'd be in the mess it's in today if its citizens could think? I mean really think and then act accordingly, like rational individuals. They wouldn't even have to have balls; all they'd have to do is act rationally in the privacy of the voting booth. What you don't understand, Yeager, is that they're not rational individuals; they're a bunch of fucking animals, and I'm talking about the Ph.D.s and the corporation executives as well as the cab drivers and the housewives. They don't think; they only feel and react according to a batch of conditioned reflexes."

Ryan paused to catch his breath, and then his words came more calmly: "Sure, everybody knows that there are a lot of smart people, people who can figure how to get laid or how much income tax they owe or how to make a computer do what they want it to. Problem solvers. But not rational individuals. I'll give you an example: that *Illustrated Sunday Herald* article on the Jews by Churchill you mentioned being so impressed by. Don't you realize that right wingers have been reprinting and distributing that article for more than 70 years, without making even the slightest dent in the fortunes of the Jews? My father first gave me a copy of that to read nearly 40 years ago, when I was a teenager. If people were rational, they would have done something about the facts in that article. They would at the very least have quarantined the Jews, put them back into ghettos with strict limitations on their activities, the way Europeans did in the Middle Ages. That was rational, although it's passed off as superstition and prejudice by the controlled media these days. It was based on a recognition of the danger presented by the Jews and a determination to protect the people from that danger. The popes and emperors who made the Jews stay in their ghettos were rational people, who recognized facts and acted on them.

"I'll give you another example. For you the Jewish control of the mass media is a big, new discovery. But it's nothing new to anyone in the government. It's one of the most widely recognized facts of life in Washington. Everybody knows it, but no one does anything about it. And some of those people really do care what happens to the country, believe it or not. It's not rational. People behave exactly as if they're programmed. With very few exceptions, even those able to recognize a truth are unable to act on it if action would require climbing out of a rut of conditioned behavior and doing something new or different.

"Or, to shift the onus of irrationality from the right to the left for a moment, consider the cases of South Africa and Israel. The Palestinians in Israel and the Occupied Territories are treated infinitely worse than the niggers are in South Africa. But do you ever hear any of the bleeding-heart clergymen or movie stars who demonstrate against South Africa utter a cross word against Israel? It's not that the facts aren't known, and in most cases it's not even hypocrisy. A lot of those nigger lovers would as soon weep for Arabs as for Bantus, but they would have to overcome their conditioning first."

"Are you trying to tell me," Oscar came back with incredulity and defiance in his voice, "that there is no point in trying to educate people, that it does no good at all to point out their errors to them and give them facts?"

"I'm trying to tell you that you *can't* educate them—that is, you can't change their behavior—with pamphlets. The only way to persuade the population of this country that they need to change their ways is to give them a good, hard boot in the ass—about 600 times. They need to be reprogrammed, and that takes order and discipline, not books or leaflets."

"Ryan, you have a pretty dim view of human nature."

"Bullshit, Yeager! My view is realistic. I know how people function, both as individuals and in the mass. Making people do what I want them to do, whether they're violent criminals in a hostage situation or my own subordinates in the Bureau, has been my job for nearly as long as you've been alive, and the reason I've been successful at it is because I've been realistic about human nature. I'm even a little bit of an optimist, which is why I'm enthusiastic about my new job. I think I may be able to do some good."

"By kicking people in the ass?" The sarcasm in Oscar's voice was heavy.

Ryan looked at Oscar for a moment, sighed, shook his head, and said, "I'm really amazed that you did such good work on Kaplan and Feldman. If I didn't know it was you who'd taken them out, I wouldn't believe you capable of it. You talk like a goddamned intellectual, the worst sort of intellectual, the kind who can't face life as it really is. I've just told you a few of the facts of life. Instead of being grateful to me you're resentful."

He paused, then continued, "Let me give you a real nugget of wisdom: Whatever is necessary is good. Whatever the good Lord designed into our world is good. Try to change the things that are changeable, if you think they need to be changed. But don't be resentful toward the things which by their very nature are unchangeable.

"You think it's terrible that people aren't rational, that they behave like animals and have to be manipulated like animals. You want everyone to be like you. But that's childishly egocentric. If everyone were like you there could be no society, no civilization. Everything would fly apart. If there were only a thousand men like you in this country it would be ungovernable. It was just a fluke that I caught you, after half the Bureau had been tearing its hair out for months because of you. If there were 50 of you at work in Washington, 50 in Chicago, 100 in New York ... we'd be utterly incapable of dealing with the situation. You'd bring the government down.

"If you like to read books, then you should be grateful that most men aren't rational, because it takes a pretty big herd of irrational animals to provide the infrastructure for just one printing press. To

be able to afford one philosopher we need a million drones operating
on their conditioned reflexes. So be happy that people have to be
manipulated instead of educated. That's the way the Lord designed
things. The government accepts that and acts accordingly—at least,
this part of the government does," he said, tapping his chest with his
thumb. "So do the Jews.

"If it offends your humanist sensibilities to reform the behavior
of the American people with hunger and the toe of a boot and the
threat of a bullet, then there are gentler methods, more 'educational'
methods. If you had the television networks under your control you
could feed the public a new brand of pablum and accomplish in 20
or 30 years a part of what needs to be done. That is, you could change
the content of the 'ideas' that they parrot back and forth to each
other. You could have them wringing their hands over what's
happening to the Palestinians and demanding a boycott of Israel,
instead of demonstrating against South Africa. You could chase the
queers and the other freaks back into the closet. You could cut race
mixing down to almost nothing.

"You could do all that—you could partly reprogram the herd—
by changing the plots of the soap operas and the biases of the
talk-show hosts, by reworking the dialogue and being careful about
the complexions of the characters in the animated cartoons for the
kiddies, by telling your anchormen when to sneer and when not to
while they're reading the evening news. Of course, you'd still need
to give the majority of the people a good kick in the ass to make
them break a lot of the bad habits they've picked up." Ryan placed
his hand on Oscar's arm and assumed a fatherly tone. "Anyway,
since you don't control the television networks, we're going to have
to do things my way. Be glad that you have a chance to help. It's
not often in history that two rational men are able to work together
on a project so 'worthwhile. And, for Christ's sake, forget about
pamphlets."

Oscar felt stunned. He didn't want to accept what Ryan had just
told him. He fought against it. But he knew that he would end up
accepting at least a substantial part of it. He might be able to
convince himself that things weren't quite so stark as Ryan had
painted them, but the bulk of Ryan's message had the unmistakable
ring of truth. It was a truth that already had been hiding inside his
own mind, and Ryan's brutal words had simply stripped away its
cover. It was Oscar's turn to sigh. So far as his personal strategy was
concerned, it was back to the drawing board again.

Ryan glanced at his watch, then smiled and patted Oscar's arm.
"I'm going to be very busy for a couple of weeks. You do your
homework, and I'll be calling you when I need you."

XXI

Oscar was not ready to give up his pamphleteering ambition immediately, despite the cold water Ryan had poured on it. If education were as ineffective as Ryan indicated, then Harry's organization, the National League, should have discovered that fact. The day after his meeting with Ryan he gave Harry a call and received an invitation to attend a meeting of local members being held at eight o'clock the following evening, a Friday.

Persuading Adelaide to go with him was not difficult, although she made him promise that he would take her out to dinner afterward. The meeting was in the home of a member whose address Harry had given him. It was a much larger house than Harry's and was located in a wooded neighborhood of Arlington with large lots and expensive homes. Only a dozen other persons—nine men and three women, including Harry and Colleen—were present when he and Adelaide arrived.

The meeting itself lasted only a little over an hour and consisted mainly of informal progress reports of their activities by the members, followed in each case by a brief discussion, with questions or suggestions from the others. One man reported on his success in obtaining a mailing list of nearly 50,000 buyers of historical books from a commercial source which initially had refused to rent the list to the League on political grounds. Another reported on the preparations being made to mail League book catalogs and other promotional materials to the list.

A woman member, who was a commercial artist, showed an art poster she had just completed and sketches for several possible new posters. The completed poster seemed very striking to Oscar. Under the slogan 'Save the Endangered Species' it portrayed various endangered animals: On one side a surfaced whale was being attacked with harpoons from a whaling ship. On the other side, in the foreground, a leopard in a jungle setting was being shot by a Black poacher, while in the background there was a New York fur store with a leopard-skin coat in the window and a greasy-looking proprietor in the doorway counting a handful of money. And in the center, larger than the rest, was a White family—a man, a woman with a baby in her arms, and a small child, all with handsome, Nordic features and coloring. The Whites were standing huddled together on a boulder, distress and fear evident on their faces, while all around them pressed a threatening, packed mass of non-Whites, like a rising tide about to engulf them, with brown and black and yellow arms stretching up to grasp their legs. The opinion was expressed that all of the large environmental organizations would be afraid to touch the poster, but that it might sell well to students, many of whom would buy it because of its controversial theme.

Three other members were working on a video drama. One, who had written the script and would do the directing, was presently involved in the casting and appealed to the others present to provide him with an actor for one role as yet unfilled. Another, his wife, was making the wardrobe. A third was building sets in his garage.

When the business of the meeting was concluded, Harry introduced Oscar and Adelaide to the others present, including Kevin Linden, a broadcast engineer, who was the coordinator of the local group. Harry apologized for the fact that Saul Rogers, whom he especially had wanted Oscar to meet, was not present. "Saul's a schoolteacher, and he's often burdened with extracurricular duties. Tonight they've got him frisking students for drugs and weapons at a school basketball game," Harry explained.

Oscar commented on the high degree of professionalism among the members he had met. "Not exactly what I had expected a gang of wild-eyed, neo-Nazi revolutionaries to be like," he joked.

"The people we're interested in now—in fact the only kind of people we can use—are those who are willing and able to *do* things," Kevin told him. "And since the main thing we're doing is propagating facts and ideas, our people tend to be ones who have specific skills which are useful for that work. Actually that covers a pretty wide range, from writers and artists to engineers and businessmen, but it is true that in this phase of our program we have a rather high percentage of professionals and relatively few street fighters and bomb throwers, despite the image of us painted by the controlled news media. In fact, Harry is the only real bomb thrower here tonight," he finished with a grin and then excused himself.

Oscar turned to Harry and asked, "What do you think the Horowitz Act will do to your ability to continue producing and distributing your materials?"

"Some operations will have to go underground, but most of what we're doing probably won't be affected right away," Harry responded. "We've always taken a pretty positive approach, with an emphasis on raising the racial consciousness of our own people, instead of pointing out the shortcomings of others. The list of books we distribute starts off with the *Aeneid* and *Beowulf* and includes many of the other classics of Western history and legend. Much of it's the sort of thing that every graduate from our better universities used to be familiar with, before democracy came to the academy and the standards were lowered so that the Hottentots and wetbacks could get degrees too. Then, of course, there was a deliberate weeding out by the egalitarians of books which were considered to be written from the viewpoint of the White male—racist and sexist, you know," Harry added primly, larding his tone with an affected self-righteousness. Then he switched to sarcasm: "Unless a book was written by a militant lesbian, a revanchist American Indian, or a Negress with AIDS who'd converted to Judaism, it was suspect. The exception was anything about the 'Holocaust,' for which Jewish male authors, even those of the heterosexual persuasion, were acceptable.

"Now some of the classics are hard to find, even in the universities, and so we perform a useful service by making them available from a single source. I don't think that the government is ready yet to start locking people up for reading the *Iliad.* There are some books we carry which deal with the Jews which they might try to ban, if that were all we carried. We also have books which provide more historically accurate versions of 'sensitive' historical subjects—the Second World War, for example—than the officially approved books, and they'd really love to consign those to the flames. I doubt that they'll go after any of our books now, however. I think they'll be afraid that if they attack us for any one title we carry, that'll just attract attention to the rest of our books and raise some issues they'd prefer to avoid for the time being.

"What they'll do first is go after the surviving Klan groups and the publishers of low-brow racial or anti-Jewish material: things like *The Protocols of the Learned Elders of Zion* or some of the crude anti-Black material that's floating around. The pseudo-intellectual libertarian types won't squawk about banning that, and it'll allow the book-burners to establish useful legal precedents. Then, in three or four years, they'll come after us, but we'll worry about that as the time approaches. For right now we're establishing alternate channels of distribution for our most vulnerable material—mainly our original video tapes. We have a few dramatic productions on tape that are quite powerful, and the Jews are itching to keep them out of circulation. Since we produce those ourselves, though, and aren't dependent on any outside suppliers, we have a lot of freedom in changing the way we do things in order to make it much harder for the government to stop us."

Harry paused for a moment and chuckled. "Actually it's ironic. The material the government will be banning with the Horowitz Act for the next few years will be stuff the Jews aren't afraid of, for the most part; they're not especially worried by *The Protocols* or by religious tracts which purport to prove that they're actually the descendants of Satan. What really scares the bastards is the

Aeneid—and our other books which help White people understand who they are. They know that if enough of us ever develop a historical sense and an interest in our racial roots, and those things grow into a feeling of racial identity and racial responsibility, we'll snap out of the brotherhood-and-equality spell they've so carefully woven around us, and then their goose will be cooked. That's why they've waged such a campaign against the Western classics in the universities."

"You're an optimist, Harry. It's fine to educate people, to wake them up, to raise their consciousness. I've been thinking along those lines myself: making some of the interesting materials I've run across in my study project on the Jews more widely available, perhaps by working together with the League, since your people seem to have some experience with publishing—although recently I've been having some doubt about the effectiveness of such efforts. The more I think about it, the more it seems to me that no more than a fraction of a per cent of the White people in this country can be pried away from their TV sets long enough to read even a pamphlet, much less the *Aeneid*. But even if we educated everyone who's educable, what could they do as long as they remained disorganized? As soon as you start trying to organize people, the government will use the Horowitz Act to put you out of business."

"You must be referring to the provision which outlaws all organizations with racial qualifications for membership," Harry responded. "That really doesn't bother us, since we're not a membership organization."

"What do you mean, you're not a membership organization? Who're these other people here tonight? And the last time we were together you told me about at least two other people you described as members of this unit," Oscar replied somewhat indignantly.

"That was last time," Harry chuckled. "Have you heard me use the word 'member' in referring to anyone tonight?"

Oscar was impatient: "Come on, what kind of word game are you trying to play with me?"

"It's the game of survival," Harry answered, his tone now serious. "These people here are simply my friends. We get together every now and then to discuss matters of common interest. If you were a government police agent, you could never find a piece of evidence to prove otherwise."

"Sure, I could," Oscar replied belligerently. "I would just apply for membership. Then, after I received my membership card, I'd go before a Federal grand jury. The officers of the League would be subpoenaed and questioned. If they denied that it was a racially discriminatory organization, they'd be ordered to produce the names of all of the Black, Jewish, and Asian members. When they couldn't name anyone, that would be the end of the League."

"Wrong," Harry explained patiently. "First, you wouldn't get a membership card. Second, the officers, if subpoenaed, would refuse to answer all questions, citing the Fifth Amendment. They could, if they were so inclined, explain to the grand jury that the League is simply a non-profit corporation without members, and all of the official records would substantiate that. But, as a matter of principle, we refuse to answer questions for grand juries. The government could continue to pursue the matter if it chose to do so, but it wouldn't find anything that could lead to a successful prosecution."

"But what about members' dues payments? All they'd have to do is check your bank records. And what about some fellow out in the boonies that no other member has ever met? How can he join without sending in an application form or something like that to indicate that he wants to become a member?" Oscar persisted stubbornly.

"There are no dues payments, because there are no members," Harry continued his explanation. "Of course, we ask our friends to support the League's work by sending in donations regularly. The corporation accepts all donations and uses the money to pay for printing, postage, and other expenses, including staff salaries. If a friend were remiss in his donations, another friend would speak to him about it.

"As for the fellow out in the boonies who wants to apply for membership . . . ah, excuse me, who wants to participate in our work, we'd have someone correspond with him to make a preliminary evaluation. If it seemed likely that he could fit into one of our little local circles of friends or even participate on a solo basis, we'd arrange for an interview. But there wouldn't be any forms to fill out—and no records, or at least none the government would ever be likely to get its hands on. Believe me, Oscar, our legal advisers have been busy on this, even before the Horowitz Act became law. They've gone over just about every possibility and worked out ways for us to adapt to the new conditions without disrupting any of our programs."

Oscar shook his head. "Maybe you'll be able to stay out of jail, but what's the point? You'll never be able to build a politically significant organization under such constraints."

"Politically significant? What made you think we're trying to do anything politically significant?" Harry paused, smiled, then continued. "Well, of course, we are, in the long run. But if you're thinking of public demonstrations and marches with lots of people, of election campaigns and so on, that will take another organization.

We'll build it when the time comes. But right now we're trying to do something different."

He paused again, "A couple of minutes ago you estimated that fewer than one per cent of the White people in this country are interested enough in what's happening in the world around them to read a pamphlet. That's not far off the mark. Most of our fellow citizens have absolutely no sense of civic or racial responsibility. It's as if they believed that the world outside their own skins is only a sideshow for their personal amusement. What do you call that—solipsism?

"Anyway, nearly all the ones who do get involved politically are just conforming to the social pressures on their particular segment of society; they shout the same slogans that the people around them are shouting, and just as mindlessly. Almost no one is involved in a cause because he has carefully considered the situation, decided that something needs to be done, and taken upon himself the responsibility to do it, either independently or as part of a group. To me that's what defines a human being: his acceptance of responsibility. By that standard most people are simply animals thinking animals, but still animals, without the essence of humanity."

Oscar felt the hairs rising on the back of his neck as Harry's words recalled those he had so recently heard from Ryan. It was uncanny, he thought, that two men as different as William Ryan and Harry Keller—one a sworn defender of the regime, eager to use the most extreme measures against its enemies, and the other dedicated to the overthrow of that regime because of its racially destructive policies—should express the same, shockingly unorthodox view of the great bulk of their fellow men. And that he should have lived 40 years without hearing such a view, then suddenly have it thrust in his face twice within the span of a few days!

While Oscar marvelled to himself over this coincidence, Harry continued speaking: "Our task now is to educate and recruit human beings—only human beings. We don't need a mass movement for that. In fact, we can't build or control a mass movement until we have a much stronger organization of responsible people . . . ah, excuse me again, until we have many more responsible friends working together. So it's that fraction of a per cent we're after now, the few who're a little closer to the threshold than the rest."

"Threshold?" Oscar asked.

"In the Nietzschean sense," Harry replied. "The threshold between animal and man—or between man and higher man, if you prefer. In any case, between the unconscious and irresponsible on one side and the conscious, responsible preparers of the way for the Superman on the other side."

"I see," Oscar nodded. "But I suppose the Nietzschean term which seems to me more fitting is 'abyss'—the *Abgrund* which man must cross between the animal and the Superman. My impression is that the transition is not so sharp as 'threshold' implies, but rather that it's more strung out, like Zarathustra's 'rope over an abyss.' In myself, for example, I recognize a mixture of the unconscious and the conscious. Sometimes when I'm searching for the truth I feel as if I'm groping through a dense fog. Everything isn't completely dark; I'm conscious of some things. But other things are so dim that I can hardly make them out; I can't quite grasp them in my consciousness. I suspect that there are a lot of other people out there to whom it would be inaccurate to refer as 'animals,' because they have at least the barest glimmerings of consciousness, the barest beginnings of a sense of responsibility—some more and some less."

As Oscar spoke, a broad smile lit Harry's face. "So! A fellow Nietzschean!" He grasped Oscar's arm, genuinely pleased.

A momentary smile flitted across Oscar's face in response to Harry's reaction, but it immediately gave way to a frown, and he said, "I believe also that I prefer to think of the more irresponsible members of our race as children instead of as animals. You say that the possession of a sense of responsibility is what distinguishes the human being from the animal, but one can make the same distinction between adults and children instead."

"If you wish," Harry waved his hand. "But a child normally grows into adulthood. Most members of the generation alive today will go to their graves with no more sense of responsibility than when they were born."

"Perhaps, perhaps," Oscar conceded. Then he returned to his former concern: "The fact remains, there are others out there like me—at least to the extent that they are educable, that they are groping for the truth and are capable of becoming responsible adults—and I suspect that you haven't yet located most of them. It wasn't because of any of your recruiting efforts that I found out about you; if Carl hadn't introduced us, I wouldn't be here tonight. Now, with the Horowitz Act, your recruiting certainly won't go any better."

"On the contrary," Harry interrupted. "The Horowitz Act should help a lot. Many people are aware of us and our goals, but they've put off taking any action. The Horowitz Act will make them realize how late the hour is. Already we're getting more inquiries from people who've decided that the time finally has come to act."

"Enough to succeed?" Oscar queried.

Harry shrugged, and when he spoke the worry was audible in his voice: "No one can guarantee us success. But what we're attempting is necessary, and because it's necessary we must believe it is possible and do our best to succeed. If it's impossible, we'll die trying."

"So will the race," Oscar added grimly.

"What are you two arguing about so seriously?" asked Adelaide, who had just walked over and slipped her arm around Oscar's waist. Throughout his conversation with Harry he had been eyeing her with an anxiety he hoped did not show, as she chatted gaily on the other side of the room with a circle of five men who had gathered around her like moths attracted to a flame. It was clear that a couple of the other women at the meeting were irritated, and Adelaide eventually had noticed this and had broken away from her circle of admirers.

"I'm just trying to convince Harry that his organization has to buy the CBS television network away from that gang of Jews who own it in order to reach more people with his message," Oscar answered lightly.

"That would do it," Harry agreed. "We dream about that sort of thing. Some of our rasher mem . . . er, friends have proposed seizing a broadcasting studio of one of the networks during a live broadcast of a major sports event and sending a taped message up to the satellite and into 40 million living rooms. They figure we could hold off the cops for half an hour while our tape was broadcast. And believe me, we'd try it if we thought it would have a major effect. But a single broadcast, no matter how well done, won't make much of an impression on the public. The only way to get a new idea into people's heads or to change old ideas is through endless repetition. The first time they don't even realize what you've said. After the thousandth time they begin to get the idea. And after the ten thousandth time they're convinced."

"Well, now, finally you've told me that you have some members who've been thinking along the same lines I have," Oscar responded with a grin. "How do I sign up?"

"Are you serious?" asked Kevin Linden, who had just rejoined their circle.

"Yes," Oscar answered. "I get a little impatient with Harry's lectures sometimes, but it's seldom that I meet a man who is able to stimulate my thinking as much as he does. I need to talk to him on a more regular basis, and so it would only be fair for me to pay my dues for the privilege. Besides, I really have been thinking seriously about changing my activities more toward the sort of things the League is doing."

"And what have you been doing until now?" Kevin asked.

"Ah, well, mostly it's been what you might call one-on-one persuasion, delivering the racial message to individuals or couples—although on one occasion I believe I may have influenced the thinking of a larger group. But I really find that method is too slow and would like to explore ways in which the mass media might be used to reach more people," Oscar answered somewhat lamely.

"We'll be happy to count you among our circle of friends in this area," Kevin said, extending his hand to Oscar. "Harry will get some personal data from you. He'll also notify you of meetings and will discuss with you an appropriate schedule of donations."

"Hey, me too," Adelaide chimed in.

XXII

Oscar took his new commitment to the National League very seriously, despite his growing misgivings about the value of educational work at such a desperate hour in his race's struggle for survival. Fueling his fervor for the organization's work was his inability to think of anything more effective he could do. He was inclined to believe Ryan's assertion that a thousand men like himself could bring the government down, but the problem was to find them and recruit them; then, perhaps, would be the time to return to his former activities. Until then the League seemed the best available medium for finding the other 999 men needed for that sort of work to be conclusive in its effects.

His obsession was to find a way to utilize the mass media for the League's message. He understood Harry's argument about the need to reach and recruit a sufficient number of superior people before trying to move the masses, but he chafed with impatience at the slowness of the results the League was obtaining, and he was afraid of the dangers involved in such a narrow strategy. The League's lawyers might be entirely correct, in a textbook sense, about the inability of the government to prosecute the organization under the Horowitz Act, but they were assuming that the government would be bound by its own rules. They did not realize, as he did, that in the future the government would be relying more and more on men like Ryan to protect itself: men who did not play by the rules. The only way an organization could protect itself from a government served by such men was to mobilize large masses of people—masses who could be sent howling into the streets when necessary. So instead of more history books, he began bringing books on mass communications home from the library. And he began watching more than the news programs on television; he spent dozens of hours with Adelaide watching even the most mind-numbingly insipid programs, from the game shows, with their gongs, buzzers, raucous laughter, and imbecilely grinning contestants, to the rant and cant of the faith-healing evangelists, and then analyzing with her the factors that gave them their appeal to a mass audience. He had not lost his interest in investigating the Jews' role in the affairs of his race, from biblical times to the present, but he already knew that something had to be done about them, regardless of what his continued historical studies might reveal to him about their schemes and their motives. Their control of the news and entertainment media alone demanded immediate action.

Adelaide also was an enthusiastic League member. Not only did her membership in the organization seem a worthwhile activity in itself, but she was doubly pleased by its effects on Oscar. Whatever it was that he had been brooding over in the past seemed to be bothering him less now. There were fewer evenings when he made excuses for not being able to be with her, and they were together more. He was even beginning to talk with her in a definite way about marriage. They already had decided that she would give up her apartment and move in with him in June, when she had a vacation scheduled.

Three weeks after they had joined the League, and a week after their second League meeting, Harry invited Oscar and Adelaide over to meet fellow members Saul and Emily Rogers. When they arrived at the Kellers' house Colleen ushered them down to the basement recreation room. At the foot of the stairs Oscar was startled by the appearance of the man who confronted him from the other side of the large room: he was a veritable giant, whose huge, craggy-featured, bearded head nearly brushed the ceiling, and whose piercing, blue eyes seemed to have a luminous quality to them as they transfixed Oscar in the doorway. Never before had he seen such an imposing figure.

By the time introductions had been made and everyone was seated, Oscar had recovered from his astonishment and begun to size Saul up. The man probably was between 40 and 45 years old, although his beard made him look older; at least, it emphasized an air of sternness and authority about him which usually was associated with greater age. His voice was deep and strong and had a strange, arresting quality. It was hard to imagine such a man as a schoolteacher, although he certainly would have an advantage in dealing with some of the unruly classroom punks who infested the public schools these days, Oscar thought.

Saul's wife Emily was tall and thin, in her early thirties, blonde, and rather pretty. She also was a teacher. The couple had no children.

After initial pleasantries Oscar took an aggressive stance in his conversation with his new associate: "What did your parents have against you when they gave you the name 'Saul'?" he queried with a mischievous smile.

Saul leaned as far back in his chair as he could and stretched his legs straight out, while he contemplated the ceiling for a moment. "Well, Oscar, they were what you would call 'thumpers': very devout Fundamentalists. All of the kids in the family were stuck with names from the Old Testament. Don't feel sorry for me; grieve for my brother Abinadab. Actually, the Jewish names were the least of our burdens; it was the endless readings from the Bible which nearly killed all of us. Not just on Sundays, but every damned day. There was no way to get away from it."

Suddenly Saul leaped to his feet as if electrified, his huge frame erect and rigid, making him seem to loom even taller than his six and a half feet. With his arms raised over his head and his eyes blazing, with his head tilted back and his beard thrust out at an angle from his chest, he looked the very image of all of those Sunday school classroom pictures of an Old Testament prophet in a state of incipient frenzy, about to let loose with a revelation from on high. He flung his right arm toward Oscar, his index finger pointing accusingly, and roared, "Behold, I shall smite the unbeliever. Yea, I shall lay waste to him; I shall destroy him utterly, and I shall make his household a desolation; I shall wipe out the memory of his seed from under heaven. I shall make his name an abomination among all the tribes of Israel, for he hath forsaken the Holy One."

The thunder of his first words seemed to his listeners still to be rolling and crashing around the room when he lowered his voice and finished in a tone somewhat gentler, but carrying no less authority, "Thus saith the Lord."

Foam flecked Saul's lips. The fire in his eyes died as he slowly relaxed and brought his arms down to his sides. The room remained silent.

Oscar was the first to find his voice: "Jesus, Emily, what's he been drinking?" Although Oscar's question was meant as a jest, the awe in his voice was unmistakable.

Emily forced a nervous laugh. "He's cold sober. Just be thankful. Sometimes when he's had a couple of drinks, he'll keep up the fire and brimstone for half an hour. It's amazing what comes out of the man's mouth."

"Really?" Oscar was interested now. "Hey, Saul, give us another demonstration."

"Oscar, please don't get him started!" Emily begged.

"But he's really good! I've never seen anything like it. Where did you learn to do that, Saul?"

Saul laughed to hide his reaction to Oscar's flattery. "Actually, when I was a kid that was my way of coping with the forced doses of Bible reading we had to listen to from my father. I would go out into the garage when no one was around and do my Isaiah imitation. Or Jesus. Or God. I would improvise and spout out everything which had been pumped into me, but with a few new twists of my own. It became sort of a game, in which I would make up the most outlandish things to say as I pretended to be a Biblical figure calling down the lightning onto the idolators. But I think it was really a sort of therapy for me too. Anyway, I got to be fairly good at it. I've always been a frustrated actor, you know."

"Would you mind performing just a little more now? I'd like to see what you can do when you set your mind to it. You've given me an idea."

"Shall I give you my version of the Sermon on the Mount?" Saul asked, not really convinced that Oscar's request was serious.

"Whatever. Just spew out some more and wave your arms a bit."

Saul stood up again, slowly this time, and hesitated. Then, with a serene, distant look on his face, he raised his arm in a gesture of blessing and began, his voice calm and quiet, but powerful: "Verily, my children, I say unto you, he that suffereth for my sake shall be a horse's ass, for I am not the way, the truth, or the life. He that hungereth after righteousness shall starve, for my father in heaven hath . . . ."

As Saul spoke, the fact that he was babbling nonsense seemed almost not to matter. The richly resonant tones of his voice and the expressiveness of his face, his gestures, and his stance carried such utter conviction that Oscar and the others easily could imagine him wearing a flowing, white robe instead of a business suit, standing on an outcropping of rock in the desert before a multitude of flea-bitten Israelites instead of on the carpet in the Kellers' recreation room. Not much more imagination was required to see a golden halo of light about six inches above his head. Saul's voice went on and on, as melodious and soothing now as it had been harsh and commanding before. He was never at a loss for words, and all of his words sounded like something his listeners thought they could vaguely remember reading in the King James Bible in childhood, although Saul was making most of it up as he went along. There was an overwhelming intensity about the man as he spoke, together with a powerful sense of presence.

Oscar finally broke the spell by standing up. "Saul," he said, hardly able to suppress the excitement he felt, "we have a job for you!"

"You're going to have him stand on the sidewalk in front of the Capitol and preach a crusade against the reprobates inside," Emily laughed.

"He'll preach a crusade, all right, but it will be to more than the tourists outside the Capitol. I believe that we have the answer to Billy Gresham, Jerry Caldwell, Jimmy Braggart, Pat Robinson, Moral Richards, and the rest of that sleazy crew of Jew worshippers. Saul, do you know anything about the Christian Identity doctrine?"

"Oh, yeah, a little. I read a piece in the Sunday *New York Times* a few weeks ago about the people who follow that line. And I'd

heard about them a couple of times before that. They've taken the
basic Fundamentalist doctrine and turned it around. They teach that
we are the 'chosen' people, and the Jews are impostors. The people
of the Old Testament were really Aryans instead of Semites. And
the Jews' god—they call him 'Yahweh'—made his special covenant
with our ancestors, not the Hebrews, or something like that. The
people at the *New York Times* really hate their guts—call them
neo-Nazis and everything else."

"Okay, good. I read the same article you did, but I've done a little
research since then. I read everything about them I could find in the
library, which wasn't much, and I even wrote to one of their churches
and got some of their literature. The really important thing about
them is that they are having pretty good success in recruiting
conventional Christians. They are strongest in rural areas. A lot of
farmers in the Midwest have bought their line. They've grown a lot
in the last few years, despite the fact that they have no mass medium
for their message. I'm convinced that the only thing holding them
back is that all of their leaders and spokesmen are working-class
people who aren't sophisticated enough to compete with the big-
time Christian hucksters like Caldwell. On a one-to-one basis,
though, they seem to be doing all right, and I'm sure it's because
their doctrine has a powerful appeal to Fundamentalists."

"The reason they can't recruit anyone but uneducated hicks is
that their doctrine is crazy," Harry chimed in. "I've actually met and
talked to one of them. He drove a truck for the company I was with
before I went to the Pentagon. They have this completely nutty
version of history, which no one who's paid attention in his high
school history class can believe."

"Crazier than the doctrine of Transubstantiation or the Immacu-
late Conception?" Oscar quickly came back. "Do you think that
people who believe Jesus walked on water and rose from the dead
can't accept a nutty version of history? Not all of those people are
uneducated hicks, although being uneducated must help. The point
is that there are somewhere around a hundred million White folks
in this country who already believe things no more bizarre than the
Identity doctrine. With Saul as a spokesman and network television
as a medium, the Identity movement could bowl Caldwell and the
rest right over."

"It won't work," Harry rejoined. "One thing I do know something
about is network television. The only reason Caldwell and the others
are able to use it so effectively is that they work hand in glove with
the Jews. If one of those TV evangelists had even the faintest whiff
of Identity about him, he'd never be allowed near a TV camera."

"Hey, I'm not a simpleton," Oscar replied, a trace of exasperation showing in his voice. "I've been spending a lot of time thinking about the fact that the TV evangelists have forty million Americans convinced that whatever the Jews want the Jews should have—that it's the worst sort of wickedness to oppose the Jews' slightest wish. It's these forty million Fundamentalist morons, even more than the Jews themselves, who are responsible for America's suicidal policy in the Middle East, for example. They are willing to bring a nuclear holocaust down on our heads in order to insure Israel's continued territorial expansion; in fact, they even *hope* for a nuclear holocaust. They've been convinced it will be the fulfillment of Bible prophecy. They also believe that they'll personally escape the holocaust by being gently wafted up to the pearly gates at the last moment: 'the rapture,' they call it.

"Now, I know that one can't simply start preaching against the Jews on television. And I didn't mean to imply that Saul should preach the Identity doctrine, now or ever. But there is a phenomenon out there which I believe we can use. Forty million people literally believe whatever Caldwell and the other evangelists tell them; believe it so strongly that they not only give enormous sums of money to the hucksters, but they vote in accord with their beliefs and are willing to commit mass murder in furtherance of them.

"Sure, if the hucksters start leading their flock in a direction the Jews don't like, they'll have their water turned off in a hurry. But there are ways around that. The problem that I didn't see a way around was that of competing effectively with the hucksters for the attention of the sheep. I mean, Caldwell and the others are no dummies; they know their business, and they're damned good at it. I've spent hours watching them. But now, by God, we've got somebody who's better!"

Colleen had been listening quietly, but now she spoke up: "Oscar, it's not that easy. I've spent all of my adult life in television broadcasting. The Jews control every aspect of it, and they pay close attention to it. They are fully aware of the power it gives them, and they are also aware of the danger it could be to them if an enemy were able to use it against them. They are always on the lookout. Nobody, but *nobody*, gets a network audience before the Jews have checked him out thoroughly and are completely convinced that he's tame. I've seen it happen over and over again. They have a huge secret-police network, the B'nai B'rith, which keeps computerized files of every 'anti-Semitic' incident in the country. If Joe Blow tells a Jewish joke at a Rotary Club meeting, and a Jewish member hears about it, the B'nai B'rith's Anti-Defamation League soon will have a dossier on Joe Blow. If Joe ever tries to become a talk-show host, the first thing a Jewish station owner will do is check him out with the ADL. And he won't get the job. If the station owner is a Gentile, and he hires Joe, the network his station is affiliated with will check with the ADL. And the word will come back to the owner: get rid of Joe—or else.

"Besides, even if Joe Blow is completely clean, breaking into television will be no easy matter for him. There's big money in TV, and a whole lot of people besides Joe would like to get their hands on it. You don't get in on the basis of talent, although that undoubtedly helps a little. It's who you know; it's who'll do you a favor. An outsider really doesn't have a chance."

"Colleen, 1 appreciate your concern. I'm sure that you know the business. We'll need a lot of advice from you. But I've got a couple of tricks up my sleeve, and I'm convinced we have a good chance to get Saul on the air. I'm also convinced that Saul is so damned good that once he's on, the Jews will have a hard time getting him off, because he'll get a real hook into the sheep in a hurry. We'll have to be very careful, of course, and play our cards just right. But I'm certain we have to try this. A gift like Saul hasn't been dropped into our laps for nothing."

Harry snorted, "Hell, Oscar, you're beginning to sound like one of the sheep yourself. What do you mean when you say Saul is a 'gift'? A gift from Yahweh, maybe?"

Oscar blushed, then glanced at his watch. "I know it's getting late, folks, but I need to check a couple of things with Colleen before we give up for the evening. You may not be convinced yet, but this project is going to be a big thing for us, and I intend to get started on it now."

XXIII

Oscar's excitement continued to run high during the next few days. Although his initial consultation with Colleen had revealed more unforeseen obstacles than opportunities, he was nevertheless able to formulate a tentative plan of action which both Harry and Colleen grudgingly admitted just might succeed in getting Saul on the air. And his further meetings and discussions with Saul reinforced his initial impression of the latter's unique talent.

Oscar's scheme, in basic outline, was to attach Saul to the coattails of an established television evangelist by letting one of them see just enough of Saul's preaching ability to be convinced Saul would be useful, but not enough for him to realize that Saul could overshadow him. After being launched into the public consciousness with the evangelist's facilities, Saul would be cut loose from the coattails and allowed to develop his own following. Then—and only then—would he begin leading his flock along a new path.

The biggest initial problem was convincing Saul. It wasn't so much that he doubted his own ability as that going along with Oscar's plan would mean crossing a personal Rubicon for which he hadn't prepared. He could hardly count on ever going back to teaching again, after being in the public spotlight and causing the sort of furor Oscar had in mind. Emily was distraught when Saul began seriously turning over Oscar's proposal in his mind. She threatened to leave him if he went through with it. But for Saul the plan had a certain fatal fascination, because it depended in a crucial way on his peculiar talent and appealed at the same time to his long-suppressed urge to perform before an audience.

The break came when Jerry Caldwell, the number-two man among the television evangelists, agreed to give Saul an audition. Harry had instigated that offer. The company for which he moonlighted sold television-studio lighting equipment, among other things, and Caldwell was a customer. He dropped by Caldwell's studio during a taping session of his "New Time Gospel Hour," which boasted a weekly television audience of eight million, ostensibly to see how his company's equipment was working. Caldwell's customary program format required the participation of several auxiliary preachers—sometimes as many as five—in addition to himself, and there was a fairly rapid turnover among these auxiliaries.

After the session was over, Harry told Caldwell about Saul, saying that he had seen the latter preaching on a local station in another state and had been very impressed by his ability. Saul was now looking for a larger audience, Harry said, and certainly would jump at the chance to work with a real professional like Caldwell. The flattery worked, and Caldwell told Harry to send Saul to see him.

After Saul was hired as an auxiliary by Caldwell, he had to tread a thin line. He needed to put on a good enough show to keep Caldwell convinced of his value, but he dared not let his light shine at anywhere near its full brilliance. To do so would focus the attention of the television audience on himself instead of Caldwell, and then he would be canned in an instant. Nor was there ordinarily an opportunity to catch Caldwell off guard with a *fait accompli*, because the sermons nearly always were taped in advance. It was not at all uncommon for Caldwell to demand extensive editing or even an entire retake, if he was not satisfied when he viewed the tape.

Even with Saul carefully restraining himself and maintaining a mien of humility the going was a bit sticky sometimes. He was a good nine inches taller than Caldwell and had a much more commanding appearance. Because of this, he and Caldwell could not appear on the screen at the same time, except by employing camera trickery of one sort or another, so that the difference in height was not apparent to the viewers.

It was clear to Saul that his employer had mixed feelings about him. On the one hand Caldwell recognized his assistant's audience appeal—Saul already had attracted favorable remarks from several Fundamentalist commentators—and he was not one to pass up any opportunity to increase his share of the Fundamentalist television audience. But he was a careful, calculating man, and the last thing he wanted to do was help a rival—or a potential rival. Saul wondered how long the relationship would last.

He shared his worry with Oscar, and they decided that their best chance for success in launching Saul on an independent career was to act as soon as possible—which meant the next time Caldwell gave a live broadcast. Actually, these occurred four or five times a year, generally on special occasions, such as Easter or Christmas or a political event, and Saul already had participated in one, just three weeks after he began working for Caldwell. An Easter sunrise service was coming up in a little more than a month.

"Well, what shall I do to get the rubes' attention?" Saul wanted to know. "The service will be outdoors. Perhaps I can call down a lightning bolt from heaven onto Jerry's head and then take over his pulpit."

"I'm afraid our special-effects department can't provide lightning bolts on demand," Oscar replied, "but there are some things we can do. How about a halo for you during your part of the service? Think that'll wow 'em?"

"Can you really do that?"

"Maybe. I've been thinking about it, but I still need to try a couple of things. I'll know in a day or two. Meanwhile, you can be thinking about how you'll handle your mini-sermon."

It was the middle of the following week before Oscar was ready to try out his artificial halo on Saul. It was really just a tiny, high-intensity light bulb in a special fitting Oscar had made in his shop. It was designed to take advantage of Saul's unique complement of hair. Although thinning, there still was enough hair on Saul's head to constitute a fairly lush if entirely disorderly mop, with sparse, iron-gray tufts thrusting out in every direction. The light was energized by a battery belt, similar to those used by news cameramen, connected by a thin wire which ran from Saul's scalp down inside his collar.

Oscar carefully positioned the fitting close to the center of Saul's scalp, anchored it with a dab of sticky wax, and then combed his hair back in place over it. It could not be seen unless one looked directly down on Saul's head from above, and even then it was unlikely to be noticed by a casual observer. Oscar positioned himself some 15 feet in front of Saul, about where the television camera would be when he was behind the pulpit, and then had Saul close a switch on the battery belt, activating an electronic circuit which smoothly increased the power to the bulb to its maximum value.

"Eureka!" Oscar cried. "Your hair looks like it's on fire. It diffuses the light just enough to give the impression of a nimbus. Of course, it's too bright in the center, and there's no light at the sides, but we can fix that."

Suddenly Saul's hair *was* on fire, and a thin wisp of acrid smoke curled upward from the center of his head, even though Saul already had opened the switch. Fortunately, the damage was limited to a few dozen strands of hair immediately above the hot bulb, and Saul's scalp was not burned.

"We'll have to watch that," was Oscar's reaction. "The bulb is putting out 150 watts when it's on. You'll have to keep the most dramatic passage of your sermon down to about five seconds, including about a second each for the power-up and power-down sequences. And we'll have to use a hair stiffener with more body, so the heat doesn't cause your hair to wilt and contact the hot bulb."

"You might also put a little more insulation between the fitting and my scalp," Saul suggested. "It got uncomfortably hot. And while you're looking for a stiffer hair spray, why don't you find something that's fireproof? Otherwise, I might end up doing an impromptu imitation of Moses' burning bush."

Oscar spent the better part of the next two weeks refining his gadget, and Saul went through another four test runs with it before Oscar was completely satisfied. The final version consisted of three separate bulbs, and two hours of painstaking effort was required to position them and arrange Saul's hair after they were in place. The switch was moved from the battery belt down to Saul's knee joint, inside his trousers. He could turn it on and off unobtrusively by pressing his knees together. The power-up sequence was shortened to half a second, while the power- down sequence was stretched out to nearly two seconds to give the right effect.

"When the big day comes we'll have to start to work on you at least three hours before you're due to go on camera, and then you'll have to dodge Jerry's regular makeup man. It might seem like a lot of trouble just to light up your hair for a few seconds, but it could make a big difference in the way the television audience perceives you," Oscar commented, as he jotted down notes to serve as remind ers during the final installation of the lights.

XXIV

66This had better be worth getting up for," Adelaide grumbled in mock irritation, as Oscar adjusted the color and brightness on the television screen in their motel room. She propped herself up in bed and pulled the covers to her chin. Oscar had just returned from Saul's room a few minutes earlier. It was 5:00 AM, and Caldwell's Easter service was about to begin. On Saturday Adelaide and Oscar had driven up from Washington to the small Maryland town where Caldwell's church and television studio were located.

"Quit complaining," Oscar admonished her as he dropped the last of his clothes onto a chair and slipped into the bed beside her. "I've been up all night."

"Don't I know it!" Adelaide exclaimed, maintaining her pretense at anger. "You talk me into going off with you for a romantic weekend in a motel, and then you leave me in the motel by myself the whole night. Some romance!"

"Tell you what, sweetheart. I'll give you as much romance as you can handle in just a minute—if this caper comes off without a hitch. Otherwise I'll shoot myself."

For the first time since he had known her he was oblivious to the feel of Adelaide's naked body next to his. Despite her warmth and her intoxicating nearness, he was cold and tense. There was a tight knot in his stomach. He had the sickening intuition that this whole stunt with Saul was a terrible and foolish mistake. There were just too many things which could go wrong. How could he have been so naive, so childish, as to believe that he could pull off a deception like this with millions of people watching! Almost certainly some of Caldwell's people around Saul would spot the trickery immediately and expose it. He began to perspire, and the desperate thought flashed into his mind that perhaps there still was some way he could get word to Saul telling him not to go through with it.

But, no, it was too late! On the screen another of Caldwell's assistants, who had just finished leading the singing of a hymn, already was introducing Saul. Oscar was so apprehensive he could hardly bear to watch as Saul swung into his mini-sermon. He stole a quick glance at Adelaide's face. She was absorbed in what was happening on the screen. Oscar had not told her about the gadgetry with which he had equipped Saul. She only knew that Saul was to try to steal the show from Caldwell this morning by departing from his script and pouring on the histrionics. He turned back to the television screen.

"And, my brothers and sisters, our Lord Jesus commanded us all to love one another as brothers and sisters, no matter what our station in life, no matter what our color or race, no matter what our nationality; yes, he did: that was his message to us." Saul still was mouthing his lines with a sort of beatifically vacant smile. It was almost time for him to wind up and turn the pulpit over to Caldwell.

Suddenly Saul's voice came to a strangled halt in mid-platitude, as if he had tried to swallow a large chicken bone and it had stuck in his throat. His body froze in an awkward, twisted stance, and the smile on his face was instantly replaced by an intense expression which seemed a blend of awe and fear, as of a man staring with irresistible fascination into the white-hot mouth of an erupting volcano which he knew was about to incinerate him.

Then Saul spoke again, but this time in a croaking, hoarse whisper: "My God, the power, *the power!*" He seemed completely overwhelmed by something that only he could see. But this phase lasted only a few seconds. Then the stiffness and awkwardness passed from his body as quickly as they had come, and he stretched himself to his full, imposing height. It was as if he suddenly had become physically larger. The expression on his face now was completely changed. In place of the fear there was serenity; in place of the awe there was majesty. He turned his piercing eyes, now flashing with the fire that Saul knew how to summon up from his depths, directly on his television audience. He slowly raised his arms. And Oscar flinched as he saw the lights go on in Saul's hair.

Saul's voice—but a voice entirely different from the one in which he had been giving his sermon—boomed out: "Behold! I am come again unto you, that you might live. Through this, my servant, I will speak to you." Saul swung his right arm in toward his chest. "Hearken to me, and obey."

With these last words, which went rolling out over the open-air assembly like a thunderclap echoing and reechoing off distant mountains, the lights in his hair dimmed out. The expression on his face changed once again, from majesty back to awe, but this time mixed with wonder instead of fear. And he seemed at the same time to shrink an inch or so in stature. He stood speechless and apparently confused for another moment, then he turned and stumbled away from the pulpit, while a stricken-faced Jerry Caldwell hastened to take his place.

"My God!" exclaimed Adelaide. "Was that really Saul?" She was visibly shaken.

"Yep," answered Oscar, feeling immensely better than he had just a minute earlier, "that was our Saul."

"But there was light streaming from his head! He looked like a god!"

Oscar turned to look at Adelaide again. She appeared almost as stricken as Caldwell. To Oscar's critical eye the halo effect had looked painfully tinny, just barely passable. He had not seen anything streaming from Saul's head, just some lights going on in his hair which caused it to look a bit luminous. But Adelaide, not knowing the trickery involved, thought she had seen more. Apparently the power of suggestion had been at work with her. He hoped it had been at work with the rest of the television viewers as well.

Adelaide, still staring at the television screen, where Caldwell was awkwardly and woodenly attempting to recapture the audience, started to say something else, but Oscar quickly placed a hand over her mouth. Gently but firmly, he pushed her back down into the pillows. Then he pulled the blanket down, exposing the glorious swell of her breasts. His mouth hungrily sought one of her nipples, while his free hand reached under the blanket about her hips and tenderly caressed and probed her. In a few seconds she relaxed and then began responding eagerly to his caresses.

XXV

"Well, Saul, how do you plan to top last Sunday's performance?" Harry wanted to know, when Oscar, Saul, Colleen, and he met in Oscar's house three days later. "Will you levitate a mountain to impress the rubes the next time you're on the air?"

"He's going to take it easy on the miracles for a while," Oscar answered. "The main thing we've got to do is get him established with his own program and build up his audience. I don't want to risk blowing the whole thing with any more cheap tricks now. Caldwell is furious and is threatening to denounce Saul as a fraud if he goes into competition with him."

"Oh, did Jerry figure out how you did your halo trick?" Harry turned to Saul. "Doesn't he believe that you were really a medium for Jesus during your sermon?"

"That cynical little turd doesn't believe anything, except that he was had," Saul grinned. "Even though he was watching my part of the service on his backstage monitor, he hasn't figured out what happened. He had to take the pulpit after me, and I headed straight for the rest room and got Oscar's gadgetry out of my hair. Then I pretended I wasn't feeling well and went home. After the service Caldwell was fit to be tied. The main thing he's afraid of is that I'll start my own program and drain off some of his donations. The phones at his place have been ringing off the hook around the clock ever since Sunday morning, with the faithful calling in to express their gratitude to Jerry for letting them hear Jesus speak through me. He knows what an effect I had on them, but he doesn't know what to do about it. All he could say to me was, 'God damn you, Rogers, god damn your ass, I'll get even with you if you try to take advantage of this thing, god damn you!' He's still so mad he's incoherent. I've been getting regular reports from one of his secretaries, who is convinced now that I am the true mouthpiece for Jesus."

"Well, don't disabuse her of that conviction," Oscar laughed. "She can be useful. Now, Colleen, tell us what you've found out about getting Saul on the air."

"Washington has been my one big success," she replied. "There's an empty Sunday-evening slot at WZY-TV, and they're willing to sell the time to Saul. But besides that, I've been talking with Carl Hollis, who's the sales manager for the Gospel Time Network. I believe that we can lease their satellite transponder for an hour of prime time a week, although Hollis hasn't given me a firm answer yet. He says the network directors want to have an interview with

Saul first, but it's the one Christian network in the country that's actually run by Christians, and I believe Saul will be able to get by them—especially since the network is having real financial problems now, and they need the money. If it goes, that'll put us on about 370 local television stations around the country, but they're nearly all very small stations, with rural and small-town audiences. They also have access to nearly 100 local cable systems, through their arrangement with Acme Cablevision and half a dozen smaller cable networks.

"The problem is getting Saul on the powerful independent stations in the big metropolitan areas—places like Chicago, Los Angeles, Nashville, Atlanta, where the biggest Fundamentalist audiences are. There's real interest in Saul around the country now, but the stations in most of the big metro areas are being very cautious. They all know there's some kind of hokum involved with Saul. It's not that they object to hokum. They carry Moral Richards, and he pretends to cure cripples, restore sight, and perform other 'miracles' on his show. It's just that Saul is an unknown factor. The Jews know that Richards is under control. He's one of Israel's biggest boosters. He has a vested interest in maintaining his pro-Israel line. But they don't know about Saul, and they aren't going to let him on the air until they're sure he's not dangerous to them. The green light at WZY was just a fluke. I've been dealing with the station manager there for years, and I vouched for Saul. That won't work with the other big stations. It's just like I was telling you at first."

"Okay, so we'll have to convince them. But I don't see why that should be so hard. After all, Saul has been preaching with Caldwell, who phones the Israeli Embassy for permission to go to the bathroom."

"He was with Caldwell for less than three months," Colleen interjected. "He doesn't have a vested interest in continuing to follow Caldwell's line. What the Jews want is people who have the same interests they have. That's the only way they'll trust anyone."

"Okay, we'll have Saul make a tape in which he crawls on his belly for the Jews the way Caldwell and Richards and Braggart and all the others do. We'll cook up a sermon for him in which he spells out his own theological position, and it'll be a position even more subservient to the Jews than that of the rest of the evangelist pack. You can send the tape to the stations we want to sign up. We'll make Saul so pro-Jewish that the thought of his turning on them will be inconceivable."

"Aren't you in danger of painting Saul into a corner if you do that?" Harry asked. "I mean, if Saul really does come on strong with the standard Judeo-Christian line, he'd lose his credibility if he suddenly switched and started talking out of the other side of his mouth."

"Saul's not going to pull a switch on the Jews," Oscar retorted. "Jesus is. Besides, you're really not talking about Christian Fundamentalists when you worry about being ideologically consistent. They're perfectly capable of absorbing the wildest inconsistencies you can dream up, without batting an eyelash."

Saul stroked his beard thoughtfully. "I think I can see a reasonable scenario for what you have in mind. But it seems to me that timing will be the most important factor for us. We need to get on the air now, while I'm still hot. But then we'll also need to get Jesus back into the act very soon too. If I just keep dishing out the standard Caldwell pap for very long, I won't stay hot. We can't keep paying for air time forever, unless we keep the rubes on the edge of their seats. We'll go broke."

"You don't give yourself enough credit. Caldwell and the rest are keeping the rubes' attention with that same old pap, and they're raking in hundreds of millions of dollars."

"Billions," Harry corrected Oscar. "Television evangelism is a six-billion-dollar industry."

"Now, suppose we do get our own racket set up the way Caldwell has his, and the audience is willing to keep paying for the pap," Saul continued. "We don't know anything about the business end of Caldwell's operation. He didn't establish himself overnight. He spent years building his organization and learning the tricks of his trade. I may be able to preach circles around him, but there's a lot more to it than that. Our own studio facilities are fine for what we do, but they're not up to Caldwell's standard; they're not really adapted for commercial broadcast work at all. To make the tape you want to send to the Jewish station owners—which should be as slick as possible—we'd have to use a commercial studio and crew. Where's the money for that coming from?"

"I don't know all the answers yet," Oscar replied. "Keep the line open to Caldwell's secretary. She should be able to give us some advice. I don't see why we can't hire a commercial studio for the first tape, then get the additional equipment we need to use our own studio for the broadcast tapes. Eventually, we'll need our own studio crew anyway, if we're to try any more special effects. As for an initial shot of money to get things started, there are some people I can call." Actually, there weren't; he had no definite ideas for raising money, but he was willing to do whatever might be necessary.

The conference lasted another three hours. It ended with a detailed assignment of responsibilities. Oscar was to raise at least

$200,000 for production expenses and buying air time. Colleen was to continue negotiating with the religious network people and the independent station owners. Harry was to make the arrangements for studio facilities and begin rounding up the equipment Saul would need for their own studio. Saul was to work on a series of sermons.

Oscar was determined to push as hard as possible to win a major share of the Christian evangelical television audience for Saul within the next two or three months. He felt that an important part of their strategy was to pull listeners away from the other evangelists, to change their loyalties, before trying to change their ideas about Jews and other matters. If Saul came on too strong too soon, a lot of people might be influenced momentarily by him, but Caldwell and the other evangelists would still have their ears and would be able to convince many of them that Saul was a false prophet. Oscar wanted to weaken the opposition as much as possible before the real shooting started, so that Caldwell and the others would be preaching to empty pews.

Besides, as soon as Saul began hitting the Jews things would start happening fast, things that would keep Oscar very busy. He wanted to take care of some other matters, besides raising the seed money for Saul, first. One of those things was an assignment Ryan had given him in a telephone call two days before Easter.

XXVI

The Agency for Public Security—"the Agency" as Ryan always referred to it now, just as he always had referred to the FBI as "the Bureau" before—had made rapid strides since its creation and Ryan's appointment a little over four months ago. He had taken some 800 special agents and nearly 1,000 clerical and other support personnel from the FBI—virtually the entire Anti-Terrorism Section—as the nucleus of his new organization, giving him instant operational capability.

And he had made extraordinarily skilful use of the news media, holding weekly press conferences at which he gave dramatic accounts of his activity. They were staged almost like wartime Army General Staff briefings, with Ryan giving the latest battlefield summary of the Agency's war on terrorism during the past week, then calling in his battle-group commanders to give sector reports. Ryan himself carefully avoided any appearance of grandstanding; he maintained a sober, almost grim demeanor and came across on the television screen as a self-effacing but highly capable and energetic military commander waging a determined war of annihilation against the sinister forces of terror which threatened the nation. It was clear to Oscar that Ryan's immediate aim was to make himself and the Agency seem indispensable and at the same time to convince everyone that they posed no threat to right-thinking, law-abiding citizens or to the established power structure.

Oscar marveled at how well Ryan already had succeeded in this aim. In just a few months he had managed to magnify the specter of terrorism in the public mind to such a degree that most people accepted the need for a special governmental body to combat it the same way they accepted the need for a fire department to put out fires. In accomplishing this feat he had made the best possible use both of the few genuine opportunities for suppressing terrorism which existed and of the remarkable freedom from restraints under which the Agency operated in order to create additional opportunities. And he had exercised diplomatic finesse in choosing his targets, balancing the interests and prejudices of various groups.

He had staged a spectacular raid on a nightclub which served as the headquarters of an organized-crime gang in New York City whose members were all Israeli or Soviet Jewish emigres and which heretofore had operated with impunity, depending upon protection from corrupt officials in New York and Washington. The FBI, ever wary of offending Jews, had held back from taking action against the gang, even though it had become notorious for the magnitude of some of its rackets and the ruthless brutality it displayed in killing witnesses and potential informers. But because it engaged in some activities which Ryan interpreted as "terroristic" and therefore within his purview, his men had gone in with shotguns and assault rifles blazing, killing 14 of the gang members and taking more than 30 captive, while television teams recorded it all for the evening news.

Two days later, just as the complaints about "excessive force" and "police brutality" were picking up volume, his agents arrested nine members of a Palestinian group in Detroit, nearly killing two in the process, and Ryan appeared on television that evening showing off a small arsenal of captured weapons and claiming that the Palestinians had been preparing to assassinate Jewish leaders in the United States. As if by magic the whining about the Agency's alleged civil rights violations in the New York raid stopped.

Then there was a shootout in Chicago with a heavily armed White supremacist who was wanted for questioning about an attack on a mixed couple. He had barricaded himself in his home, and both he and his wife were killed in the ensuing exchange of fire with Ryan's men. In the press conference which followed, Ryan said that the Agency had evidence that the man had traveled to Washington several times in recent months. He was believed to have been in Washington at the times of both the Horowitz assassination and the bombing of the People's Committee Against Hate and was, therefore, a prime suspect in both of those terrorist acts. Oscar took note of how neatly Ryan had wrapped up those loose ends. Dead men make such convenient scapegoats—and they tell no tales.

There were a few persistent media critics of Ryan and the Agency—commentators who still questioned the wisdom of putting such unrestrained police power into the hands of the Federal government—but the man in the street had no such qualms. Neither the violence of Ryan's operations nor his freedom from the restraints under which other police agencies operated seemed to bother the average citizen; in fact, John Q. Public loved it. For too long, it seemed to him, the bad guys had been getting away with murder; now the time had come to take off the gloves and do whatever needed to be done to restore law and order. Ryan's own sentiments on that matter seemed an accurate reflection of the public's.

Ryan, of course, had a lot more in mind for the future than merely cracking down on terrorists. One of his principal worries now was that he might run out of terrorists—and justification for the continued buildup of the Agency. His solution to that problem was to have Oscar begin striking Mossad targets and leaving clues that would

implicate Palestinian groups. When the Mossad hit back at the
Palestinians, as it inevitably would, Ryan would have a pretext for
a massive move against the Israeli organization. Meanwhile, a terror
campaign between Israelis and Palestinians waged in the streets of
America's cities certainly couldn't hurt his plans.

In his telephone call, Ryan had told Oscar to choose half a dozen
or so Mossad agents and offices and take them out in a high-profile
manner that would guarantee plenty of media coverage. Ryan's final
words to him had been: "You can stretch this thing out over a couple
of months if you have to. It'll take me at least that long to solidify
my position enough to be able to take on the Mossad. But get started
on it right away. And, Yeager! Be careful, but make it as messy as
you can: lots of property damage, innocent bystanders, and so forth.
I want as much public outrage as we can get. And don't be too slick;
make it look amateurish, if you can. That's the way those dumb
Arabs do things."

Oscar was not happy to have this assignment. He considered the
possibility of terminating his partnership with Ryan. Unfortunately,
that would be much more difficult to do safely now than it would
have been before Ryan became head of the Agency. Ryan could
have him killed fairly easily, but it was no longer so easy for Oscar
to get to Ryan. Besides, Ryan clearly was headed upward, and the
connection might be very valuable in the future.

He thought it over for a week before making up his mind on the
matter. His decision was to go with the Mossad project and to get it
over with as soon as possible, before Adelaide moved in with
him—and before the television project with Saul started occupying
even more of his time. He also decided that it was about time for the
partnership to begin providing some help with his own plans. He
called Ryan back early on Friday and told him that he was ready to
proceed but would need operating funds.

"No problem," Ryan responded. "You can have $50,000."

"Not enough," Oscar replied. "I'll need $250,000." He had added
what he needed for Saul to what seemed a reasonable amount for
dealing with the Mossad.

There was silence at the other end for a few seconds, then Ryan
answered tersely: "You've got it."

In another call that evening Oscar was directed to a pickup point
where he found a large package containing not only 25 banded
bundles with 100 used $100 bills in each, but also three radio-con-
trolled detonating devices, a dozen time-delay detonators, a kit of
high-tech burglar tools, a large set of master keys for vehicles of
various makes and vintages, and several other useful odds and ends
of gadgetry. Finally in the package were a ball-point pen with an

imprint in Arabic on it, three Syrian coins, and a tattered pocket edition of the Koran in Arabic: items to be discreetly left at the scenes of one or more of the actions. Oscar was impressed by Ryan's thoroughness and by his speed in delivering the requested money.

Over the weekend he went carefully through the dossier Ryan had given him earlier and tentatively chose as his first target an office-supplies store in downtown Washington which served as a reporting point for the Mossad's many non-Israeli spies in the area, primarily Jews with U.S. citizenship who worked for the Federal government or for government contractors and had copied or stolen documents or other information of interest to the Israelis. To avoid an embarrassingly heavy traffic into the Israeli embassy, they took their information to a complex of offices in the back of George's Stationery on K Street, where a dozen Mossad agents worked full time debriefing them and handing out new espionage assignments.

It was a large, modern store with lots of plate glass, Oscar noted during a reconnaissance visit on Monday. It would be fairly easy to surreptitiously leave a briefcase full of explosives in one of the aisles, but the layout was such that probably not much damage would be done to the rear offices. A more daring approach would be to actually take a bomb into one of the Mossad offices, but he didn't like the risks involved in that. There were a couple of sharp-eyed characters near the back of the store, ostensibly rearranging stock on the shelves but actually scrutinizing everyone who approached the door leading into the rear hallway. During the three or four minutes that Oscar pretended to be examining an automatic telephone-answering device on display he saw five men and three women go into that hallway, most of them distinctly Jewish looking. All had come in from the street, and four were carrying attache cases. Two of them were stopped by the pseudo-employees. One was permitted to proceed almost immediately, but the other was detained until one of the door-watchers had gone into the rear and returned, apparently with an okay for the visitor.

Oscar was amazed at the size of the operation. The arrogance of the Israelis, carrying on their espionage activities on such a scale right under the nose of their *goyische* benefactor and supposed "ally" was breathtaking. They must be pretty sure that they had the fix in and would not be called to account. He felt his resolve harden: it would be satisfying to teach these uppity aliens a little humility.

He went outside and walked around the corner and into the narrow alleyway which ran behind the stores on the block. Making his way around huge, metal trash bins and delivery trucks with engines idling, he found George's delivery entrance in a recess just large enough to accommodate a medium-size truck. The door was sheathed in steel and locked, with a push button beside it to summon an employee. To the left of the door was a small, grimy window protected by steel bars. Beginning about 25 feet to the right of the parking recess were eight much larger windows, also barred, all of them with tightly closed venetian blinds. He took a quick look into the small window. He could see the shelves of a the store's stock-room, with a double swinging door leading out onto the display floor. To the right he could see a wall of the stockroom, about where the larger windows began. So they had to open into the offices used by the Mossad; it was the only thing that made sense. It took him only a few more seconds to finish sizing up the job and make his decision: Ryan wanted a high-profile operation, and so high-profile it would be.

XXVII

The next day Oscar busied himself with preparations both for the stationery store job and for Saul's program. First, with an eye toward the future when he would be sharing his house with Adelaide, he drove out to Manassas, in the Virginia countryside some 25 miles west of Washington, where he rented a nice, sturdy double garage.

Then he bought himself a used Chevrolet pickup. With the pickup he drove to a large feed and fertilizer store on the edge of town and bought 15 bags of fertilizer-grade ammonium nitrate. He would have bought more, but 1,500 pounds was about as much as he estimated he could manage in one load without damaging his truck. After unloading that in the garage, he stopped at a hardware and farm-supply store and bought two 50-pound cases of Tovex cartridges and a box of electric detonators. Tovex was an aluminized water-gel dynamite commonly used by farmers and contractors for blasting stumps and boulders.

He knew he would have to show a driver's license and have his name, address, and social-security number recorded when he made that last purchase, and so he had used the license he had taken from David Kaplan's wallet three months earlier. He also had worn the brunette wig he had bought for the Horowitz job, but Kaplan's photograph on the license still bore very little resemblance to Oscar. That discrepancy gave the clerk no pause, however.

These preliminaries done, he gave Harry a call to schedule a meeting and headed back toward Washington. He would need the better part of a day to prepare his bomb, and he would have to steal a suitable truck to pack it in first. Perhaps he could handle those things tomorrow, if he got an early start. Meanwhile, he was eager to push ahead with Saul's television career.

When Harry looked into the paper bag Oscar handed him and saw that it was full of $100 bills, he was speechless for a few seconds. He dumped the money out onto the coffee table, quickly estimated the amount, and whistled. "How did you raise 200 grand so quickly?" he asked, his voice conveying mixed feelings of awe, elation, and dark suspicion.

"A friend owed it to me for some contract work I'm doing for him and finally paid me off the other night," Oscar answered unconvincingly.

"Does he always pay you in cash?"

"Actually, the less said about that the better. Just take my word for it: the money's real. How've you been doing with the preparations for Saul's introductory tape?"

"We can do it in a day or two—as soon as Saul and I can set aside two or three hours on the same evening for the taping. Maybe tomorrow. Saul has been rehearsing his material and is ready to go. I've been talking with Capitol Productions, and they can schedule us almost anytime. They do top-quality work, and I've known the people there for years. They're expensive, but it looks like we can swing their fee now." Harry grinned. He apparently had decided not to worry about how Oscar had gotten his money. "The financing is really all we were waiting for."

They discussed related matters for nearly an hour, and Oscar was pleased by the progress which was being made. Harry estimated that with a portion of the money Oscar had brought he could have the League's video recording studio up to broadcast standards within ten days. He was so confident of that, in fact, that he would have Colleen schedule Saul's first broadcast on Washington's WZY-TV for two Sundays hence.

One of the most important developments, Oscar learned, was that reporters for the tabloids had been trying to reach Saul. Caldwell's secretary had received more than a dozen calls from the *National Enquirer* and three or four of the other checkout-stand papers which specialized in the bizarre and the sensational. So far Saul had not returned their calls.

Oscar called Saul from Harry's house. "Hey, this is a great opportunity for us. Have you thought about what you should say to the reporters?"

"Do you really think I should talk to those jerks? Don't you think it'll lower our credibility if we get a big write-up in the cretin papers?"

"Listen, Saul. The people who believe the stories in the *National Enquirer* are exactly the ones who'll believe that Jesus has returned to cleanse the nation. If you play it right, you should be able to get front-page publicity where it'll do the most good and still keep a certain amount of your dignity. And it certainly won't hurt our campaign to get you on as many stations as possible."

"So you believe I should act like a simple, sober soul who is still shaken by his experience on Easter morning and doesn't know why Jesus chose him as a medium?"

"Exactly! You can even give 'em a detailed description of what it felt like when Jesus took over your body at the microphone. Just act a little shy and embarrassed by the whole thing, but nevertheless determined to keep spreading the word to the boobs—and even to let Jesus speak through you again if he wants to. You know: sort of a combination of 'Why me, oh Lord?' and 'Thy will be done.'"

"Okay. I'll call them back tonight. I'll tell them I couldn't call sooner because I was fasting and meditating. How's that?"

"Right on!"

Later that evening with Adelaide he watched the national television news. The latest unemployment figures had just been released and were causing a stir: there had been an increase of seven-tenths of a per cent last month, to 7.9 per cent. Some members of the Congress were charging that the actual unemployment rate was even higher and that the Hedges administration was juggling the figures to keep the public from knowing how bad things were. The economic analysts were predicting that as much as ten percent of the work force would be unemployed by mid-summer and that no improvement was in sight. Furthermore, the trade deficit and inflation were both up sharply, making an exceedingly grim overall picture.

Ryan was in the news again too. He announced the arrests of 42 members of a militant anti-abortion group, the Pro-Life Commando, which was suspected in the bombing of several abortion clinics and a Planned Parenthood office. Elsewhere on the terrorism front, an interracial couple had been gunned down by an unknown sniper in Chicago, and Blacks were rioting in a Miami suburb, after ambushing and killing two White policemen.

It would be interesting to see how Ryan would deal with that last situation. Heretofore he had gone after individuals and organized groups; he had not yet had to counter unplanned mob violence. Oscar was confident, however, that very shortly the rioting Blacks in Miami would be wondering what had hit them. Ryan clearly was a cop who meant business and knew how to get results. It was amazing to Oscar what foresight the man had. People had been making gloomy economic forecasts for years, but not with the definiteness Ryan had when he had told Oscar back at the end of last November that the economy would be out of control by this summer. It looked now as if he would be right on target. Would that I had asked him what stocks I should invest in, Oscar thought ruefully.

XXVIII

Oscar wasted four hours the next day looking without success for a delivery van or a light truck he could steal for his bomb, but he did manage to round up all of the other supplies he needed. He also studied his sheaf of Mossad dossiers again and began thinking about later targets.

He had dinner at Adelaide's apartment, then left at ten o'clock and resumed his search for a truck. Finally, around midnight, he spotted a suitable van in the parking lot of a shopping mall with a 24-hour supermarket. Leaving his own car several rows away and using the set of master keys Ryan had provided him, he quickly entered the van and drove away. The space in the back was adequate for his need, but the garish, red lettering on the side of the bright-yellow truck—"Dino's Specialty Wall Coverings"—made him feel self-conscious. He decided to drive immediately to Manassas rather than take the risk involved in leaving such a conspicuous vehicle parked in the open overnight.

In his rented garage he removed several five-gallon cans of wallpaper adhesive and dozens of rolls of wallpaper from the back of the van, replaced them with four 40-gallon plastic trash barrels he had purchased earlier in the day, and spent the next three hours emptying sacks of ammonium nitrate into the barrels and stirring a fuel-oil sensitizer into the white pellets. The barrels were closely grouped around one of his 50-pound cases of Tovex. It was after four o'clock in the morning when he finally was ready to place a time-delay detonator in the Tovex.

He lay down as well as he could in the front seat of the van and slept fitfully until 8:30 AM. Then he drove out of the garage and joined the tail end of the stream of rush-hour traffic headed into Washington. At 9:50 AM he turned into the alley which ran behind George's Stationery. He pulled up as close to the bricks as he could, directly outside two of the tightly curtained windows in George's rear wall. He leaned back into the cargo area just long enough to set the detonator for five minutes and start it counting down. Then he stepped out into the alley, locked the door of the van, and made his way back to the busy sidewalk. He turned the corner and walked back toward the front entrance of George's, stopping two doors away to watch the traffic go by.

The explosion came at 9:57 according to his watch. The shock was stronger than he had expected, and he staggered, nearly falling before recovering his balance. George's plate-glass windows had been transformed into a deadly hail of glittering shards, which had cut down four pedestrians on the sidewalk in front of the store. Dense smoke poured from the interior of the building. No one could survive inside, he realized with a sinking heart; if the blast had not killed them already, the smoke soon would. How many were there? If Monday had been typical, there would be about a dozen customers and clerks in the store.

The smoke and dust were still heavy in the air in the alley, and even with a handkerchief over his nose and mouth he coughed and gagged as he made his way back to the blast site to survey the damage. Where the van had been was a gaping crater a dozen feet across. Apparently there had been a basement of some sort under the store which had extended out beneath the alley. About 40 feet of the rear wall of the store was gone, and most of the interior walls of the Mossad offices were gone as well. He counted the remains of six, maybe seven, persons in the wreckage of the offices. Undoubtedly others were buried under the rubble.

Papers were floating down from the sky and fluttering about in the alley. He picked up one and noted that it was typed in Hebrew characters. With the metropolitan police as well as the FBI and the Agency involved in the investigation of the bombing, it would be hard to hush up the nature of the business which had been conducted in George's rear offices. Another little embarrassment for those who believe that the "chosen people" can do no wrong.

A second blast rocked Oscar, and he felt a flash of heat on his back. The fuel tank of a burning truck about 30 yards away had exploded. Still coughing, he stumbled back out to the sidewalk and walked rapidly away from the devastated area. He hailed a taxi. During the ride back to the shopping mall in Virginia where he had left his car he found himself appalled at what he had done. He had not regretted the bombing of the People's Committee, but here, in contrast, many of the victims were innocent bystanders. He knew that in every war most of the victims were non-combatants, but he still did not like it. Ryan, on the other hand, probably would be very pleased.

What, he wondered, had the crews of the bombers which had carpet-bombed German cities during the Second World War felt? Were they pumped so full of Jewish hate propaganda that they were happy for all the White civilians they were killing, or did they instead hate themselves for what they were doing: for obeying orders they knew were immoral and for not having the courage to speak out against them? On the other hand, perhaps Ryan and Keller were right: perhaps nearly all of them were simply animals and were unmoved by ethical questions; perhaps they were only concerned with how their fellows regarded them and had no moral compasses of their own. Perhaps the more sophisticated of them just memorized one of the cliches of justification the Jews provided them with—"No, I didn't hate the German women and children I was killing and maiming with my bombs, but we had to do it to stop Hitler"—while the less sophisticated didn't even worry about the pretense of justification.

At home Oscar slept until midafternoon. Over a late lunch he thought about his various responsibilities. Although he was spending about a dozen hours a week on their television project, for the time being Saul seemed to be in good hands with the Kellers. It would probably be another six or eight weeks before he would need to become much more closely involved in that project again.

It was five weeks until Adelaide would be moving in; she was a well-organized girl and was handling most of the logistics of that task quite well by herself. She had even told him which pieces of his own furniture would have to go. He would hardly have to do more than provide the muscle when the time for moving the heavy things came.

The Air Force was satisfied for now and wouldn't be expecting anything else from him until mid-August. He would start worrying about that around August 10. God, what a cozy setup it was being a Defense Department consultant, he thought. If he wanted, he could work a lot harder, get more contracts, and make more money, but as long as he was satisfied with the $50,000 or so per year he was getting now, he had 90 per cent of his time free to spend on other things.

Ryan's assignment still was his most immediate concern. More than that, it was his one responsibility which worried him. The danger of the work was a consideration as was the problem involved in keeping it secret from Adelaide, but the real worry was that it was not under his control, and he had serious misgivings about the motivation behind it and where it was leading him. Still, his admiration for Ryan's abilities, already substantial, was growing, and he sympathized with the man to a degree.

Killing Mossad agents, for example, certainly was something that needed to be done. Even Ryan's strategy of provoking a terrorist war between the Arabs and the Israelis on American turf seemed justifiable: tough on the poor Arabs, of course, but after the Israeli problem was solved the Arabs needed to be booted out anyway. He would be happy to see all of those greasy, Middle Eastern types go.

After having time to think about it and become accustomed to the idea, he even found himself with a certain grudging sympathy for Ryan's program of reform-through-trauma for improving the character of the American people.

The arrangement between himself and Ryan had undeniable value for his work with the League—not to mention the extra $200,000 he had just received—and it might become even more valuable in the future. Nevertheless, the man made him uneasy. For Oscar to be comfortable with their relationship he needed to have a clearer idea of just where Ryan was headed and whether or not he really wanted to go along on that particular ride.

For now, however, he was inclined to push ahead with the Mossad project and get it done as soon as he could. He had tentatively selected as his next target one Sheldon Schwartz, a Congressional aide, the chief of staff for the Senate minority leader. The man was an American-born Jew, but he had lived in Israel for five years during the 1970s. He was believed to carry the rank of colonel in the Mossad.

His nominal superior on the U.S. government's payroll, Senator Howard Carter, was a WASP from an immensely wealthy and prominent New England family. He also was one of the country's most powerful politicians, heading the Senate Foreign Relations Committee among other things. He had declared himself unavailable as the Republican candidate for the Presidency in next year's elections but was considered the most likely choice five years from now. His public image was a dignified one, as befitted the power he wielded, but his FBI dossier revealed that although married he was a homosexual and a pederast.

Oscar was shocked by this revelation. No wonder Ryan was such a cynic!

Carter was very careful to keep his perversions from becoming public knowledge, but he apparently was ruled by them. Schwartz served him not only as a legislative aide, but also as a discreet procurer of young boys. This dual role undoubtedly gave Schwartz a strong hold on Carter and put the Mossad agent in a position where he was privy to the nation's most closely guarded secrets of state and could exert decisive influence on key legislation of interest to Israel. Perhaps in this lay the explanation for Carter's 100 per cent rating with the Israeli lobby.

Oscar studied Schwarz's own dossier attentively and considered the ways in which the man might be killed. After today's bombing the Mossad would be taking extraordinary precautions to protect its key people, and so Schwartz's residence probably would be under observation. Perhaps it would be easiest to get at him while he was at work. He could hardly risk calling attention to himself by having his fellow Mossad agents guarding him in his Senate office. Or could he? With the Israelis no degree of arrogance seemed excessive.

Oscar noted that it was nearly 3:30 PM—a bit late to make a trip over to Capitol Hill today. On the other hand, he hated to waste even part of a day. It took three telephone calls, posing as a newspaper reporter, to find out that Schwarz's office was on the third floor of the Senate's Hart Office Building, that Schwarz had stepped out for a moment but would be back shortly, and that he was expected to be in until six o'clock.

Oscar spent half an hour arranging his wig and applying his facial makeup; then he put on a suit, slipped his silenced pistol into its holster, and headed for Capitol Hill. There he observed that most of the people going into the Hart Office Building were either wearing plastic identity badges or were fumbling in their purses or pockets for them at the doors.

To get a better look at the security arrangements, Oscar walked up to a door and asked the two Black guards seated at a table just inside, "Excuse me, but is this the Dirksen Office Building?" He noted that there was a metal detector that all persons entering the building had to walk through. The guards were talking with each other and seemed bored and inattentive. One of them pointed vaguely to the west and said impatiently, "Next building on Constitution Avenue," then returned to his banter with his fellow.

During the time Oscar was at the door three persons edged their way around him and walked through the metal detector. Their badges got only cursory glances from the guards. One woman who entered was carrying a purse, which she merely held open where the guards could look into it if they bothered to do so as she walked by.

Oscar had a hunch that if he could get inside the building it would be easy to get to Schwarz with no further interference. But how to get in? There was another entrance being used at the other end of the building, but it undoubtedly had the same security arrangements as this one. He walked the three blocks back to his car to consider the matter. On his way he observed the stream of vehicles coming from the parking area under the building and being directed into the rush-hour traffic by policemen. That must be where all the VIPs parked their cars, and it looked like it wouldn't be easy to get in there.

As Oscar approached his car, parked illegally beyond the last metered space before an intersection, he saw that the car ahead of his, against whose rear bumper his own front bumper was tightly pressed, was trying to get out. The driver had his head out the window and was looking back at Oscar's car as he jockeyed his own car back and forth and swore to himself. Oscar walked up to the other driver's window to tell him that relief had arrived: "Hey, sorry I blocked you. I'll move my car now."

The other man glared up at him from a sallow, pockmarked face, and Oscar suddenly noticed that he had a plastic badge clipped to his breast pocket. Under the photograph the legend "U.S. Senate Staff" caught Oscar's eye. "You work in the Hart Building too?" Oscar asked in a friendly manner. "Parking around here's a bitch, isn't it?"

"Yeah," the other replied, somewhat mollified by the impression that Oscar was a fellow Senate staffer. "I'm new here, but next month I'll get a spot in the lot over on Third Street."

Having quickly noted that there were no other pedestrians on his side of the street at the moment, Oscar made an instant decision. While he opened the car's door with his left hand, he drew his pistol with his right hand and, pressed in close to the car so that his action could not be seen from the street, shot the man in the forehead twice. As the driver slumped silently over his steering wheel, Oscar deftly unclipped his badge, then pushed his body down in the seat, with his head under the glove compartment where it would be less visible.

Oscar moved his own car to a metered space which had opened up at the other end of the block. He stashed his holstered pistol under his seat and reached up to his sun visor for a long, plastic letter opener which was clipped there. It actually was a razor-sharp knife made of a tough, hard, fiber-reinforced resin. He tucked the knife into his belt where it would be hidden by his coat, then headed back toward the Hart Office Building. On the way he looked at the identity badge he had taken. The slain man's name was Joseph Isaacson, and his accent had sounded New Yorkish. Did that mean he was a Jew? Oscar didn't know. He had had to force himself to kill the fellow, and he probably would have done it in any case—but the man's appearance and his accent probably had made it a little easier.

He looked at his watch as he went through the metal detector. It was exactly 4:30, and the hall was full of people headed toward the exit. He did not look directly at the guards, but he could see from the corner of his eye that they gave him no more than a cursory glance as he went by.

By the time Oscar had made his way to the third floor and oriented himself, the hallways were nearly empty, except for a group waiting for the next elevator. Schwarz's office, unfortunately, was part of a large suite assigned to Carter. The main door from the hall was open, and two women were at desks in the palatial anteroom. Three other doors led from the anteroom to inner offices. One was open, but from the hall Oscar couldn't see into it. He didn't know what else to do, so he stooped and pretended to be tying his shoelace in order to gain a few seconds to think. As he rose again a man about 30, obviously not Schwartz, came out of the open office and closed the door behind him as he put on his coat. Oscar saw him nod his head toward one of the other closed doors and heard him ask one of the women, "The Senator left yet?"

"No," she answered, "he's still in conference with Shelly."

"Well, good night. Don't let him make you work too late," the man said cheerfully as he stepped into the hall.

Oscar already was walking toward a side corridor which intersected the main hall about 50 feet from the entrance to the suite. Surely a big shot like Carter didn't have to come and go from his office through the front door, where he would be forced to rub elbows with the *hoi polloi*. There *must* be a private rear door.

Sure enough, a dozen yards or so around the corner there was an unmarked door in the wall of the side corridor, which bounded the Carter suite. Just beyond was an elevator door bearing a placard which read, "For Senators Only."

Did he dare? Oscar felt the icy perspiration in his armpits. He stepped up to the unmarked door and tried the knob. It was locked. He slipped his lethal letter opener from his belt and rapped on one of the solid, oaken panels with his knuckles.

There was no immediate response. He spotted a trash receptacle a few yards away and filched an empty envelope from it. He rapped on the door again and immediately slid the envelope under it. That should catch someone's attention, if there were anyone in the room beyond the door. Within a few seconds the door swung inward, and Oscar found himself looking into the annoyed and suspicious eyes of a man whose features were familiar to him from the photograph in the dossier he had been studying very recently.

The knife slipped easily into Sheldon Schwartz's belly, and Oscar ripped savagely upward with it, spilling the man's entrails onto the carpet. The eviscerated Schwartz could utter no more than a long, wheezing gasp as his knees buckled and he fell forward.

Oscar reached out with his left hand to ease the dying man to the floor, but he was not fast enough to avoid getting the front of his trousers smeared with gore. He quickly stepped into the room and closed the door behind him, at the same time calling out, "Give me a hand, will you, Senator. I believe Shelly is sick."

The door was in an alcove concealed by a pair of strategically placed flag stands. Oscar brushed aside the flags and saw Carter's back as the legislator rose from the chair behind his desk about 30 feet away. Carter was a tall, heavily built man with a large head of silvery hair and sagging jowls. He moved his bulk with slow, imperial dignity. He and Oscar were only a dozen feet apart when he saw the knife in Oscar's hand. The questioning smile on his august face turned to an expression of horror, and he froze in mid-stride. His last words were, "Oh, shit!"

"Yep, and that's all she wrote, faggot," was Oscar's response as he plunged the ten-inch blade into the center of Carter's chest. He grabbed the falling man, so that the body would not hit the floor with an audible crash. He left the knife in him and quickly checked his pulse to be sure that his heart had stopped. On his way out he carefully dropped the ballpoint pen with the Arab markings into the bloody mess in the alcove.

He stopped at home only long enough to shower and change his clothes, then drove to Adelaide's apartment for dinner. It was after midnight when he pulled into his garage again. As soon as he turned off his ignition he could hear the telephone in the house ringing. It was Ryan.

"Where the hell have you been? I've been trying to reach you for four hours," came the exasperated voice from the other end. "For Christ's sake, don't do anything else until I tell you to! What do you think you are—a fucking one-man army?"

"Well, I thought you wanted me to . . . ."

Oscar was cut off in mid-sentence by another outburst from Ryan: "God damn it, when I said I wanted you to generate some public outrage I didn't mean for you to turn the whole country upside down. Have you been watching the news this evening?"

"Sorry, I've been too busy. Am I getting much coverage?"

"Coverage? They're going wild. They're hysterical. The President was on. The Vice President was on. The Speaker of the House was on. A dozen senators were on. They're calling for martial law. Nothing like you did today—yesterday—has ever happened before in this country. Damn, man! It's really hit the fan.

"You know, what I *thought* you'd do is pop one or two of those Yids with your gun, maybe wire a stick of dynamite to a starter or two, toss a satchel charge into somebody's office. That's what I was *counting* on. A slow build-up of hostilities between the kikes and the camel jockeys. Give me time to work the press a little and then move in hard on both of 'em.

"But no, you start off by dropping your blockbuster on their number-one facility this morning and wiping out a third of the Mossad's cadre in the Washington area, using about a thousand per cent overkill. Then, before they've even had time to catch their breath from that, you butcher their top—I mean their *top*—agent in the country and kill their top *goy* politician besides, not to mention miscellaneous government employees. You've escalated things to the thermonuclear stage before I could even get into the act."

Oscar did not respond, and there was silence on the line for a few seconds before Ryan continued, somewhat cooler. "I was planning to let this scenario develop much more slowly, while I worked on some other things, such as Black rioters. One good thing about the way you've started it off, though, is that you've panicked the Israelis. They're usually pretty levelheaded, and one of my fears was that they'd figure out it wasn't really the Palestinians who were knocking off their guys. But now you've got them so paranoid that they feel forced to take drastic action immediately, and that'll be their undoing.

"The Agency is intercepting most of their communications, and we know they've already called in a team of 20 of their trained killers from Israel, who'll be flying here Sunday. Better yet, they're planning to kidnap Abu Kareem, the chief of staff in the PLO Mission to the UN in New York. They intend to drug him, pack him in a crate, and ship him back to Israel on an El Al flight just the way they did Adolf Eichmann, so they can torture him and find out who snuffed Schwartz and blew up their debriefing center on K Street. If we're lucky both of those operations will take place simultaneously, and we can nab 'em in the act. Then, if I'm able to work the media just right, we can go after the rest of their crew. But I can't afford to have any more surprises until that's done, Yeager, so just take that quarter of a million you gouged out of me and have yourself a nice, long vacation. Understand? Don't do *anything* else now."

"Gotcha, partner. Say, did they find my Koran? I left it in the glove compartment, but it looked to me like there wasn't enough left of that van to put in a matchbox."

"Yeah. We found the engine and most of the front end of the van in the basement, and one of our men spotted your Koran almost as soon as we had hoisted the wreckage back up onto the pavement and started going through it. The Israelis were looking over our shoulders the whole time, of course."

Then Ryan chuckled, "Probably the best thing you did today was something that wasn't even part of your assignment, and that was killing Carter. More than anything else, that'll guarantee me a free hand, with no interference from the bleeding-heart liberals in Congress. Not that Carter was especially liberal, but the one kind of crime those bastards are in favor of cracking down on is crime against themselves. If you or I get knifed by a Black mugger, their main concern is that the cops don't violate the mugger's civil rights. But if one of *them* gets knifed—well, that's a different story."

XXIX

Oscar followed Ryan's advice, more or less, for the next four weeks. Instead of taking a vacation, though, he turned his attention toward his project with Saul and began spending much more time with it. The maiden broadcast over WZY-TV on May 10 was an enormous success. Within days it led to positive answers from several of the big Midwestern stations Colleen had been attempting to get Saul on.

More and more, Saul's message was tailored by Oscar, who was attempting to coordinate his plans for building Saul's public power base with other developments more or less beyond his control—namely, those involving Ryan. It was much clearer to Oscar now than it had been six months ago that the country was headed for some major changes in the near future. He wanted to have Saul in position to make a decisive move at the right moment. For the time being, however, he was careful not to let his premonitions of things to come carry him too far too fast.

Saul's theme was more austere than Caldwell's, but it was not really a radically different one. He preached of the danger of God's punishment striking America soon because of its sins. He chastised the government for its corruption and its inability to curb the country's continued decline. Other evangelists had gone over much of the same ground in the past, although in recent years they had accommodated themselves to the generally fat-and-happy mood of the country by going easy on the brimstone and appealing more to middle-class materialism and self-indulgence. They were not privy to Oscar's inside information on the suddenness and severity with which hard times were likely to strike again, and they also were slow to sense the new tide of foreboding and worry which already was beginning to creep into the public consciousness.

Saul's real point of departure from the evangelist pack was the undertone of imminent change, the recurring hint of big things to come, which ran through his sermons. A few of the flakier evangelists far out on the fringe had occasionally predicted that Judgment Day was at hand or that some great catastrophe was about to overwhelm the world, but Saul wore the mantle of prophecy differently, not only with more dignity but also with more credibility. His credibility was due in part to his indefiniteness and in part to his affected humility. He was making no specific predictions nor even claiming that he knew what was coming; instead, in keeping with his role of medium, he merely asserted that a great turning point in the affairs of men was at hand, that his evidence for his assertion was his own experience on Easter morning, and that he, along with everyone else, would find out the details only when Jesus chose to utilize him as a medium once again: "I do not know what our Lord will reveal to us or demand of us. I only know that he will speak to us again soon, and that the world will not be the same after that."

Saul's oratorical magic gave an aura of mystery and suspense to this simple statement that left his television audience on the edges of their chairs. Oscar was concerned that the hint of a revelation to come might cause the Jewish media moguls to prick up their ears and be more wary of giving Saul access to that portion of the airwaves they controlled, but his initial audience ratings, together with his strongly pro-Jewish and pro-Israel introductory tape, seemed to overcome any misgivings on their part. Colleen was able to buy as much air time as their initial budget would allow. By May 24 Saul's share of the total evangelists' viewership had reached just under 50 per cent. The mail donations were beginning to roll in, and it seemed clear that they had a going thing

Both Oscar and Adelaide pitched in and helped with the fast-growing secretarial work load. Emily, who had been on the verge of filing for divorce a few weeks earlier, quit her job and devoted all her time to attempting to handle her husband's torrent of correspondence. The real break came when Saul was able to persuade his secretarial ally in Caldwell's camp to leave her former employer and take charge of his own office affairs.

During this time Oscar did not forget about Ryan or the other phase of his own activity. For that matter, few Americans did. Ryan and his affairs were in the public eye almost continually from the end of April. One of the strongest impressions he made was four days after Oscar's two blows against the Mossad. The big news on that Monday evening was the Agency's gunfire-punctuated raid on an El Al airliner at Kennedy International Airport, from which a crate containing the drugged body of Abu Kareem was seized after a shootout which left eight Mossad guards and four other Jewish air passengers dead. Ryan really made a show of it, with television cameras recording the scene as the crate was opened and the unconscious, tightly trussed Palestinian was removed. Then the cameras scanned the hypodermic syringes and bottles of drugs found on one of the slain Mossad guards. It was the sort of chilling display which knocked a big hole in the Jew-as-blameless-victim myth which had been so carefully maintained by much of the media to that point, and it made it very hard for even Israel's most slavish Gentile boosters to complain about the rough way in which the raid was conducted.

Ryan followed up that same evening with a number of coordinated arrests of members of the Mossad assassination team which had flown in the previous day. Like the El Al raid, the arrests were as violent as Ryan could make them without being obvious about it, and news cameramen accompanied all of the arrest teams. For balance he also had his agents haul in a dozen luckless Palestinians. Afterward he had a lineup of the Israelis and Palestinians who had survived the arrests. As the camera went down the line and halted on each face, filling the screen with a battered and disheveled mug over a number board hung around the man's neck, a list of aliases and alleged terrorist activities was read off by an Agency spokesman. Then the camera moved to a table on which the weapons seized with the Mossad agents were laid out. The spokesman carefully pointed out the silencers, the poisoned darts, and other grisly tools of the assassin's trade.

Finally Ryan himself came on and grimly summarized things. For too long, he said, Americans had tolerated the terrorist war being waged in their midst by the ruthless hirelings of foreign powers. He briskly detailed several bombings of Arab offices in the United States which had taken place over the past five years, none of which had received much news coverage at the time it had happened. In each case scenes of the damage were shown to emphasize the gravity of the act. Then he moved on smoothly to recent events: the bombing of the Mossad offices in the rear of George's Stationery, the stabbing of Senator Carter, the kidnapping of Abu Kareem, and the influx of professional killers from Israel. He gave a continuity to all of these happenings which left the viewer with the clear impression that the latest outrages were the outgrowth of the earlier bombings and that Israel's agents really had started the whole process. He concluded his summary by saying that he had been charged with the responsibility for bringing this terrorist war to an end, and he intended to do it, using whatever degree of force was necessary.

Oscar could imagine the cheering and clapping which must have followed this announcement in working-class bars and middle-class living rooms all over America. Ryan had stage-managed things perfectly, neatly pulling the rug out from under all those who might otherwise have opposed the wholesale roundup of Israel's agents which the Agency carried out during the next few days.

The Agency held back from becoming involved in the Black rioting in Miami for more than a week. The governor of Florida had called in National Guard troops to patrol the riot area. They were able to arrest some looters and disperse some crowds, but sniping and arson continued. On the eighth day of the disorders Black youths stopped a car on a highway bounding the riot-stricken neighborhood

by throwing a cement block through its windshield from an over-
pass. They swarmed over the car and beat the White man who had
been driving it almost to death, then pulled two teenaged White girls
from the back seat and carried them screaming into a nearby housing
project.

After the mother of the girls made a tearful plea on television
that evening, the governor called on the Federal government for
help.

The next morning more than 600 men from the Agency were in
the riot area, equipped with helmets, flak jackets, and M-16s. Ryan
himself was there with them, directing operations from a hastily set
up field headquarters. They swept through apartment block after
apartment block, blasting the locks off doors and shooting down
anyone who did not respond instantly to their orders. By nightfall
they had arrested more than 400 Blacks, killed 123, seriously
wounded 200 or so, and completely quelled the disorder. It turned
out later that Ryan had sent in a dozen Black undercover agents—
every Black, in fact, who had come over to the Agency with the
Bureau's former Anti-Terrorism Section—as soon as the rioting had
begun; then, while waiting for the most politically opportune time
to apply muscle, he had gathered all of the information on the local
Black community—in particular, on the key figures who were
keeping the riot going—needed to use that muscle decisively.

The fallout from this action was by no means uniformly favorable
to Ryan. Black groups complained long and loud, and they were
predictably joined by much of the White clergy. Jews, uncharacteristically, were divided: many smaller groups, especially those with
a leftist orientation, and individual Jewish columnists and editors
denounced the Agency's repression of the riot, but the Jewish
establishment, including the top media bosses, either remained
silent or gave a restrained applause to the restoration of order. The
reaction of the White public was so overwhelmingly and enthusiastically favorable, however, that the dissenting voices were thoroughly drowned out. In their eyes it was the first time the
government had handled Black rioters the way they deserved to be
handled.

Ryan was becoming a bit of a popular White hero, no matter how
hard he tried to avoid that role. It was clear to Oscar that Ryan
realized the disadvantage of being perceived as politically ambi-
tious. He needed the cooperation of the media, and he wanted the
approval of the public, but most of all he had to retain the confidence
of the power structure. He had to seem the perfect guardian of their
own interests, nothing more—at least, at this stage of the game.

Ten days after his Miami action Ryan made another balancing movement by rounding up 35 members of a White survivalist community in a remote part of Idaho. His men came crashing in at dawn in armored personnel carriers while helicopter gunships circled overhead. Camera crews and reporters were everywhere as the sleepy families were hustled roughly out of their cabins and handcuffed. The cameras watched Ryan's agents unearth a plastic-wrapped footlocker full of firearms and ammunition while an ex-member-turned-informer who had showed them where to dig skulked in the background.

No direct allegations of terrorism—or even of illegality—were made against the arrested community members; it was all by insinuation. One of the agents who opened the footlocker took a weapon from it and held it up to the camera. "Here's a machine gun that'll never be used for terrorism," he said. Oscar's experienced eye recognized the weapon as a semi-automatic rifle of a common model, but millions of other television viewers would believe that it was a machine gun intended for terrorist acts. The media people were even more prejudicial in their comments, referring without fail to the community members as "terrorists." The local sheriff and a representative from a Jewish organization in Boise were interviewed, and they both commended the Agency for helping to end the danger of terrorism in Idaho, again without mentioning any specific crime the community members were alleged to have committed. Their real crimes, it seemed to Oscar, were that they were White, they were armed, and they had opted out of the great multiracial social experiment everyone else in the country was participating in.

On June 1 the unemployment figures for April were announced. Overall unemployment was up to 9.2 per cent, after the largest one-month increase since the Second World War.

XXX

Having Adelaide living with him definitely mellowed Oscar. He could not help but have a more positive outlook now that her lithe, warm body was snuggled up against his seven nights a week instead of two or three and her laughter and grace were present at every meal.

Did it also take away some of his edge? he asked himself. He thought back over some of the wild things he had done in the past few months and wondered that he had been so daring. Now he hoped fervently that Ryan would not call on him again for any special activity. Was Adelaide to be blamed for this excess of caution? Was he overly fearful of losing the joy that she had brought to his life?

Perhaps. And perhaps it was at least as much something else: Before he had been striking out from a sense of helplessness, of frustration at not being able to do anything else about the hateful things he saw happening all around him, he lived in a world which had become so intolerable that it did not really matter what he did to it. But now he had a plan, or at least the beginning of one; now he had just a glimmering of hope that he might be able to make a difference, that he might be able to make a better world. And that hope made him cautious. Even the faintest possibility that he might be able to accomplish something of lasting value was too precious to be jeopardized by recklessness.

The new possibility for the future lay in Saul, of course. Through him Oscar had the ears of millions; through him those millions might be stirred into decisive action at a critical moment. Even before that moment Saul could be used—carefully—as a medium for constructive ideas, a medium with much greater carrying potential than anything else he or the League might reasonably hope to develop with their present resources. For weeks he had been thinking about the ideas which might be propagated through Saul, considering not only strategic feasibility—i.e., which ideas might be slipped past the Jews without alarming them and causing them to sever Saul's connection to his audience—but also intrinsic value: Which were the ideas that it was really important to get into the public mind, or into that segment of it to which Saul had access?

He talked with Harry about ideas too. Toward the end of June, with the business end of Saul's operation more or less under control, they had time for several discussions. One of these took place in Oscar's house on a Sunday afternoon after they, together with Adelaide, Colleen, and Saul, had previewed the tape of Saul's sermon which would be broadcast that evening. Oscar had suggested that the time had come to begin using the sermons to raise the racial consciousness of Saul's audience.

Harry was skeptical: "What's the point? I mean, what do you want to accomplish by that?"

The question irritated Oscar, and his irritation showed in his tone. "The point is that our race is going down the drain, and one of the biggest reasons is that White people have such a low level of racial consciousness. We should do whatever we can to rectify that situation."

Harry sighed as if he were about to explain something for the tenth time to a slow learner. "Sure. Our aim is to keep the race from going down the drain, if we can. More than that, it's to get the race back on an upward path again, to get it back to work preparing the way for a higher race to come. Consciousness is one of the prerequisites for doing that. But consciousness must be based on knowledge, and Saul's audience is singularly unknowledgeable. I don't know that it's even feasible to try to do anything about that. I mean, these are Christian Fundamentalists. They're excitable, certainly—but educable? Barely if at all, I think. It seems to me we should try to take advantage of their excitability and forget about trying to educate them."

"I guess I don't share your pessimism," Oscar replied. "I know there are a lot of superstitious dimwits out there, but surely it's possible to teach them something. After all, most of them have learned a certain amount about the Bible, so we should be able to teach them a little about racial history and the present racial situation. One thing that I'm unclear about, though, is your distinction between knowledge and consciousness."

"Knowledge is a collection of data—organized data, presumably—in someone's mind, together with a system for making sense of it. Knowledge is what one acquires when one studies French or learns how to operate a computer—or hears a lecture on the history of the race. If one has the capacity for it, then one also acquires a certain degree of understanding along with the raw data.

"But consciousness is a higher state of development. Consciousness is knowledge plus awareness plus motivation. Knowledge involves only the mental faculty; consciousness involves a coupling of the mental and spiritual faculties. Knowledge resides in the mind, in the depths; consciousness becomes a part of the personality; it resides on the surface as well as in the depths; it permeates the being.

"If I study the history of my race, then after a while I may be racially knowledgeable. I may be able to quote you a lot of facts, to tell you the ethnic makeups of the opposing armies at the

Catalaunian Fields in 451 and at Tours in 732, or list two dozen
genetically based differences between Blacks and Whites besides
skin color. But that does not make me racially conscious. There are
many racially knowledgeable people on the faculties of our universities, but virtually no racially conscious ones. To become racially
conscious one must elevate one's racial knowledge to such a degree
that it actually governs one's thoughts and behavior; one must have
a constant awareness of it; one must *feel* it. One can gain knowledge
from reading books or listening to sermons, but achieving and
maintaining consciousness generally involves changing the way one
lives."

"Wow!" Oscar responded. "You must have given that little
lecture before." He reflected for a moment on what Harry had said,
then continued. "I guess I agree with your distinction, but I still don't
see why we shouldn't try to illuminate Saul's audience and gradually bring at least a portion of them around to some level of racial
consciousness. They may not be everything we could hope for in
the way of pupils, but they're what we have to work with. The
Identity preachers have re educated exactly the same kind of people
and then built a consciousness of sorts in them. Why can't we work
a few lessons about race into Saul's sermons and then prod his
audience into taking them to heart enough so that they become what
you would call 'conscious'? We wouldn't have to say anything
about the Jews at all. They might decide that Saul is a 'racist,' but
so long as there was no direct threat to them they probably wouldn't
go so far as to shut him down."

"Oscar, one doesn't give people consciousness so easily. The
Jews aren't as conscious as they are just from studying the factual
history of their people. What makes and keeps them conscious is the
constant tension between themselves and the non-Jewish world.
Most of what they are taught about Jewish history—by their families, their rabbis, their Jewish periodicals and books—is calculated
to increase that tension. It's a deliberately distorted history: for
example, their famous 'gas chamber' myths of the Second World
War. What they're taught is that the world is out to get them, and
that the only way for them to survive is to get the world first. The
theme that they hammer into their kids over and over again is
persecution, persecution, persecution. The history they've concocted is a record of how they survived one persecution after another
by getting the better of the host peoples among whom they lived;
their principal holidays are celebrations of the survival of one
persecution or another—and the way in which they got revenge on
the alleged persecutor involved. Young Jews grow up regarding the
Gentiles around them as enemies who must be outsmarted—or else.

They are taught that the world hates them. And, of course, with such attitudes, their worst suspicions and fears tend to come true. *That*'s what gives them their consciousness. *That*'s what makes it so strong.

"And the Identity Christians, to the extent that they have a consciousness, get it in a somewhat similar way. That is, they, like the Jews, regard themselves as the 'chosen people,' the heirs of the ancient Israelites who made the deal with Yahweh. They believe that they have been cheated out of their inheritance by the Jews, who are the minions of Satan. The Jews in turn have used the mass media to denigrate the Identity people; they've sicced the government on them; they've tried to make pariahs of them. That has put them on the defensive and made them feel like a persecuted minority—at least to some degree, although certainly not as much as the Jews. And from the resulting tension has come a degree of consciousness. It worked the same way for the Mormons, at least in the beginning. It works the same way for every group of true believers, if they manage to make themselves unpopular enough.

"But it's hard to make that work for the majority—and Saul's audience feels itself a part of the majority. They may feel that they're surrounded by sinners to a certain extent, but they don't feel persecuted, they don't have the awareness of hostility and danger that it takes to build group consciousness."

"Well, what about us?" Oscar blurted out, frustrated. "How did we develop our racial consciousness?"

Harry laughed. "Sure, we do have some degree of consciousness. I only wish it came near to being as strong as that of the Jews! Our consciousness, instead of being based on a feeling of personal danger, of personal threat, depends on our capacity for abstraction. We perceive the threat to everything which is beautiful and good in the world. Some of us might state that a little differently, perhaps a little more personally, and say that we perceive in the mindless push toward an ever more inclusive egalitarianism, an ever more debased democracy, and all the consequences those things entail—more and more ugliness, more and more disorder, more and more racial degradation—a threat to the meaning of our existence. We're not threatened personally and physically, but the thing we identify with, the thing which gives meaning and purpose to our lives, is threatened. We identify with our race, with an idealization of our race— more than that, with the process of which our race is the principal agent, the process of higher organization, the process which is the active principle of God."

Harry blushed ever so slightly, perhaps because he had bared his soul to his listeners more than he intended. Oscar looked at him intensely and then said quietly, "I didn't realize that you were a religious man, Harry."

Harry laughed again, this time to cover his embarrassment. "There are no atheists in this fight, to paraphrase what someone else said." Then he continued, in a serious tone again: "I don't want to imply that the people who watch Saul's broadcasts aren't capable of developing some degree of racial consciousness, even without feeling personally threatened. I just believe that it will be a very hard job and the result won't be enough to make a decisive difference. Remember, this used to be Caldwell's audience. Their religion is not based on idealism. It's based on the idea of getting into heaven, of getting a share of the pie in the sky, by and by. They've been taught that Jesus hates racists, that racists don't go to heaven. You would not only have to turn that belief around, but you would have to make idealists out of people who are essentially self-indulgent materialists.

"And there's more to it than that. To serve our cause effectively, people need more than knowledge and consciousness; they also need discipline. There's no way Saul can give discipline to people who have grown up without it. Self-discipline, self-control, comes from a lifelong process, a process which requires not only the self-training of the will, but which in nearly every case requires growing up in an environment which imposes a certain degree of external discipline. Without discipline, people may *want* to serve a cause, but they don't have sufficient control over their own resources to be able to do it effectively.

"What all of this leads to is that Saul's viewers can be used in certain ways naturally and easily—namely, in the ways which suit their nature. They can be persuaded to vote for a certain candidate: the candidate that Jesus wants them to vote for. They might be persuaded to boycott certain products in the stores. They might be persuaded to write a flood of letters to Washington opposing or supporting some legislation that Saul tells them Jesus feels strongly about. They might even be provoked into causing some sort of civil disorder, if Jesus spoke to them through Saul in forceful terms.

"But to try to change them and make them do things which are not easy and natural for them—that's a task of an entirely different magnitude. We need to know what we want to do with the power Saul has. Do we want to swing an election? Or do we want to build an army of warriors for the White race? Before we try to do the latter, let's be sure that it makes sense, that it fits into our overall strategy."

There was silence for more than a minute. Oscar found himself amazed once again by the striking similarity between the things two men as different as William Ryan and Harry Keller had said to him.

Reflecting on it, however, he also had a strong feeling that there was an important difference between the views of the two men: a difference that he couldn't quite put his finger on, but which made it easier for him to swallow what Harry said than to accept the same, or a very similar, truth expressed by Ryan.

"All right," Oscar finally said. "All right. Maybe I do get a little ahead of myself sometimes. I guess the thing I worry about is that in the long run we *have* to change the public's ideas; we *have* to build a sense of racial consciousness in the average citizen. Otherwise, swinging an election or starting a riot can't have a lasting effect."

"You're right, of course," Harry replied. "But remember that the Jews have spent decades swinging public attitudes around to what they are now, and to do that they've had a much bigger input than a single television program once a week. In order to give the public a new orientation we'll need a comparable input ourselves. Perhaps if we use Saul wisely we can gain a bigger input. Perhaps eventually we can gain a big enough input to compete effectively with the Jews for the hearts and minds of our people. My concern is about using him for a small and ineffective input now and maybe losing our chance of getting a much bigger and more effective input later."

"Other than the experience we're gaining now with the use of the television broadcast medium, how do you think we can use Saul's broadcasts to gain a bigger input to the public?"

"I don't know. I can think of several possibilities, but right now I believe we have to feel our way along and be ready to take advantage of new opportunities which may arise. The fact that so much money is coming in from Saul's broadcasts promises to give us more ability to do new things than we've ever had before. We could easily have $100 million in the bank a year from now if things keep going the way they are. Then we could think seriously about buying a couple of big-city newspapers. But it's a tricky business. We might spend $100 million on newspapers and then find ourselves losing $50 million a year on them if the Jews got wise to us and launched an advertising boycott against our papers. We'd end up having to sell out at an enormous loss. The advantage they have is that they're organized in depth. Before they took over the media, they established a firm hold on the sources of the largest part of the media's advertising revenue. We can't hope to duplicate that."

"Which, it seems to me, is why we should be working to get our ideas out to the public now," Oscar replied. "We can't do things the way the Jews did it. We can't do it with money alone. But we might be able to do it with ideas, with inspiration. I understand, of course, that we're getting ideas out to individuals now with our books and videotapes. I understand the importance of that; the people we're reaching now are more intelligent, better educated, and better able to participate in our efforts than any of the people in Saul's audience. But we can't afford to continue letting the public drift in the direction the Jews have got them headed."

He paused for a moment, then leaned forward as the glimmerings of a plan began to take shape in his mind. "Suppose we start with something that's subtle enough that it can't pose any danger to Saul's program, but which begins to lay a basis for more obvious ideas later on. For instance, we might get them to thinking about roots. We might begin countering the Jewish line that everyone is nothing but an individual, with no roots and no responsibility except to himself."

Saul, who had been only a listener until now, suddenly spoke up. "Like this?" he asked, and then began declaiming: "Brothers and sisters, is a man only an atom? Are you adrift in this world all by yourself? No, my brothers and sisters, you are not. God teaches us in the Bible that a man is like a link in a chain. You are the link which joins the past to the future. You are the link between all the generations which have gone before and those which will come after. You are what you are because of what your ancestors were and the way they behaved, the way they chose their wives and husbands. What your descendants are like will depend on the way you behave now. In other words, brothers and sisters, God gave us the responsibility for determining what the world will be like in the future. He expects us to take this responsibility very seriously. Because God loves the world, and he wants us to take care of it for him. Yes, he does, brothers and sisters. In the Bible Jesus himself tells us, 'God so loved the world that he gave his only begotten son.' That's what Jesus said. And so when we bring our own children into the world, we'd better pay attention to what we're doing. We'd better make sure that they appear fair in the eyes of the Lord, that they're the kind of children that'll please God and make him feel that we're taking our responsibility seriously."

"Exactly, Saul, exactly!" Oscar responded excitedly. "That bit about appearing 'fair' may raise a few squawks from the race-mixers and the darker-hued brethren, but I think we can get by with anything that's no less subtle than that."

"Of course, I'll have to whip up a mess of parables to illustrate that message. The brothers and sisters can't understand anything unless it's got plenty of parables in it. But I like the basic idea. You know, I grew up in the Fundamentalist milieu. Those people tend to be simple, but they're not bad people. I felt a little uncomfortable with treating them all like a herd of animals that we'd stampede in a certain direction when the right time came. I feel much better about including them in the race along with the somewhat more advanced folks we sell our books to. I'm sure that with sufficient time and patience we can undo a lot of the damage that's been done to them and bring their better instincts to the fore again. It's just a shame that we have to use a Jewish religion and Jewish scriptures to do it, instead of pulling them up out of that mire altogether."

"Well, first things first, Saul," Oscar replied. "Before they can free themselves from a lifetime of alien superstition, they have to learn to think along new directions. We have to give them a new framework for viewing the world and themselves. We have to help them gain a sense of racial identity, a better understanding of their relationship to the rest of the cosmos, and a sense of purpose in their lives."

Harry had been looking thoughtful while Saul and Oscar were speaking. Now he spoke again: "I don't see anything wrong with what you have in mind. It could be five years, even longer, before we're ready to do anything exciting with Saul's audience. In that time we might bring some of them a long way. Certainly not all of them, or even most of them. Christianity is a slave religion, and that suits the nature of a lot of White people, unfortunately. They can't get along without the idea of a Big Daddy in the sky to watch over them. They'll never be taught to stand on their own feet, to think like aristocrats, to have an aristocratic religion. But some of them will, and those may become an important source of new recruits for us. But we'll have to be very careful with the way we try to swing them around, so that we don't lose the bulk of them or arouse the suspicion of the Jews."

"The Jews are bound to be suspicious," Oscar came back. "They'd be suspicious even if we didn't try to put a racial message into Saul's sermons. Being suspicious is their nature. But if we keep it subliminal and if we're careful not to attack any of their more immediate interests, such as Israel, I think we can get away with it. Saul's ratings are so good now that they love him. He's pulling the viewers in and making money for them as well as for us. And remember, we plan to develop Saul into a multi-media operation, just like Caldwell and the others. The ones who respond well to his television message can be carried further with mailings of printed materials. That'll allow us gradually to separate the goats from the sheep without going further than the sheep are capable of going."

Three days later, on July 1, the unemployment figures for May were released. Total unemployment had risen half a per cent since April, to 9.7 per cent, but the increase for the month was less than half the previous month's increase, and government spokesmen

declared unemployment "under control" and predicted confidently
that it would be dropping again soon.

XXXI

Actually, the government didn't have things under quite as firm control as it would have liked. The crime rate had been rising right along with unemployment. Muggings, burglaries, and auto theft were up sharply, month after month. Labor disturbances also were a growing problem. For the most part these were localized, but on the Fourth of July there were huge demonstrations by unemployed workers in New York, Washington, Detroit, San Francisco, and half-a-dozen other major cities. In both Washington and San Francisco the demonstrations became violent, with smashed plate glass and overturned, burning vehicles littering the demonstration areas. Looting of stores by Blacks in Washington became heavy. When the police tried to stop it, the Blacks turned to arson. By the evening of the fifth, 20 square blocks of the capital were in flames, and snipers were holding the fire fighters at bay.

Again Ryan held back, waiting for the right moment to use his muscle, when he could count on both official and public approval for his actions. That moment came after the wind had shifted during the night and carried the smoke from the burning area over the White residential sections of the city to the west. A thermal inversion, very rare for Washington, kept the smoke close to the ground. The dense, choking pall was especially heavy in Georgetown, where many legislators, diplomats, and officials had apartments or town houses. A panicky attempt at exodus via automobile quickly jammed the narrow streets, and coughing motorists abandoned their vehicles, forcing other drivers behind them to do the same. Rescue teams had to go in on foot with gas masks to lead thousands of other residents to safety. The next morning Congressional leaders were furious and demanded strong action immediately. The President called Ryan at 11 o'clock.

Ryan was ready. As in Miami he had been gathering information from his undercover agents since the beginning of the disturbance. In his "war room" at Agency headquarters the locations of all fires, street barricades, gatherings of Black rioters, and reported snipers were indicated on a huge, electronic wall map of the city, which was updated second by second.

He went in just before noon with a dozen helicopter gunships, each carrying a team of heavily armed agents and a television news crew. Buildings from which sniper fire had been reported were rocketed and raked repeatedly with 20-mm. cannon fire before flak-jacketed agents with assault rifles were lowered to their roofs.

Other helicopters swooped over groups of Blacks on the streets and dropped specially rigged clusters of concussion grenades into their midst. This tactic had spectacular results and made especially entertaining viewing for those watching the live television coverage of the Agency's assault on the rioters. One moment the telescreen showed hundreds of Blacks in the street below, shaking their fists defiantly at the helicopter above and shouting obscenities. Then there were a hundred practically instantaneous flashes scattered among the crowd and a deafening, staccato explosion. All that could be seen after that were horizontal Black bodies strewn grotesquely on the pavement. Finally, about half of the bodies would struggle to their feet and begin running in every direction as fast as their legs would carry them. A few of the others would begin crawling or attempting to drag themselves away, while the rest remained still. An Agency spokesman referred to the grenade-dropping devices the helicopters were equipped with as "riot busters." They had been newly developed by the Agency and were expected to be standard equipment in the future.

Within two hours the Agency assault had suppressed the sniping completely and virtually cleared the streets of Blacks in the riot area, except in two large vacant lots, where more than a thousand prisoners had been herded until they could be bussed away. All the fires were out by nightfall.

The image the public had of the Agency's suppression of the Washington riot was one of decisiveness, professionalism, and irresistible force. The contrast with the ineffective tactics of the Washington police was inescapable. Just as after the Miami riot two months earlier, opinion surveys found an overwhelming White approval for the Agency, with churchmen being the only White dissenters worth mentioning. Comments expressed in letters to editors and on radio talk shows ranged from the prissily conservative "the government must be firm with lawless elements" to the robust "we've finally got somebody in Washington who knows how to deal with niggers." The 312 Blacks killed by Ryan's agents in putting down the riot were a mere statistic on the inside pages, cited by no one except angry Black leaders, who made comparisons with the 1960 shooting of Black rioters by South African police at Sharpville.

On July 22 the Congress approved a supplemental appropriation for the Agency allowing it to hire and train an additional 2,500 agents and 1,500 support personnel—more than doubling its strength.

On July 24 the Bureau of Labor Statistics announced a revision in its unemployment figures for April and May, raising both totals by nearly one percentage point. On August 3 the figures for June were released: the total for that month was 13.6 per cent. It was estimated that the figure for July might have gone as high as 15 per cent.

On the same day the President signed an Executive Order indefinitely suspending the civil rights of persons suspected of conspiring to engage in activities which might cause a riot or other public disorder.

Other news had held the public's attention during July, but the first reports of seizures and prosecutions under the Horowitz Act began appearing then as well. Just as Harry had predicted seven months earlier, it was the Ku Klux Klan and a few ragtag neo-Nazi groups which were the initial targets of the Board of Examination set up to examine and approve or disapprove suspect books and other printed materials. The civil libertarians kept their mouths shut, and the impression given by the controlled media was one of a nearly unanimous public approval for the suppression of the "hate" groups and the burning of their literature.

The only noteworthy dissent occurred in August when the Board recommended the banning of a newly published book on AIDS— *The Growing Threat of AIDS in America*—and the prosecution of its author and publisher. The book, written in a semi-popular fashion by Dr Harvey Crossland, a prominent medical researcher at Johns Hopkins University, analyzed the ways in which the disease was infecting heterosexual Whites, who until recently had remained nearly free of it. He placed a heavy blame on bisexuals, who acted as carriers of the HIV virus from its reservoir in the homosexual population to the relatively uninfected heterosexual population; and on promiscuous White persons who engaged in sex both with Blacks, who formed another reservoir for the virus, and with Whites. He pointed out that the only really effective way to prevent the further spread of the deadly disease would be to check everyone for the virus and then quarantine those who had it.

The book was already on the *New York Times* list of non-fiction best sellers when the interdict was issued, and an immediate storm of protest assailed the Board of Examiners. For a period of several weeks the storm grew in intensity, as publicists, educators, writers, legal experts, politicians, and spokesmen for various minority groups jumped into the fray on one side or the other. A number of cooler heads among the original supporters of the Horowitz Act tried quietly to persuade the Board to withdraw its interdict, but their initial efforts were fruitless.

The Board's dozen examiners had been selected by a White House staffer from the surviving members of the People's Committee Against Hate, with the obligatory balancing: there were a Catho-

lic bishop, a rabbi, a Protestant minister, a Black civil rights lobbyist, a militant feminist, an American Indian, a Gypsy, a male homosexual activist, and so on. It was the last named examiner who had insisted that the Board act against the AIDS book. He was infuriated by the book's implication that homosexuals were a health threat to the rest of society and that many of them should be quarantined. He was able to persuade the Black member that Blacks as a whole also were defamed by the book. The feminist, who was rumored to be a switch hitter, was a natural ally. So was the Protestant minister, for the same reason. The four of them steamrollered three other examiners into voting for the interdict, on the basis that the book incited hatred by stigmatizing interracial sex.

The ruckus finally was settled when the President himself intervened and pressured two of the examiners to change their votes. Before that, however, rowdy demonstrations of homosexuals were occurring on a daily basis outside the New York offices of the book's publisher, Harmon House. There was an especially nasty incident during the second week of demonstrations, when two of the homosexuals sloshed containers of AIDS-infected blood over a Harmon House secretary as she left her office.

The next morning there was much more AIDS-infected blood on the sidewalk, when the secretary's husband pulled his car up to the curb 10 yards from a group of the demonstrators, poked the barrel of a 12-gauge autoloading shotgun out the window, and fired seven loads of No. 4 buckshot into them, then reloaded and fired seven more times.

Amazingly, while the avenging husband was thumbing fresh cartridges into his shotgun the 30 or so policemen who had been assigned to keep order at the demonstration site failed to intervene. When one rookie assumed a combat stance with his pistol pointed at the man's head and began shouting for him to drop his weapon, the sergeant in charge knocked the young policeman's arm aside and spoke words to him that caused him to blush deeply and return his pistol quickly to its holster. The sergeant gestured angrily, with the same effect, at another cop who had drawn a bead on the shotgunner.

Several of the policemen turned their weapons toward bloodied demonstrators who were attempting to flee and forced them to drop to the pavement where they were, being careful to avoid contact with them. Other fleeing demonstrators tripped over these and went sprawling. The resulting pileups presented easy targets when the shooting resumed a few seconds later.

After the second barrage the sergeant sighed, ambled over to the car, gently took the man's shotgun from him, and handcuffed him.

Five of the sodomites died quietly on the spot, but 11 others screamed and bled for more than an hour, while ambulance crews refused to touch them until special protective suits with gloves and hoods were provided. The *New York Times*, reflecting the sentiments of the homosexual community, was furious and demanded the prosecution of the policemen, but there was never any serious likelihood of that happening. The official explanation was that the primary responsibility of the police had been to protect the public by preventing the blood-spattered homosexuals from leaving the immediate area of the shooting and possibly infecting others with their blood.

The public agreed vehemently and almost unanimously, as indicated both by informal polls and by actions. When a homosexual spokesman announced plans for a march to protest police behavior and attitudes, someone firebombed his office. When a dozen of his fellows appeared in front of City Hall with placards, a group of street workers attacked them with pipes and shovels, beating them senseless. The throwing of the contaminated blood on the secretary had caught the public's imagination in a way the homosexuals themselves could not have imagined; it had awakened a deep horror and revulsion, which would not easily be repressed again by media admonitions against "intolerance." This was reflected at one level by a sharp rise across the country in the number of assaults on homosexuals by skinheads and others.

There also were demands that Crossland and Harmon House be charged with conspiring to cause the disturbances in front of the latter's offices, but nothing came of these demands either.

There were several official consequences of the affair, however. For one thing, the President quietly reconstituted the Board of Examiners, replacing all of those who had voted for the interdiction of the Crossland book with more pragmatic appointees.

In Congress the most rabid supporters of the Horowitz Act moved in the opposite direction by introducing new legislation to give the Board a greatly expanded authority. Instead of merely acting on complaints about specific books which already had been published, it would exercise prior censorship; all publishers would be required to submit the texts of new books to the Board for approval before proceeding with publication.

It is conceivable that before the fuss about Dr. Crossland's book such legislation might have been enacted, but there was no chance of that now. The spell had been broken. The media-orchestrated hysteria that had allowed the passage of the Horowitz Act in the first place had died down. People had dared to speak out against the heavy-handed censorship of the Board, even at the risk of seeming to favor "hate." There was no move to roll back the Act or to restore rights to such pariahs as Klansmen and neo-Nazis, but the spell would have to be carefully re-woven before the government would be able to move to ensure that no new books would be published which might offend some favored minority.

The Horowitz Act supporters did win one victory, though. They succeeded in transferring responsibility for its enforcement from the FBI to the Agency. Their argument was that "hate" literature and "hate" organizations were associated with terrorism and so should come under the Agency's jurisdiction. They cited the recent shooting of the homosexual demonstrators as a terroristic consequence of the publication of a book which should have been banned. Their real motivation was their anticipation of more vigorous enforcement by Ryan's Agency than by the FBI.

XXXII

66Don't these fags realize that all of the hatred they're causing to
be built up against them may come boiling out of the public one
of these days and scald them all to death? Do they really think they
can keep rubbing the average guy's nose in their filth indefinitely,
and there'll never be any payback?" Oscar asked.

He, Harry, and Saul were in the Kellers' recreation room having
another Sunday-afternoon planning session for Saul's program. For
the last ten weeks Saul had been delivering consciousness-raising
sermons, very carefully designing them to embody a racial message
without actually mentioning race. The viewers received the message
surprisingly well, and his ratings were continuing to rise. Two
Sundays after the latest Nielsen ratings were announced, showing
that Saul's share of the Fundamentalist audience had risen to 55 per
cent, Caldwell, Braggart, and Richards simultaneously accused Saul
of being a "racist" and denounced his sermons as "un-Christian" and
"divisive."

Saul, of course, vehemently denied the charges and kept his
sermons right on course. The week after he was attacked he had
given his most daring sermon yet, beginning with the Old Testament
account of Ezra's measures to keep his fellow Jews from intermar-
rying with their Gentile neighbors and finishing with an admonition
to his audience not to undo what Jehovah had so carefully done:
"God didn't spend a thousand generations to make you what you
are, just for you to mess it all up. He wants me to tell you the same
thing today he had Ezra tell the Israelites 1,500 years ago. He made
them get rid of all their 'strange wives' and of the children they had
by those wives too. If they weren't pure-blooded Israelites they had
to go. That's what God wanted. You young people, think about what
your parents and your grandparents are like. Think about the way
they look and act, and then you pick yourself a mate who looks and
acts that way too." And still there was no explicit mention of race.
Saul could have just as well been speaking to a Black audience as a
White one. The controversy resulting from the attack by his fellow
evangelists caused his ratings to shoot even higher.

Oscar's comment about homosexuals stemmed from a discussion they were having of a news item in that day's *Washington Post*.
The National Education Association had just endorsed a model bill
which would require the schools in those states where the bill
became law to have a course titled "Alternative Sexual Orienta-
tions" for all students. The purported purpose of the bill, which had

been drawn up by a coalition of homosexual groups working with the Anti-Defamation League of B'nai B'rith, would be to "combat bigotry" and reduce the likelihood of further "tragedies" like the recent sidewalk slaughter in New York. The course of study outlined in the bill would "help young people understand that persons with a sexual orientation different from their own" are just as "normal" as anyone else, and that no specific "orientation" is more moral or more desirable than any other.

"Some of them must realize it," Harry replied, "but queers are really not rational. They're a lot like Jews in some ways: they don't know when to stop pushing. In fact, a lot of them *are* Jews. But you're an optimist if you believe that the public is anywhere near ready to start stamping the vermin out. That business with the blood-throwing up in New York was given a big play by the media, and it horrified a lot of folks, but it was only a fluke. You just watch; they'll hardly raise a squawk six months or a year from now when their kids are forced to take classes in which they're told that the gender of their sex partners is irrelevant and that the very worst thing they can do is hurt the feelings of someone with AIDS."

"C'mon, Harry," Oscar responded testily, "you don't really believe we're the only people in the country who give a damn."

"No, I don't. Millions of people—maybe as much as a quarter of the White population—are very unhappy about the way things are going. Not everyone believes what he's told to believe. A lot of them would cheer if the earth would open and swallow every queer, every Jew, and every Black—but not one in ten thousand has the gumption or the guts to *do* anything to make that happen. They'll make no sacrifices and take no chances, so what they believe isn't all that important. It's not for lack of the right ideas that our race is going under; it's for lack of character."

"I won't argue with your last statement," Oscar responded, "but I don't agree with your statistics. I don't believe that men like that secretary's husband with the shotgun are as rare as you think. I believe that there're thousands more like him, and that they'd respond just as forcefully if we could motivate them. And then, after those thousands had set the example, hundreds of thousands more would come out of the woodwork."

"Well, I may be a little too pessimistic, but you're way too optimistic," Harry came back. "The only time you'll find hundreds of thousands of White Americans turning on their enemies is when they're convinced that it's absolutely safe to do so. When there's a Jew hanging from every lamp post, and they're sure there's no danger and it won't cost them anything, they'll come out and spit on the bodies, but that's about all you can count on them for."

"You know," Saul spoke up, "it's not entirely a question of how many White men still have any character. It's the right conditions as much as the right stuff inside a man that make him do the right thing. Under the right conditions the most miserable coward may become a hero and the most selfish egoist may sacrifice himself for a cause. There's not much we can do to improve the American character in the time we've got. That's a job that'll take generations—after the revolution. But we may be able to do something about conditions, and it seems to me that's what we ought to be thinking about."

"Unless you know something the rest of us don't, we're going to have about as hard a time trying to change conditions in this country as character," Harry replied. "What do you think we can do?"

"Well, I'm not sure," was Saul's answer. "But we already have changed the ideological climate a little. Who would have thought just three months ago that we'd have nearly nine million Christian Fundamentalists, who've been taught for the last 30 years that God wants them to go to bed with niggers, actually beginning to feel proud that they're White and developing a real interest in their racial roots in Europe? Have you seen some of the mail we've been getting?"

"Yeah. I am surprised at how well those thumpers have taken to your message. I think the opposition is too, but it won't be very long before they recover from their surprise and start taking countermeasures. I hate to knock success, but I think we've moved way too fast. We should've spent two years doing what you've done in ten weeks, and we should have been a lot more subtle about it. Most of your audience may be absorbing your message without realizing where you're headed, but you sure as hell aren't fooling the Jews. I'm afraid we've blown our cover now and are going to have a lot harder time expanding our media resources. In fact, we may have a hard time holding on to what we've got. Listen to this." Harry then read a clipping he had cut from the latest issue of the *Jewish Week*. It excoriated Saul's program, not only for its subliminal racial message but for what were called the "anti-Semitic overtones" of his sermon on Ezra.

"Heck, I didn't say anything that should be construed as anti-Semitic," Saul protested.

"Sure you did," Harry replied. "You said, in effect, that if it's good for the Jews to avoid intermarriage, then it's good for us too. You're elevating us *goyim* to the same exalted level as the Chosen People. They regard that as *lese majeste*, the very worst sort of anti-Semitism, and they're not about to forgive you for it."

The discussion continued for another hour, but Oscar took a less vigorous part in it than was his wont. He found himself agreeing with Harry's judgment that they had moved too fast. Well, damn it, he would have been more cautious if he hadn't felt that Harry was dragging his feet on the whole concept of using Saul's program for ideological indoctrination. Harry had made him get his back up and push Saul just a bit harder than he otherwise would have, in order to prove his concept.

The program could hardly be doing better. The mail and the money were pouring in. They'd had to hire another dozen women for processing the incoming mail, and two more of the Alliance's local members were now involved full time in preparing the printed material which was sent out in response, ranging from computer-generated thank-you notes that looked like they had been handwritten by Saul himself to more serious reading material for those members of the television audience who seemed ready to have their consciousness raised further. One of Oscar's most vexing chores recently had been to figure out what to do with all the money. He put most of it into six-month certificates of deposit for the time being, while he considered various mutual-fund and stock investment possibilities.

At the back of Oscar's mind, however, was the nagging fear that the whole enterprise was in jeopardy. They had gotten themselves into an exposed position without having any clear notion of what to do next. Saul's comment about changing conditions in the country intrigued him, but he was as much at a loss as Saul was about how to do it, other than to continue cautiously raising the racial consciousness of a few million Christians. He went home that evening mildly depressed and worried.

XXXIII

Although Oscar already had seen tapes of Saul's latest sermon three times at various stages of its development, he watched it again when it was broadcast over WZY-TV at eight o'clock, propped up in bed beside Adelaide. The racial message was slightly more subliminal this time than it had been the week before. Saul took the worsening drug situation as his theme, blaming the growing use of drugs in part on the loss of a sense of racial identity by Americans—again without actually mentioning race.

The essence of his sermon was: "People used to feel that they belonged to a group of other people who were related to them in some way, people who looked like them and thought like them, people they felt a kinship to, whether it was a village or a whole nation back in Europe. That's the way God designed the world. And people felt that they had an obligation to the group they were part of, certain standards of behavior they had to uphold. The whole group had pretty much the same values, the same standards. That's the way God wanted it to be. But it's no longer that way in America, unfortunately. A few evil but powerful men didn't like God's way. They decided America ought to become a 'mixing pot' of all different kinds of peoples, with every kind of behavior you can imagine. And that's what it has become, because these evil men were able to pull the strings to make that happen. They defied God. And the result is that there are no longer any standards. No one feels any obligations. Everyone does just what he wants or what he thinks he can get away with. And that includes taking drugs. And that's why the drug problem will be with us as long as we remain a 'mixing pot.' We'll have the scourge of drugs until we go back to God's way."

That message was reinforced by the national news program which immediately followed Saul. There were two unusually sensational drug stories. One was about a running gun battle in Washington that afternoon between drug enforcement agents and Black and Colombian members of a drug gang. When their headquarters was raided several members of the gang fled in an automobile, with government agents in hot pursuit. The chase led down Pennsylvania Avenue past the White House, where the gang's car, its tires shot out, jumped the curb and crashed into the White House fence. Two of the gang members leaped from the car, seized a group of gawking tourists as hostages, and forced their way through the broken fence onto the White House grounds, where they immediately came under fire from Secret Service guards. In the ensuing shootout, all captured by the television cameras, the gang members and five of the tourists were killed.

The other story involved the arrests of four of the highest ranking officers of the Florida State Police on charges of providing protection for drug smugglers in return for bribes. The arrests were the culmination of a yearlong undercover investigation by the DEA. The four had helped to keep open a route which brought an estimated three billion dollars a year in drugs into the state from the Caribbean by providing the smugglers with full information on all relevant drug enforcement operations, and for their help they were paid millions of dollars by the drug cartel.

The timing of the news could hardly have been better, Oscar thought with satisfaction.

The final news story of the night was about the Middle East. The Israelis had committed another atrocity. After a group of Palestinian children had thrown stones at a car driven by a Jewish settler, he had enlisted the help of other armed settlers and conducted a vigilante raid on a nearby Palestinian village, killing more than a dozen of the inhabitants. The raid was during the day, when the Palestinian men were away at work, and so the victims were all women and children. The Jews were as self-righteous as usual about the incident, saying that they would use whatever degree of force they thought necessary to keep their Palestinian subjects pacified and that it was no business of the rest of the world anyway.

Comments on the atrocity were sought from various spokesmen. The White House and the State Department hemmed and hawed, said that they regretted any acts of violence, and refused to condemn the Israelis. Then, surprisingly, spokesmen for two groups hostile to Israeli policies were interviewed. One was a former U.S. senator of Lebanese descent representing an Arab-American group; he merely repeated his oft-heard call for a cutoff of U.S. economic and military aid to Israel. The other was a left-wing British cleric, representing a Christian-Islamic interfaith group, who announced an international boycott of American-made goods, which was to last as long as the United States continued to supply Israel with money and weapons. "Moral men and women, whether Christian or Islamic, will no longer tolerate the affront to their consciences that support, no matter how indirect, for those who slaughter and oppress Palestinians entails. As long as the U.S. government finances that slaughter, all people of conscience will take pains to avoid financing the United States," the cleric said. The interviewer did not seem to regard this boycott threat as anything to worry about: the organization behind it apparently was neither large nor powerful.

The clergyman's words stuck in Oscar's mind, however, and he felt the germ of an idea beginning to sprout, when Adelaide threw aside the sheet, crawled to the foot of the bed, and stretched to turn off the TV. The view thus presented of her bare, smoothly rounded buttocks a mere yard before his face immediately drove all thoughts but one from his mind.

The germ remained, however, and at the breakfast table the next morning he asked: "What do you think would happen, baby, if ten million Christians suddenly announced that they weren't going to pay their taxes and were going to buy imported goods instead of U.S.-made goods whenever they had a choice—that they weren't going to file 1040s if they were self-employed, that they were going to file for full refunds of everything withheld if they were wage earners, and that they were going to buy Hondas and Datsuns instead of Fords and Chevrolets—until the government promised never to send another cent to Israel?"

"I suppose you're talking about Saul's audience. But how'd it get up to ten million? I thought it was more like seven and a half million."

"That was a month ago, before Caldwell and the rest jumped on him. I think it's pretty close to ten million now. Nine and a half anyway."

After brief reflection Adelaide responded: "In normal times I doubt that it'd have much effect. But with things as tight as they are now, if that many people stopped buying U.S.-made cars it might bump unemployment up another fraction of a per cent. If they really didn't pay their taxes, that might also push inflation up a little. Overall, I don't think it would hurt the government enough to cause a change in policy toward Israel. But it might generate a commotion, especially when the government started putting so many people in jail for not paying taxes."

"Well, suppose there were an international boycott of U.S. products at the same time. Don't you think that six or seven million Americans joining the boycott would give it a big boost and persuade a lot more foreigners to support it too?"

"Maybe. Probably. If it reduced U.S. exports as much as, say, 25 per cent, it would push unemployment up another couple of points, and that would really hurt the government. But you aren't thinking seriously about doing that, are you? I thought you went to a lot of effort to convince the Jews that Saul was pro-Israel, so he could get on the air. Won't they cut him off right away if he comes out against Israel?"

"I'm sure they would. But they may cut him off anyway. All I'm doing now is exploring various possibilities."

Oscar dropped the subject and turned the conversation to more concrete concerns: "Sweetheart, I think you should give the Pentagon your two-weeks notice today. I've got so many things that I need your help with now that it doesn't make sense for you to keep your job."

"That's fine with me. But if you believe Saul's program may not last, don't you think it would be risky for me to quit now? Shouldn't I wait until we're sure the money will keep coming in?"

"Considering the times and what we're doing, we can never be sure of anything more than a few days down the road, baby. We're playing for big stakes now, and the 30 grand a year the government is paying you just doesn't count for much. I've got more than eight million bucks in CDs stashed away from Saul's broadcasts so far, and even if the Jews tried to cut him off next week we'd get another four or five million in donations before everything dried up."

"But that's the League's money. If we have a baby, it'd be nice to have some savings of our own."

"Sure it would, sweetheart. Actually, the money belongs to the American Faith Hour, Incorporated. That's a non-profit corporation we set up just for Saul's program, and I'm the chairman of the board. So far I haven't drawn any salary, because we haven't needed it. But we could put you on the payroll at the same salary you're getting from the Pentagon, and then you could put it all in the bank. The principal consideration is that we're at a decisive moment in history now, and we can't afford to spend our time on anything irrelevant, anything that doesn't make a difference. We have a chance now, maybe just a slim chance, to change the way things are going, to change the whole outcome. We have to give it everything we've got."

As he went about his work during the day Oscar's mind was on other, more predictable and familiar matters: writing checks, planning the taping schedule for the next few broadcasts, interviewing a prospective new employee. It took a call from Colleen in the middle of the afternoon to bring him back to the mood of reckless urgency he had felt earlier.

"They're shutting us down, Oscar." There was a tone of despair and resignation in Colleen's voice.

"Like hell they are! Tell me what you know."

Both Colleen and Harry had left their former employment and were spending all their time on Saul's program and related work. Colleen was the liaison agent with the television stations over which Saul's sermons were broadcast. Colleen gave Oscar the details: "I've gotten eight calls so far today: Los Angeles, WARJ in Chicago, Seattle, and a lot more; they all say that they're terminating their contracts with us. The Jews apparently have launched a coordinated, surprise raid on us. They've actually sent people around personally to threaten the non-Jewish station owners. They're all caving in."

"What about the Gospel Time Network? They're still with us, aren't they?"

"I'm sorry, Oscar. I'm so upset I forgot to mention them. Carl Hollis was the first to call this morning. He was too embarrassed to say much, but he was quite definite: the Gospel Time Network will carry no more of Saul's sermons. He *did* say that the Jews had threatened to bankrupt the network if they didn't cut Saul off."

"Well, what the hell! They can't unilaterally cancel our contracts. We've paid most of them in advance."

"Technically, most of them can't. They're bound to give us the rest of the time specified in the contracts; then they can cancel. But I'm afraid that they'll go ahead and try to cut us off now anyway, even if we threaten to sue them. They're really frightened."

"All right, dammit! We'll have their asses if they try that. I'll talk to Bill right away."

Bill Carpenter was the League's legal counselor. He already had gone over the contracts Oscar had with the broadcasters at the time they were negotiated. Oscar explained the situation briefly to him by telephone and then headed for his office. By the time he arrived Bill already had called two of the broadcasters and spoken to their lawyers. "I was pretty hard on them. I told them that we'd use every means at our disposal to hold them to their contracts, and that we'd pursue their assets to the ends of the earth if they screwed us. WMAB in Los Angeles was pretty hard-nosed; some foul-mouthed Jew lawyer there essentially told me to go fuck myself. The Gospel Time people were more reasonable. Their lawyer said he believed the board of directors would be willing to honor the existing contract, which runs for eight more weeks. He's supposed to call me back before five. Overall, though, I suspect we're going to have a hard time making stations stick to their commitments; most of them would rather face a lawsuit from us than a boycott by the Jews."

"Come on, Bill! There has to be something we can do that'll force even the hardest cases into line," Oscar shot back.

"Well, we could get court injunctions against them. I doubt that anyone would buck an injunction," Bill laughed.

"Then let's do it!"

Bill looked at him quizzically. "Are you serious? Do you realize what's involved in that?"

"I don't care what's involved. There's a great deal at stake here. We have to do whatever it takes to insure that Saul gets at least one more Sunday on the air from every outlet we've got signed up. Let's use every resource we have to get that result. Don't let any consideration of effort or cost hold us back."

"Hell, man, you've got 216 different contracts here. You expect me to get you injunctions for all of those?"

"Hire 215 more lawyers to help you if you have to. Just get the job done. We can't lose this one."

Bill sighed and thought for a minute. Then talking more to himself than to Oscar he said, "Of course, we could invoke the long-arm statute. If we did that we'd only have to go into the Federal district court here and claim jurisdiction over all the contractees, because they're all parties to contracts with us. We also could allege a conspiracy by all of the broadcasters. The fact that they're all moving against us simultaneously lends credence to such an allegation. We might hit 'em all with a single complaint. It'll still be a tricky job, but we might be able to do it."

"What are our chances of getting the injunctions?"

Bill turned his idea over in his head for another minute before answering: "Actually, pretty good. The facts are not really disputed here. The broadcasters want to break clear, unambiguous contracts they have with you. You can credibly claim that you will suffer an irreparable injury if they do. They can hardly make a similar claim. I mean, they certainly wouldn't dare to come into court and say that the Jews would retaliate against them if they gave you what's due you under their contracts. And what else is there for them to say? I think we'll get the injunctions if we apply for them in time. Now, you realize that going for injunctions against these folks will be regarded by them as hostile acts. If they're not already mad at you they will be. Which ones do you want to enjoin?"

"Let's not take any chances on the waverers changing their minds at the last minute. Enjoin them all. If we can get on the air next Sunday, I don't care how mad at us they are after that."

"You know, it's a good thing that this is Monday instead of Friday," Bill answered as he poured himself a cup of coffee and prepared for a long evening of work. "If the Jews had been smarter they would have waited until Thursday or Friday to apply the pressure to the broadcasters. Then there wouldn't have been time for us to get into court."

Oscar used Bill's phone to call Saul and set up a meeting for five o'clock. Before he could leave Bill's office Colleen called to tell him that four more stations had cancelled.

At Saul and Emily's house he outlined what he had in mind for next Sunday: "We've got to hit them with our best shot. We came on a little too strong before and got ourselves into the present jam, but now we have to overwhelm them. We *may* be able to force most of our stations to let us stay on the air until our contracts are up, and we'll use whatever time we get as effectively as we can. But this Sunday is the only thing we can be reasonably *sure* of. And because we may not have a chance for much follow-up, we need to use a little judo: we need to get other people to carry our ball for us, if we can. I think the Middle East is the issue which gives us the best opportunity for that."

"So you think it's time for Jesus to tell the faithful to stop sending their tax dollars to Israel to support the Christ-killers?" Saul surmised.

"Something like that," Oscar agreed. "There are a helluva lot of people who're already in favor of shutting off the pipeline to Israel. The Jews have been able to deny them an effective voice so far—and to control their representatives in Washington. We want to try to hit that issue hard enough to inspire some of the intimidated millions to speak up. It would also be good if we could tie into the boycott that some of the more liberal Christians in Europe are backing."

"Well, I'm a little hesitant to get into economic and political complexities with my audience," Saul responded. "I'm not sure that I could make them understand how buying Jap cars would hurt the Christ-killers without doing a lot of explaining, and I don't think it would look good for Jesus to give them a lecture on economics. On the other hand, I might just keep Jesus' part of it simple and apodictic, and then I could add a little explanation myself. Let me work on it. How much time do we have?"

"Hours, man, hours," Oscar came back grimly. "Fortunately, we were a little behind schedule with the tape you've already recorded for next Sunday, and we didn't mail the copies out last Saturday the way we usually do. Colleen was planning to take them to the post office this morning, when the cancellations began coming in. We really should record tonight and mail in the morning, although I suppose we could record as late as tomorrow morning and mail tomorrow afternoon. Remember, it'll take us about four hours to make all the copies and get them ready for mailing."

"That's a little tight, but I'll do the best I can. I already have a couple of ideas."

"I'm sure you can do it, Saul. This is one time you won't have to be subtle. You can minimize the subliminal hints and maximize the histrionics, which is your strong point. The harder you hit the Jews the better. We'd like to provoke them into helping us keep the pot boiling, and there's hardly an issue on which it should be easier to make them blow their cool."

That evening Oscar and Adelaide watched the news together. The big story was the rioting in Chicago by Blacks. Actually it had started Sunday afternoon but had been kept off the Sunday night network news. Ryan's troops already were in action and were keeping the riot contained, but the Blacks were doing a lot more shooting than they had in Washington. Apparently they had some heavy weapons, because they had shot down one of Ryan's helicopter gunships. Oscar had no doubt that Ryan would knock the fight out of the rioters pretty quickly, but the situation was complicated by the fact that White vigilantes were acting on their own. Barricades had been set up to control vehicular traffic through some White neighborhoods, and cars driven by Blacks were in danger of being fired on. In addition, other Whites had taken the initiative in reducing the potential for Black disorders in their neighborhoods by burning out Blacks who had recently moved in. Initially roving gangs of skinheads with Molotov cocktails had set fire to buildings inhabited by non-Whites in mixed neighborhoods. The idea seemed good to other Whites, who decided that the time was ripe for creating a little no man's land around their own neighborhoods. Hundreds of buildings were ablaze in border areas.

XXXIV

66And now, my brothers and sisters, I must tell you this, even though it is very difficult for me: Our lord and savior came to me again seven nights ago, just after my broadcast last Sunday." Saul had spent nearly 40 minutes of the broadcast working his way up to this statement and, in effect, setting the stage for it. His dignified, almost austere delivery gave him better audience credibility to start with than his more flamboyant and folksy rivals. Their supernatural claims—visions, miracle cures, and the like—nearly always coupled as they were to appeals for funds, came across rather like tailgate pitches for snake-oil remedies. Saul had avoided any such claims between his "visitation" during Caldwell's Easter broadcast and tonight. And now he acted almost pained as he continued.

"I had gone into my library to begin preparing for tonight's talk, and suddenly I felt another presence in the room. Then, before I understood what the presence was, the room filled with light so bright that I could see nothing else, and I felt *him* place his hand on my shoulder, and I heard *his* voice." With these last words Saul's own voice cracked. He sobbed, made an effort to regain control of himself, and then went on, the strain clearly audible in his voice.

"He told me that his heart is heavy. He died for us on the cross, he said, in order that we might have eternal life. But nearly all of us have rejected this priceless gift he offered to us. We have rejected it by rejecting justice, by rejecting mercy, by rejecting decency, and by allying ourselves with the very ones who sent him to the cross—the very ones who today are crucifying other innocents in the land where *he* lived when he was on earth. He told me that we can be forgiven our sins if we accept his love, but that there is no forgiveness for those who reject his sacrifice and adhere to his enemies and even help them in the same sort of wickedness today that they were pursuing two thousand years ago."

Here Saul paused for a long moment to give his audience time to grasp what he had just said before continuing: "He told me that *I* am among those who have rejected his love, because I have adhered to his enemies and have supported their lies and their false claims, and I have not spoken out against their wickedness. And, oh, my brothers and sisters, it is true! It is true!" The anguish and grief in Saul's voice were overpowering. He broke down completely, sobbing uncontrollably.

It was a masterful performance, the best Saul had ever given. It brought tears to Oscar's eyes as he watched. Adelaide sniffed and reached to the nightstand for a Kleenex. The tapes for the broadcast had been sent out by express mail the previous Tuesday afternoon, and Bill Carpenter had succeeded in obtaining the injunctions they sought two days later. Most of the broadcasters had put up no real opposition in court, and the Jews weren't ready yet to reveal themselves publicly as the moving force behind the contract cancellations. The injunctions were good only for this broadcast, however, and the broadcasters would have a chance this week to present their arguments against making the injunctions permanent. The Jewish organizations certainly would come out from behind the scenes too and use all of their legal muscle.

The evening's climax was yet to come. Saul, sufficiently recovered from his grief to continue, began confessing his sins: "I did like all the other evangelists; I praised Israel, and I knew it was wrong. I was careful never to criticize those who crucified our lord, when I knew they should be criticized. Like all the others, I said that it was a fulfillment of prophecy when the Jews murdered the rightful inhabitants of the Holy Land and stole their birthright, and I knew that I was blaspheming when I said it; like every other Bible scholar I knew that the Jews broke their covenant with God thousands of years ago and have been cursed for it ever since, that the Bible clearly says that they long ago lost any right they may have had to the Holy Land. I knew that, but I was afraid to speak the truth. We were all afraid. We knew that in order to stay on the air we had to praise Israel, we had to blaspheme, we had to lie about God's word, we had to prostitute ourselves. We were afraid of the Jews and the power they have, their money power. The others are still afraid, and it's for good reason, let me tell you! As soon as the word began leaking out last week that I wasn't going to lie any more, that I was through protecting those who crucified our lord, they started trying to force me off the air. This very television station that you're watching now tried to keep me from speaking to you tonight. I had to go into court to make them honor their contract with me. Because they're afraid of the Jews too. And until Jesus put his hand on my shoulder last week and spoke to me, I was just as afraid as all the rest. I knew their power. But since Jesus spoke to me I've been afraid of something else even more than the power of the Jews. I've been afraid of losing the gift of love that Jesus offered to every man and every woman who would accept it. I've been afraid of losing my immortal soul."

"God, what an actor!" Oscar exclaimed, momentarily breaking the spell cast by Saul's magic. "He's the most convincing liar I've ever seen. If he'd gone into politics, he'd certainly be President now."

Adelaide, still enthralled, silently snuggled closer to Oscar, but her eyes never left the television screen.

After a pause Saul's voice, which with his last words had become a hoarse whisper, began rising in pitch and intensity: "I want Jesus' love. I want the everlasting life that only he can give. I will no longer blaspheme to protect those who hate him. I will no longer praise those who crucified him. I will no longer justify their tyranny and murder. I will speak out against their wickedness. I will not fear their power, for Jesus is with me. And I call on each of you, my brothers and sisters in Christ, to stand with me. I call on you to turn away from those who hate our lord, to withhold your support from them, to condemn their wickedness as I do. And I also call on our government to break the chains with which the Jews have bound it. I call on the officials in Washington to stop sending our taxes to murderers and tyrants and haters of Jesus. I call on them to break all their ties to the abomination which is Israel!"

Saul's voice, powered by righteous fury, was ringing out now. "Fear will not still my tongue, and those who serve Christ's enemies will not silence me. I will give you the truth that you must have in order to be saved. I will tell you how we can break the power of the Jews over our lives and over our government. I will . . . I . . . ."

There was a startled look on Saul's face as his voice broke. Then he gasped out, "He is coming again! Our lord is coming!"

His hands clung to the lectern in a death grip, as if he were afraid of being carried away bodily. Then the same sort of transformation took place in his posture that had occurred during the Easter sermon. He relaxed and at the same time seemed to grow taller. Viewers thought they sensed a change in presence. Then his halo began to glow. The effect had been much easier to arrange this time, with their own studio facilities, and it was even more impressive. Saul's voice, profoundly changed, rolled out over the recording studio, out over the television audience, out over the plains and the mountains, the fields and forests and cities of the nation, like an irresistible wave of power and serenity: "My children, I suffered greatly that you might live. Cleave not to those who persecuted me. Serve not those who hate me. Believe on me and walk in the paths of righteousness. Hearken unto my servant Saul and obey him, and you shall dwell with me in heaven forever."

The light blazing from Saul's eyes went out at the same time that the aura around his head died out, and he slumped forward onto the lectern, as if drained of energy. After a few seconds he made a visible effort of will, straightened up, and then tried several times to speak, but no sound came from his throat. Finally he found his voice again and, struggling to control his emotions, said haltingly: "I am so glad that he came again tonight and spoke to you. I was afraid that you might not believe me, but now he has shown himself to you too. Now you know. And now, my brothers and sisters, we must do as our lord has commanded us."

The timing, the gestures, the changes of posture and of voice had been perfect. No actor could have done better. Saul used the remaining minutes of his sermon to explain just what it was that Jesus wanted the faithful to do. They were to protest in the strongest possible terms to the politicians in Washington about the continued sending of money and weapons to Israel. If the politicians did not respond immediately, then they were to withhold their taxes. They were to apply pressure to the government in every way possible. If they continued to allow their tax dollars to be used to pay for the evil deeds of those who had handed Jesus over to be crucified, then their souls were in danger of eternal torment. He did not ask them to boycott American-made automobiles, because he and Oscar had decided at the last moment that that would have required too much explaining. They would keep it simple and see how people responded. Then maybe a boycott would be feasible later.

"It's a shame we have to use trickery to persuade people to do what's right," Oscar commented wryly to Adelaide after Saul's sermon. "It makes me uneasy. My instinct is to tell them right out what's wrong and what needs to be done. I know we can't do that; I know it wouldn't work. These people—most people—*have* to be tricked. They just aren't developed enough to recognize the truth or to distinguish between right and wrong. The Jews trick them, the government tricks them, the churches and the other evangelists trick them, the controlled media trick them, and we have to trick them too. They were born to be tricked all their lives. But I still think it's a shame we don't have the time to bring them around slowly to the right way of looking at things by educating them, even if we have to do it subliminally. I think Saul was getting somewhere with his sermons, helping his viewers to straighten out their thinking, before the Jews forced our hand."

He looked hard at Adelaide, laughed, and said: "Of course, it's not just that trickery runs against my grain. I'm also worried about how well it'll work. What do you think? Do you think Saul convinced most of his audience tonight?"

Adelaide hesitated for a moment before replying. "Yes, I think he did. I haven't been a Christian or a believer in the supernatural since I was a freshman, and I wasn't much of a believer even before that. Yet Saul came very close to convincing *me* tonight that Jesus was speaking through him. He was really compelling. I'm sure that most of the people who were watching tonight were very deeply moved and that they really believe now that Jesus wants them to stop sending their taxes to Israel. But . . . ."

"But what?" Oscar demanded impatiently.

"Well, I just don't know how many of them will actually *do* anything about their conviction. People are so passive. And they're so fickle, so easily swayed. I don't know how long they'll *keep* their new conviction, before the other evangelists sway them back again. If only Saul could keep talking to them, week after week! Then I'm sure he could get at least a portion of those he's convinced to actually do something."

"Yeah, dammit, that's the problem. We really had just this one shot. I'm sure we'll be able to keep Saul on some of his stations for a while longer, but after tonight the Jews will pull out all the stops in their campaign to silence him. We just can't match their economic power or their political power, and they're bound to cut our audience way down. But we'll fight 'em every inch of the way."

XXXV

Feedback on the impact of Saul's September 27 broadcast was felt immediately from the Jewish side and within the week from Saul's viewers. The Jews went literally berserk. The realization that a hated *goy* had gotten the better of them; that someone they had allowed to use one of *their* media had turned it against them as a weapon; that what they had been tricked into believing was a tame Christian had sneaked into the sheep pen behind their backs and turned loose millions of other Christians they had spent decades taming, and was now putting no telling what sort of dangerous ideas into their heads—this realization drove many Jews to such a frenzy of rage and hatred that they abandoned all caution and restraint.

On Monday morning a mob of enraged Jews burst into the studios of WFKZ, the New York City station which carried Saul's program, and ransacked it, destroying equipment and beating any employees unlucky enough to fall into their hands. One 19-year-old secretary was hospitalized with a skull fracture and internal injuries after being worked over with baseball bats. Monday night a bomb wrecked the transmitter of Saul's Los Angeles station. And screaming, cursing, spitting Jews demonstrated noisily outside a dozen of Saul's other stations in major cities across the country, terrifying employees and damaging property.

Editorial comment in the nation's newspapers was quite predictable: Saul was branded as a "hater" and a "neo-Nazi," and there were suggestions that he had exceeded the permissible limits of speech, that such sermons should no more be tolerated than the cry of "fire!" in a crowded theater. Editorial misrepresentations of what Saul had said were rife and blatant; Oscar could see in these the cold calculation that more than 20 times as many newspaper readers had not seen Saul's program as had seen it, and so most readers would not realize they were being lied to when they were told that Saul's broadcast had been filled with "Hitlerian ravings" and "anti-Semitic filth." Those who had seen it might be amazed by what they read in their newspapers, but their awakening to the fact that their newspapers were edited by liars was an acceptable loss in the frantic media campaign to limit the damage caused by Saul's broadcast.

And the other evangelists fell over each other in their eagerness to denounce Saul. Caldwell was the most vociferous. He was interviewed on Monday's NBC Evening News, where he evoked memories of concentration camps and gas chambers and lamented that the poor, blameless Jews were still being persecuted and hounded by anti-Semites like Saul. To be against continued support for Israel was to be against God, Caldwell declared; to blame the Jews for Jesus' death was to commit blasphemy.

Interestingly enough, not one of the evangelists accused Saul of fraud; not one questioned the genuineness of his experience as a medium for Jesus. They simply avoided the issue; it was clear to Oscar that the subject of faked miracles was one they preferred not to broach.

The politicians also lost no time in jumping on the bandwagon, although by the end of the week a few had jumped off again. It was a notorious fact that the Jews had at least 75 members of the U.S. Senate in their pockets: three-quarters of the Senate would sign any petition or vote for or against any bill without question or quibble if the Jews demanded it of them. Another 15 or so senators could usually be gotten into line with a little persuasion. Eighty-three of them put their names to a resolution Monday denouncing Saul and his program. In a news poll taken that afternoon it was discovered that not one of the 83 had seen Saul's broadcast.

Then the reaction from the audience began coming in. The Fundamentalists who had seen Saul's performance were solidly behind him. Their letters started arriving in Washington Wednesday. By Friday the mail was in bags stacked to the ceilings in the offices of many Bible Belt legislators. Eight senators who had signed the Jewish statement against Saul on Monday publicly withdrew their denunciations on Friday, explaining that since Monday they had viewed a tape of the broadcast and found it not so objectionable as they had been led to believe it was.

It was clear that the Jews still held the balance of power, in terms of control of the politicians, by a considerable margin. But it also was clear that among the people Saul enjoyed enough support to put up a real fight. The recognition of this latter fact served as a goad to keep the Jews' alarm at a fever pitch. In the week following Saul's broadcast the publications of various Jewish organizations were full of dire predictions of the danger which would arise if the change of attitude toward Israel which Saul had effected among his television audience were allowed to spread to other segments of the population. A prolonged fight over the issue of support for Israel would certainly lead to many additional *goyim* aligning themselves with Saul and was, therefore, to be avoided at all costs. Saul must be silenced immediately, and the issue he had raised must be put to rest at the same time—quietly.

The *Jewish Week* warned that the growing public unrest from the worsening economy could easily be transformed into a massive resurgence of anti-Jewish feeling and action. All it would take to trigger such a transformation would be a general recognition by the Gentile masses that while they were struggling to make ends meet, the Jew-controlled politicians in Washington were taxing them to provide a massive subsidy for the Jews in Israel. With the total economic and military aid to the Jewish nation running at nearly five billion dollars, that worked out to a rate of about $5,000 per year per Israeli family of four—more than enough to make a big difference for the average American family.

After this, the change in the treatment of the issue by the mass news media was as profound as it was rapid. Saul's name virtually disappeared from the newspapers. The furious battle raging in the courts over his right to remain on the air was covered by only the briefest mention in the inside pages, and even there the only explanation given was that the broadcasters objected to the "racism" in his sermons. There was no hint of Jewish involvement in the litigation.

The other side of the same coin was a flood of new tear-jerking stories about the "Holocaust" and reruns of old stories, a trick the media masters always pulled when they thought the Gentile public needed to be reminded about how much the poor Jews had suffered and what a debt the world owed to them.

Saul's program was carried by nearly two-thirds of his regular stations the Sunday after his bombshell sermon, and by a little over half of them the next Sunday. Bill Carpenter had enlisted reinforcements and was putting up a stiff fight in the courts, but it was clear that the best outcome which could be hoped for was a delay of a total blackout for a few more weeks. The Jews simply had them outgunned. The judicial system in America long ago had degenerated to the point where the letter and the spirit of the law were no longer the governing factors; money and politics carried a lot more weight than justice in the courtroom these days. The faction with more political clout or a bigger press claque had a substantial advantage over the faction which merely had more right on its side. The lawyers for all factions were utterly without scruple, and the judges themselves were much more lawyer-politicians than judicators; the rulings they handed down from the bench were at root based on personal career decisions instead of legal judgments.

While the fight lasted, however, Oscar and Saul were taking the best advantage of it they could. Saul told his viewers briefly about the situation in the Middle East: about the way the Jews, who had had virtually no presence in Palestine since Roman times, had schemed to turn the global conflict of the First World War to their advantage by using their political influence to pull the United States into the war on Britain's side in return for a pledge (the Balfour

Declaration) from the British government to establish a Jewish "homeland" in Palestine after the war; about the treachery, chicanery, and mass murder the Jews had used to leapfrog the bridgehead gained from the Balfour Declaration into a ruling position in Palestine after the Second World War (which they had had no small role in instigating); and about the campaign of genocide they had waged against the native Palestinians ever since.

He put most of his emphasis on what the Jews were doing in the United States, though. History and foreign affairs were a bit too abstract for much of his audience. Taxes, political and judicial corruption, moral and social decay, the bias of the controlled news and entertainment media, the present economic stagnation—things of which his viewers had firsthand experience, if not real understanding—were related directly in Saul's sermons to the power wielded in the United States by the tribe which had killed Christ. He kept his message simple and compelling, and his viewers took it to heart. The number of these actually grew, despite his program being dropped from many stations, as millions of non-Fundamentalists tuned in out of curiosity in the wake of the initial blast of media denunciations of Saul and then excitedly called on their friends to tune in as well when they had gotten a taste of his message. When the Nielsen ratings were released in mid-October they showed that the number of Saul's viewers had climbed from just under nine million the previous month to nearly 12 million, despite the loss of 45 per cent of his stations.

The frenzy of the Jews knew no limits. Although the mass media remained silent on the issue, their own community and organizational publications were hysterical.

Unemployment in October climbed above 17 per cent. The FBI declined to reveal the latest national figures for crime, but local figures, where published, had skyrocketed. Muggings, burglaries, and armed robberies had become such ever-present threats in the cities that Whites virtually deserted the streets at night, leaving them to the minority gangs and the police. Those whose employment forced them to go out during the hours of darkness tried to travel in groups, keeping their car doors locked and dreading a breakdown while worrying constantly about the security of the unguarded homes they had left. Shops and stores which formerly had remained open at night closed up tight at dusk and pulled down steel shutters over their display windows. People who were in the business of installing steel shutters, alarms, deadbolts, window bars, and other security devices had never before been in such demand.

Civil disorder too had become almost a daily fact of life, despite the government's draconian measures to keep it in check. The frequent marches and demonstrations to protest economic conditions very often ended in clashes with police or in other violence. Groups of unemployed squatters seized vacant buildings, and their ejection by police was seldom accomplished peacefully.

Mini-race riots also were an increasing phenomenon. Many Whites who in the past simply would have packed up and retreated further into suburbia when they came face to face with the grim reality of life with the colored brother no longer had the means to effect a retreat; they were forced to stand their ground and fight. In the last month there had been nothing else on quite the scale of the September rioting and burning in Chicago, but there had been a number of smaller racial confrontations.

Finally, genuine political terrorism seemed to be coming back into vogue. Bombings of banks and government buildings on a scale not seen since the early 1970s had developed in recent weeks, with a bewildering array of 1960s-style organizations claiming credit and issuing manifestos and ultimatums.

No doubt the situation would be much more chaotic without the efforts of the Agency for Public Security, but I soon found it amusing to contemplate the hectic pace of activity which was now Ryan's lot. He wondered whether Ryan really believed that the lid could be kept on things until the economy improved—if it improved.

XXXVI

Oscar had just turned on the late news when Ryan called. "Got an easy one for you this time, Yeager. Got a pencil and paper handy?"

"Sure. What's up?"

"Need for you to knock off a TV preacher for me."

Oscar felt his bowels churning and their contents turning to liquid; he knew before Ryan spoke again just *which* TV preacher his caller wanted killed. He listened in numbed silence as Ryan continued.

"His name is Saul Rogers. He lives at 1202 South Glendale Street in Alexandria. He has no bodyguards or other security, and he's easy to spot—a really striking looking guy. I've left an info packet on him, including a photograph, at the regular drop site. You should pick it up tonight. The job should be done right away, before he has a chance to tape another sermon. And you don't have to worry about making it look like an accident. There are so many people who want this guy dead that the police will be busy for the next five years checking out suspects."

Oscar found his voice and stammered out his question: "I . . . I don't understand. Why do you want me to kill a preacher? What does that have to do with national security?"

"Plenty. In the first place he's making a big commotion; got the true believers really riled up, thinking he's Jesus' spokesman. A lot of 'em are writing letters to their Congressmen saying they aren't going to pay any more taxes. If somebody gets them organized, we could have a tax rebellion on our hands."

"For Christ's sake, you don't shoot people for that! If he's done something illegal—incited a disorder or something—you've got the authority to have him arrested. You can hold him without bail for six months under your new powers. That'll put an end to any trouble he's causing."

"I could arrest him, Yeager, but I don't want to. I could easily enough charge him under the President's recent executive order, but I don't want to play the role of an enemy of Jesus. The man has a lot of popular support out there, and I don't want all of that support turned against me. Besides there are other reasons why we need to get rid of him."

"What reasons?" Oscar demanded.

"If you must know, every top Jewish leader in the country is screaming for his blood. They've put a lot of pressure on the

President to silence him. We're depending on these guys to keep things cool, not to encourage disorder or start criticizing the government in the media they control."

"Jews? What the hell? Have you switched sides, Ryan?"

There was a hard edge to Ryan's voice when he replied: "Listen, Yeager, I haven't got time to explain everything to you. Just take my word for it. We need the cooperation of the top Jews, whose interests at the moment happen to coincide with the government's and with mine."

"Well, I guess you're going to think I'm pretty dense and pretty stubborn," Oscar came back, "but you had me convinced earlier that your whole game was to outflank the Jews and keep them from taking over everything. Now it sounds like you're taking orders from them. I don't especially object to killing people, preachers or others, but I do like to have a rationale for what I'm doing. I like to feel that it's for a worthy cause, if you know what I mean."

"I'm getting irritated with you, Yeager. I'm not taking orders from the Jews. I'm trying to maintain order in this damned country under very trying conditions. The top Jews are smart enough to understand that if we let this economic slump result in general disorder, there's liable to be a lot of blame dumped on them, with a big rise in anti-Semitism, maybe even violence directed against Jews. In a sense we've got 'em by the balls now; we can make 'em behave themselves for once and keep the other Jews in line for us."

"For themselves, don't you mean? You understand as well as I do, Ryan, that the Jews have to go through a period of consolidation every now and then. They ordinarily thrive on disorder; they create disorder in every way they can to break a society down so they can digest it. Ever since the Second World War they've been breaking down our society, obliterating its sense of identity, turning its mores upside down, pumping it full of spiritual poison. Now it's time for them to consolidate. The new laws taking away civil liberties are designed to lock in the changes they've made, to keep Whites from undoing them. They need a fellow like you to keep fellows like me in line for a generation, until the last resistance has died down and the public thinks the new setup is the way things are supposed to be."

Ryan's voice was icy now and barely under control: "I'm not going to argue with you, Yeager. I've told you what I want done, and now you'd better do it." Then, as he had done before, Ryan relented slightly and resumed: "I suppose I should be proud of you for having come so far in your understanding of the Jews, after I got you started. But don't make the mistake of thinking you know everything. I told you a long time ago I was going to bring order to this country, and that's what I'm doing. It's not Jewish order I'm after. Its *my* order. They aren't the only people pulling the strings. I've got a good chance to get the upper hand if I can hold things together. In any case there's no point in crying over spilled milk. Sure, the Jews ruined this country. But the fact we have to face now is that it's ruined. It doesn't matter much who did it. The Whites you think are being prevented by the new laws from setting things right again would have no more chance of doing that than all the king's men had with Humpty Dumpty. All they could do is bring on total chaos, and nothing good comes from chaos. At least I'm holding together what's left and giving the American people a chance to suffer in an orderly way and maybe gain a little backbone from the experience. And, believe me, if anybody's going to slip a sack over the Jews' heads in the future, it'll be me. Just think, boy: When you pop this con-man Rogers, it'll be the Jews who'll get the blame. He's been attacking them on his program, and everybody'll assume they killed him to shut him up. Millions of evangelicals who think he's something special will hate the Jews for killing their guru."

After Oscar hung up, Adelaide, who had overheard some of what he had said to Ryan, asked with concern, "What's this about shooting people?"

"Nothing, honey. Just a rhetorical dispute with a fellow I know." Oscar made an excuse to her and drove out into the night to retrieve the information packet. He needed time to think, and he wanted to know exactly what information the Agency had on Saul.

He soon discovered that that information was minimal: name, address, place and date of birth, former occupation, physical description. All of this was on a standard Agency form, to which a photograph taken from the personnel files of the school where Saul had worked was attached. There also was a Xerox copy of a school personnel form Saul had filled out years ago. But in the space on the Agency form which asked for organizational affiliation was typed the word "unknown." Apparently the Agency was unaware of Saul's League membership.

Oscar didn't get much sleep that night. The last thing he wanted was a confrontation with Ryan. If he refused to kill Saul, Ryan probably would be willing to risk having an Agency man do it. Then not only would his relationship with Ryan be irreparably damaged, but his own life would be in danger. Furthermore, the Agency might investigate Saul further in preparation for the assassination and discover the League connection, which could jeopardize other people. The situation was bad, bad, bad.

One especially troubling thing about it was that it wasn't all one-sided. Oscar couldn't say that he really *liked* Ryan, but he had come to have a great deal of respect for the man. Tied up with Ryan's Praetorian ambition were some genuine ideals. And in fighting the Jews to determine the issue of racial survival, it seemed to Oscar that it made strategic sense to be fighting on more than one front. Certainly Ryan already was in a much better position to affect the outcome of the struggle than was the League, even if he had a somewhat different goal in mind. In fact, he was in a world-historical position, and to tamper recklessly with that seemed the worst sort of irresponsibility to Oscar. The overall situation, apart from the immediate problem of Saul, might be much, much worse with someone other than Ryan as chief Praetorian.

That was one side of the coin. The other side was that Oscar felt himself in much closer spiritual harmony with the League's approach to the struggle than with Ryan's. Oscar's nature was such that it seemed right and natural to him to fight the way they were fighting with Saul's program, by attempting to wake up and re-educate as many White people as they could, to salvage everyone who could be salvaged and then to enlist them into the common cause of racial survival; or, failing that, to take up arms and fight the way he had been fighting before Ryan caught him. He just wasn't as ready as Ryan was to opt for stasis, to write off the chance for cleaning up the racial situation and making a fresh start. If he had to choose between the stasis of Ryan's Caesarism and the uncertainty and flux of civil war, he would choose the latter.

Oscar finally drifted into a troubled sleep around three o'clock in the morning. Adelaide shook him awake at eight. After a cup of strong, hot coffee an idea gradually began forming in his mind at the breakfast table. Suppose, he thought, he faked an assassination attempt on Saul, an unsuccessful but noisy attempt. That would give Saul a plausible excuse for suddenly surrounding himself with a security screen, and the publicity would make it much more dangerous for Ryan to sic an Agency killer on him. Furthermore, it would take Oscar off the hook—sort of. He did not relish the idea of pretending to botch a job; it hurt his pride even to contemplate it. And it might make Ryan suspicious. At the very least it would badly erode Ryan's confidence in him. But it should buy some time— enough time, perhaps, for Saul to continue his program until the Jews finally succeeded in blackmailing all of his stations into cutting him off.

After breakfast he called Harry and asked him to give Saul a call from a pay phone and use some pretext—without mentioning Oscar's name—to get over to the recording studio right away. Oscar wasn't worried about his own phone being bugged, since the last thing Ryan wanted was for anyone else in the Agency to investigate

Oscar, but he was afraid that Saul's phone might not be safe. He arrived at the studio before either of the others and began planning just how he would explain things to Saul and Harry. He needed to tell them part of the truth, but he wasn't prepared to tell them the whole truth.

He began: "Listen, Saul, don't press me for details, but I happen to know that there's a contract out on you. There are some folks who want you killed as soon as possible. We're going to have to make them pull back a little—hopefully for as long as we can keep you on the air—and I think I know how to do that."

Harry looked at Oscar intently: "Hey, pal, you got connections in the Mafia?"

"No, not at all. But I am plugged into a certain grapevine. I really can't say much more than that. You'll just have to believe me. The folks who've put the contract out on Saul are heavyweight people, and they're very serious. But they're also afraid of publicity. They'll only act if they think the blame will fall on someone else; they won't take a chance on being blamed themselves. Saul needs two things now to be safe. He needs the best security force we can buy, and he needs a lot of publicity about the threat to his life. So here's what we're going to do.

"Harry, you're going to get on the phone and line up a security team. Get professionals, not League volunteers. At least a dozen, so there'll always be a couple in Saul's house, a couple to accompany him everywhere, someone to stay day and night with any vehicle he'll be using, someone to sleep in the studio—and in any other place he goes regularly. Line them up today, but they're not to report for work until tomorrow morning.

"Saul, today you'll go about your daily routine as if nothing has changed, and tonight I'll make an attempt on your life. Specifically, I'll blow up your car. I want something spectacular and noisy that'll attract as much media attention as we can get.

"Let's see, it gets dark by seven. You park whichever of your cars you've got the most insurance on outside your garage this evening, well away from your house and anything else you don't want damaged. At seven I'll attach a bomb with a radio-controlled detonator to the underside. At seven-thirty you tell Emily you're going to pop over to the studio for an hour to check out some props for your next sermon. You get in the car, start the engine, turn on the lights, then remember something you forgot. Leave the engine running and the lights on, and go back in the house as quickly as you can. That's when I'll hit the button. Got it?"

Saul looked at him doubtfully. "Oscar, are you *sure* you know what you're talking about?"

XXXVII

Ryan was not pleased. Oscar had executed the plan he had outlined to Saul and Harry, deliberately using a bomb much larger than necessary. Not only had it blown Saul's Mercedes into mangled halves fifty feet apart, but it had shattered windows in nearly every home within a two-block radius of Saul's. Police and FBI agents were swarming over the scene within minutes, and the papers and television news were full of the story the next morning.

Saul, his face bandaged where it had been cut by flying glass, explained in a network television news interview how his life had been miraculously spared by his remembering that he had left his Bible in his house. "I felt Jesus' presence as I started my car, and I heard a voice say, 'Your Bible, Saul.' If it hadn't been for that reminder, I'd have been blown to bits." Then he added, "I know that the supporters of Israel want to silence me. They're blackmailing all of the stations which carry my sermons, threatening to bankrupt them if they don't break their contracts with me. I didn't realize they'd go this far to keep me quiet. I know that the fear of the Jews has silenced many others who wanted to bring the truth to the people, but I'm not afraid because I know that Jesus is guarding my life, and he will use as many miracles as he has to while I'm serving him."

The real miracle was that Saul's statement actually went out on the news programs uncensored.

"Dammit, Yeager, you've really botched this one!" Ryan said caustically in a call that evening.

"I'm sorry, Ryan. I figured he might be planning to use his car last night when I saw it parked outside his garage. I clamped 15 pounds of Tovex under his floorboards with a magnet. I had one of those radio-controlled detonators you gave me strapped to it. Then I went back to my own car, which was parked about 200 yards away on the street, and waited. When I saw his lights come on, I pushed the button. From where I was I couldn't see that he'd hopped out of his car and gone back in his house right after he turned on his lights. I really tried to do a good job, but sometimes these things happen."

"Well, you're just going to have to try again, and the job is going to be a lot harder. The bastard has guards all around him now."

Oscar had hoped that Ryan would pull back in the face of all the publicity about the bombing and give him a breathing spell. That had been his primary goal in staging the bombing. He wanted very badly to avoid a showdown with Ryan, and when he heard Ryan's insistence on going ahead his heart sank. He had anticipated this eventuality, however, and he had prepared himself for it.

"Whatever you say. I'll just have to figure out another way to get to him. Hey, listen: I almost forgot to tell you. I found something really interesting in Rogers' car. When I was checking it out I saw a briefcase on the rear seat. The door was unlocked, so I peeked in the briefcase. I grabbed a packet of papers and stuck them in my pocket. When I got home I looked through them, and guess what! Rogers is planning to hit you in one of his sermons. He's got a bunch of stuff on you. Looks like it came from the FBI."

"What the hell are you talking about, Yeager? What stuff?" The alarm was evident in Ryan's voice.

"The papers are down in my basement. I can't remember every-thing in them, but there were several FBI investigative reports about civil-rights violations your Agency allegedly committed in putting down the nigger riots in Washington and Chicago. Rogers has gone over the reports with a fine-toothed comb, with things underlined and notes in the margin saying, 'Use this,' and so forth. He's apparently getting the information from somebody in the FBI who wants to get you. I remember one marginal note said something like, 'See Thorstein again Thursday at Hoover Building for more de-tails.'"

"Thorstein?"

"Thorstein, Thurstein, something like that."

"Thonstein! Jules Thonstein! That bastard!" Ryan exploded.

Oscar's ignorance of the spelling and pronunciation of the name was pretended. He knew quite well that Jules Thonstein was the director of the Bureau's Racketeering Section. He remembered seeing the man's name in the news reports at the time the Agency was formed; he was mentioned as a possible candidate to head the new organization. Oscar had calculated that that fact alone would make the two men rivals, and he had calculated well. Ryan re-sponded almost exactly as Oscar thought he would.

"Okay, listen, Yeager. You've got to get those papers to me right away. I can't take a chance on having them go through anybody else. I'll go to the Capri, you know that restaurant in Georgetown?"

"Yeah, I've heard of it. I think I know where it is."

"All right, I'll be there in half an hour. You be there too, with all of those papers. At exactly 8:30 I'll go into the men's room. You go in at 8:25 and pass the papers to me when I come in."

"No, no, Ryan. If I'm going to meet you again, I want it to be some place where we can sit down and talk face to face for a few minutes. If these papers are as important to you as I'm beginning to think they are, then you can figure a way to ditch your bodyguards for an hour and meet me where we can talk privately."

"What have you got in mind? You don't think you're going to blackmail me do you, Yeager?" Suspicion was heavy in Ryan's voice.

"That's the last thing in my mind. But things have changed a lot since we formed our little partnership. I need to get some things clarified, so that I'll know exactly what our relationship is going to be in the future."

There was a pause while Ryan considered the matter, then he said: "All right, Yeager. I have a boat at the marina, down on Maine Avenue. Know where that is?"

"Yep."

"My boat's in slot K-2, a big , white one with blue trim. You can't miss it. I'll go there now. You come on board between 8:30 and 8:40, and we'll talk for . . . I can give you half an hour. Okay?"

"Yeah. That'll probably be enough time."

"You just make sure you bring all of those papers you found with you—*all* of them "

When Oscar hung up he sighed. Well, Ryan had fallen into his trap very neatly. He almost wished it hadn't worked.

XXXVIII

"Come on in, Yeager." Ryan waved Oscar into the spacious but dimly lighted cabin of his 55-foot cruiser. Oscar noted that the ports were tightly shuttered. It certainly seemed an ideal place for private meetings.

While Oscar was continuing to take in his surroundings, he felt Ryan's pistol prod him in the back. "Just take it easy, Yeager. I don't know exactly what's on your mind tonight, and as I told you before I'm a careful man."

Oscar allowed himself to be expertly patted down. Ryan removed Oscar's revolver from his waistband, completed the search, then demanded, "Okay, Yeager, where are the papers?"

"There aren't any papers."

"Don't you try to jerk me around, you son of a bitch!" Ryan was angry now.

Oscar turned to face Ryan, ignoring the weapon in the other's hand, and said, "I told you I wanted to talk with you, Ryan. I made up the story about finding the papers in Rogers' car just to persuade you to meet with me for a few minutes."

"You really like to live dangerously, Yeager. I ought to kill you now and be done with you. It would make me feel good. Whatever possessed you to pull such a dumb stunt? Do you realize how busy I am?"

"Yes, I'm sure you're a very busy man," Oscar replied. "And I'm sure you're going to be even busier in the future, considering the way this country is going. So it's better that we get some things straight now rather than later. I've stuck my neck out for you, Ryan. You wouldn't be where you are today but for some of the jobs I've done for you. You may want me to do something else for you later. It seems to me that you'd regard a few minutes of quiet discussion every now and then as time well spent."

Ryan's eyes flashed and his nostrils flared at the assertion that he owed his position to Oscar. "You're too big for your britches, sonny," he shot back at Oscar. "You're nothing but a goddamned errand boy, and you'd be sitting on death row waiting for the juice right now if I hadn't decided to save your hide for better things. Sure, I know all about the battle being lost for want of a horseshoe nail, but you'd better keep in mind that you're not the only horseshoe nail around."

Having let off a little steam, Ryan shifted his tone from threatening to brusque and asked, "All right, what's on your mind tonight?" He waved Oscar to a lounge chair on one side of the cabin and took a seat for himself on the other side, on a couch. Fifteen feet and a coffee table separated the two men. Ryan glanced at his watch and then placed his pistol on the cushion beside him, within easy reach.

"Is it really necessary for Saul Rogers to be killed?" Oscar began.

"Is that what's bothering you? You don't want to finish the job on that preacher? What's the matter, Yeager? You've killed preachers before. You must've gotten a dozen of them when you blew up the People's Committee Against Hate. Maybe you believe this Rogers really is Jesus' mouthpiece, huh?"

"Come on, Ryan. You know I'm not superstitious. I've heard some of Rogers' broadcasts. I . . . uh, got some tapes from a friend who records his sermons. Rogers is saying things that need to be said. He's really on our side and can do a lot to help neutralize the Jews. I just don't see why he should be killed. Nobody else is turning so many ordinary Americans against the Jews as he is."

Ryan sighed and then began his reply in a conciliatory tone. "Look, Yeager, if it were up to me I'd be inclined to leave the guy alone, at least for now. If his followers really looked like they might make economic problems for the government, I'd bust up his act the way we used to do it all the time back in the Bureau. I'd slip an infiltrator into his operation, a seeming starry-eyed volunteer from the Bible Belt who'd offer to help out in the office for almost no salary. We'd find something to get Rogers on—irregularities in his bookkeeping, conspiracy to incite a disorder, something. And if we couldn't find what we needed we'd cook it up ourselves. Then we'd have our man go to the local cops or to the Bureau—not to the Agency—and pretend to be outraged by what he'd discovered. We put a hell of a lot of radical organizations out of business that way, on both the left and the right, back in the seventies, and we could do it to Rogers too. And we could do it in such a way that I wouldn't even get the heat from his followers.

"But, you see, I'm not the only one who's concerned about the commotion Rogers is making. If I let him keep hitting the Jews, they'll start hitting back. They'll start rocking the boat again, and I can't let that happen. Right now the smart ones, the ones at the top, know that it's in their best interests for the government to be able to keep the lid on things, to maintain order. And, believe me, they're the *only* people who can keep all the rest of the Jewboys, whose natural inclination is to make trouble, in line. If the top Jews are convinced that the government—that I—will protect them from people like Rogers, they'll stay in line and keep their wilder brethren in line as well. More than that, they'll help me keep the general

public in line. Have you noticed how calmly the media bosses have
been taking my pacification measures when the Blacks have gotten
out of line? That's no oversight on their part; it's calculated policy.
A few years ago they all would have been screaming bloody murder
if the government had gotten rough with their precious Blacks. And
if they get the idea now that I can't or won't protect them and their
interests, all hell will break loose. They'll sir up no end of trouble:
riots, strikes, demonstrations, everything to keep the White majority
off balance, everything to keep people like Rogers' followers from
organizing themselves and beginning to have some influence on
wider public opinion and governmental policy. Understand?"

"I understand all of that perfectly well, Ryan. I even understand
why you've opted for assassination instead of a frame-up. A frame-
up might take a few months, and if Rogers stays on the air that long
the Jews' position will have been severely dam . . . ."

Ryan interrupted: "You're damned right a frame-up would take
too long. This thing's got to be settled in a few days, at most."

Oscar resumed, "As I was saying, if you leave Rogers alone,
there's a good chance he'll neutralize the Jews for you, so that their
capacity for making trouble will be substantially reduced. Why not
. . . ."

Ryan interrupted again. "A good chance isn't good enough,
Yeager. And even if he did turn a majority of the people against the
Jews—which he won't; it'll be maybe 20 or 30 per cent at the most;
there are too many people in this country whose interests are tied up
with those of the Jews: the mainstream Christians, the feminists, the
queers, a lot of the big capitalists—but even if he did turn a majority
against them, they'd still be capable of making all sorts of trouble."

"Trouble you and the Agency couldn't handle?"

"Damned right! Look, I can deal with organized crime; with the
Israeli secret police, now that I've got them whittled down to size,
with your much-appreciated help; with Black rioters; and with
political terrorists of all sorts, either individually or in groups. But
I can't take on the whole country at once. At least, I'm not prepared
to do that yet. The general public has to be kept more or less pacified,
more or less in line. And it's the mass media which do that. It's the
soaps and the situation comedies and the game shows and the ball
games and their favorite news commentators. As long as the media
are telling them that they ought to put up with the present economic
difficulties without complaining, that's what most of them will do.
But if the media start telling them that they're being screwed and
that they ought to start making a fuss, there'll be hell to pay.

"And I can't do anything about that. What do you think would
happen if I started rounding up all of the Jews in the news and

entertainment media? I'll tell you what would happen. There wouldn't *be* any news and entertainment media left. There's no way I can replace all of those Jewish editors and publishers and script-writers and directors and program managers and producers—no way. The whole industry is riddled with them, at every level, and it'd take years to replace them with Gentiles. The machine would come to a halt. The TV screens would go blank. The natives would become *very* restless. I don't like it any more than you do, but I'm willing to face facts and you don't seem to be able to. And the fact is that, for better or for worse, the media *control* the vast majority of the people in this country. They tell them what to think and how to behave, and for the most part that's what the people do. Right now that's for the better. I don't want it to become for the worse."

Oscar stared intently at Ryan for a moment before answering: "Do you think it's for the better that the Jews who control the media, while telling the public to grin and bear their economic hardships, are also telling them to grin and bear the racial mixing, the un-checked flood of non-White immigrants across our borders, the continued conversion of America into a Third World slum? Do you think It's for the better that American schoolchildren are continuing to be given a falsified version of history and are continuing to be educated in a way which is calculated to suppress any feeling of racial identity or racial pride? That the general public is getting a stepped-up dose of 'Holocaust' baloney and phoney atrocity stories aimed at diverting any blame for current circumstances from the Jews? That the pro-Israel propaganda is being churned out as never before?"

He paused for only a second, then continued: "Don't you see, Ryan, that what the Jews are doing is *locking us in* to the present set of trends, and that we *cannot* and *must not* tolerate that? In return for helping you maintain order, they're maintaining the trends which surely, and not very slowly, will destroy our race. Is that really what you want?"

"You know it's not, Yeager. But damn it, man, can't you under-stand that what I want or you want is irrelevant? We have to deal with facts, not wishes and daydreams. And the fact is that we have only two choices. We could either keep muddling along the way we were, in good, old democratic fashion, just letting everything get worse and worse while everyone in the government is careful to avoid doing anything for which he might have to take the blame. Then we'd still have all the evils you've just mentioned, *and* there'd be a general breakdown of order and public morale as well. Or we can do what I'm doing now, which is to kick ass hard enough to keep the lawless elements from getting out of control, while the people as a whole learn the discipline of sacrifice and of obedience. The country may be going down the tubes, but as long as I'm running the Agency it'll go down in an orderly and disciplined manner."

Ryan chuckled and then began again before Oscar could give a rejoinder. "Actually, I don't think it's going to be half as bad as you imagine. The Jews may think they're locking us in to permanent control by themselves, but I have other thoughts. Let me tell you how it is from the viewpoint of the big boys, the ones at the top of the power structure, people like Senator Herman and the President. Right now they're really worried. They get constant feedback on the mood of the public from the opinion polls they keep going all the time. They know that the public is almost completely disaffected from the government, that the people don't really like or trust anyone in authority, and that the present civil stability is very precarious. They know that almost anything could wreck that stability. They know that they themselves have relatively little control over the situation. They know that just two forces are holding things together and safeguarding their own worthless asses: the Jews with their media, who're keeping the general public more or less ancsthotized; and I, who am ready, willing, and able to kick the pee out of anyone who tries to upset the applecart. So they're licking both our asses now. The Jews are getting more money and weapons for Israel and more 'anti-hate' laws restricting anyone who might be inclined to point the finger at them. And I'm being given a virtually free hand in dealing with anti-government elements."

Ryan leaned toward Oscar and shifted to a conspiratorial tone. "And now I'll let you in on a secret, Yeager. Very soon, my free hand will be much stronger than it is now. The big boys don't like being kept in a continual state of anxiety. They don't like having to keep licking the Jews' asses and wondering when the bastards'll stab 'em in the back. They don't like to be so dependent on me either, but at least they trust me a little more than they trust the Jews. They'd like to shift the balance of things more toward me and away from the Jews. They'd like to have stability more dependent on my police powers and less on the Jews' ability to manipulate the mood of the public. They're worried as hell about the elections coming up next year, because there are too many things which could get out of control. In particular, there are too many of their own colleagues who'll do anything, including rocking the boat, to get reelected. The Jews are looking forward to the elections, figuring that they'll get even more of their own creatures in and shift the balance toward themselves. But just between you and me there might not *be* any elections."

"What do mean by that? Certainly there would be much worse problems for the government if it tried to call off the elections. The media would raise hell."

"Right now they would. But not six months from now. Not after I put down the insurrection."

"What insurrection?"

"The one whose development I've been very carefully monitoring during the last two months. We talk about 'the public' and how the Jews have it under control, but the truth of the matter is that there are many restless factions out there which have their own agendas: the Latino revanchists, who want to take the Southwest away from the *gringos* and rejoin Mexico; many of the Christian Fundamentalists, like those who're being manipulated by Rogers now; the White supremacists, who want to kill off the minorities; the Black nationalists, who'd like to do the same thing to the White majority; and lots of others. Well, sometime in the next few weeks—probably next month—the Black nationalists are going to stage a coordinated uprising all across the country, and I'm going to smash it. But before I do it's going to do enough damage and scare the beJesus out of enough people so that the public will be happy for peace at any price. Part of that price will be no more elections, although our Jewish friends don't know that yet."

"Do they know about the uprising?"

"Not really. Not the details. What they do know is that many Black leaders are planning *something*. They don't have the sources of information in the Black community that I have. I've been tapped into the planning of this thing from the beginning, nudging it in the right direction every now and then, helping it along when necessary—all without the Blacks realizing it, of course. What the Jews know is that there's a hell of a lot more hostility to them among Black leaders—I mean the real leaders, the Black nationalists, not the Uncle Toms the Jews have set up to serve their own interests—than there is among any other segment of the population, and they're worried about it. The Black leaders all understand the Jewish domination of the media—which is something that most Whites hadn't figured out before Rogers started telling them—and they're really pissed that the media didn't raise a fuss when I cracked down on the rioters in Washington, Chicago, Miami, and a few other places. They've been preaching to the Black masses for years that the apparent Jewish sympathy for Blacks is entirely self-serving, that the Jews'll drop them whenever it suits their purpose, and now the Black masses believe it. They'll be going after Jews and Jewish businesses with a vengeance when they start the shooting and burning next month. So I won't have any interference to speak of from the media when I wipe out the Black nationalist movement once and for all. I expect the fighting will last a while, and the President will declare a state of emergency, suspend many civil liberties, and postpone the elections indefinitely. When the dust has settled, the Jews will realize that they've lost their chance to shift things in their favor, but they'll be happy enough to still be alive that they'll continue supporting the government."

"Ryan, I still don't see how that'll make the situation better. The Black nationalists aren't the ones we should be worried about. It's the tame niggers, the assimilationists, the race mixers, the ones who want to intermarry and become as much like Whites as they can who are the real threat to the race. If you put the nationalists out of business, then there won't be any separatist force, any source of separatist sentiment, left in the Black community. We sure as hell don't want that. And the Jews'll still be in control of the media, still pumping their poison into the minds and hearts of the White population."

"You must not have heard what I just said, Yeager: the elections will be postponed indefinitely. Got that? No more elections. That'll be the best damned thing that's ever happened to this country."

"Well, I'm certainly no advocate of democracy. But the country'll still have a bunch of criminals running it. The bunch in the Congress, the White House, and the courts now are about as sorry a gang of crooks as have ever come down the pike. I don't see how more elections could make things much worse."

"You're missing the point, Yeager. Two points, actually. First, it's not just that we won't be switching the crooks at the top every few years any more; we'll be changing the whole system. We'll be eliminating the four-year cycle, the old shell game of switching back and forth between Republicans and Democrats. We'll have a chance for real stability. We'll be rid of the irresponsibility, waste, and mismanagement which come when the people running the government can think and plan no further ahead than the next election. And second, it won't be the present gang who'll be running things—not really. It'll be me."

"How do you figure that, Ryan?"

Ryan answered with another question: "What's your opinion of President Hedges? What kind of man do you think he is?"

"Well, I guess you should know that better than I. I've only seen him on TV. My impression is that he's a rather shallow fellow without much character."

"You've judged him well. He's a goddamned actor, nothing more. He's absolutely hollow. Nothing inside him at all. Everything is on the surface. The man isn't even interested in power. All he

ANDREW MACDONALD

cares about is the semblance of power, the trappings of power. He thrives on being a big shot, on all the deference, the attention, the perks, the *idea* of being the leader of the nation. And he puts on a fairly good act of being President, but in reality the Cabinet runs his administration. The one good thing I can say about the man is that he's smart enough to know his own limitations, and he doesn't even try to set policy.

"The men in the Cabinet are not bad administrators, most of them, but there's only one of them besides me who has any balls."

"Hemmings, the Secretary of State?"

"Exactly. Hemmings. He's a tough little bastard. And, of course, he's entirely the Jews' man. He runs the State Department as if it were in Tel Aviv instead of Washington. But I've finally found out *why* he's the Jews' man. I've found out what they've got on the bastard, and I believe I'll be able to keep him under control. If I can't, then I'll arrange for some Black nationalist to knock him off. Or maybe I'll have you do it. But one way or another, I'm going to be the one calling the shots."

Oscar looked at the other man for a moment, then shook his head.

"Flynn, I don't know what you had to drink with your dinner tonight. You're just not making sense. You know you can't run the country by yourself. Maybe 20 years from now you could, if you spent all that time building up your machinery of control. But right now, as you admitted a few minutes ago, you've got nothing to take the place of the mass media. The Jews could pull the plug on you any time they felt like it. You can only rule at their pleasure."

"And they can survive only at mine."

"In other words, you'll have to have an alliance with them. You'll have to make deals with them: they keep the sheep from getting too restless and revolting on you, and you let them continue spreading their poison."

"It's not quite that simple, Yeager. I'll have a role to play in keeping the sheep in line too. I've been taking my own public opinion polls, and I'm not without a constituency out there. In fact, among the White working class and middle class, I'm the most popular man in the government at present. I've been keeping a fairly low profile in order to avoid jealousy, but when the Blacks do their thing next month, I'm not going to be quite so bashful. And when it's all over I'm not going to be some shadowy secret police boss behind the scenes; I'm going to have pubic exposure on a regular basis. I'm going to talk to the people. I know the Jews will be looking for an opportunity to slip a knife into my back, but I don't intend to give them one. The poison they'll be feeding the people will be no worse than that they're feeding them now. And I'll be working on building that machinery you mentioned. So, you see, any deals I'm forced to make with the Jews now don't have to be permanent. In 15 or 20 years I'll be able to shift the balance a long way in my favor."

Oscar shook his head again. "Well, Ryan, there are certain attractive features to your plan. If I were in your position I'd be a little more worried than you seem to be about making the Jews behave themselves. But aside from that I guess I can't think of anyone else I know who's better qualified to pull off your scheme and then keep things under control than you are."

Oscar paused, leaned back in his chair, stretched his limbs for a moment, then continued: "The trouble is I just can't go for any scenario which involves maintaining the present racial situation and the present Jewish media control. You may achieve stability. You may have a stronger, more smoothly running government. But the government isn't an end in itself. It's the race that's important. It's the race's mission of improving itself, of bringing forth a higher type of human being, that's important. The government should exist only to serve that purpose. Stability is only desirable when it serves that purpose. And I don't see that purpose being served at all in your vision of the future. Why can't we fight the Jews? Why can't we let Rogers keep broadcasting his message to the people? Why can't we raise the consciousness of the White people, or at least a sizable portion of them, and then send the Jews to hell? So what if there's no television for a while? So what if the rabble riot when the screens go blank? Go ahead with your Black uprising if you want, but then use the public support you gain when you put down the Blacks to get rid of the Jews, no matter what the cost. Let Rogers go ahead building support for that move. Then I can support you fully."

Ryan in his turn shook his head and then responded, "I must confess, Yeager, that there are certain aspects of your own vision that appeal to me. It's a romantic vision. But I stopped being a romantic and became a realist about the time I passed through puberty. I guess you haven't made that transition yet."

Ryan chuckled at the verbal thrust he had made, then turned serious and continued: "If you had made a serious study of history like I have you might have recognized certain very general facts of life, or perhaps I should say certain general facts of historical development. History has inertia. Any historical development, such as the one we've been going through in this country as it has changed in this century from an essentially homogeneous, White, Christian nation quite conscious of its European heritage to a heterogeneous, multi-racial, polyglot, heterodox rabble ruled by Jews and crooked lawyer-politicians in league with the Jews, has an enormous inertia.

It moves tectonically, like a crustal plate in the earth. It has built up its motion over a long period of time. That motion is driven by historical forces. There is simply no turning such a development around. The most one can hope to do is understand its dynamics and learn how best to adapt to it. That's what I intend to do. You, on the other hand, want to ignore the laws of history and charge head-on into all the forces that are carrying America in the direction she's going. In particular, you want to tackle the Jews head-on. You can't win that way."

"I don't know about your 'laws of history,' Ryan. I'm sure that the rot we can see all around us has very deep roots, but I'm not convinced that we have to sit back and be observers while the race goes down the drain. I'm inclined to agree with you that the process of decay has gone too far to be reversed, but there's still plenty of sound human material left to be salvaged. I believe that there are ways to carry out a salvage operation successfully. You could, for example, let the Black rebellion take place as planned, but then use the Agency to liquidate the Jewish leadership, the Jewish media controllers and money men, during the general confusion caused by the rebellion. The rebellion would serve as a great stimulus to White consciousness, and we could organize the salvageable elements into an effective force for cutting out the rest of the rot and isolating it. The TV screens could go blank, and the cities could burn. The more rioting by the rabble the better. At the end of a year we should have a pretty clear separation of elements, and we could start rebuilding even while completing the elimination of the rotten material."

"You're dreaming again, Yeager. You have an idealized image of the White man in your head. It's an image of what you think the White man *ought to be*, not what he *really is*, not what he *actually has become*. You imagine that when the Blacks rise up and start their wholesale burning and looting and raping and killing, hundreds of thousands of these heroic White men which exist in your mind will materialize, along with their heroic women, and you'll organize them into a disciplined force for mopping up the Jews, the queers, the feminists, the nigger-loving liberals, the politicians and the other race traitors, the nut-case Christians, the spics, the gooks, the towel-heads, and what's left of the Blacks after I've crushed their rebellion. But it won't happen, Yeager. It's only a dream.

"Just because you and I have the balls and the inclination to join such a fight doesn't mean that anyone else does. We're unique. There aren't any others like us left in this degenerate age. You'd end up with a few hundred White volunteers, and you'd find those impossible to discipline. The rest would be sitting at home waiting for their television sets to come back on and tell them what to think, running with the niggers and joining the looting and raping, or praying for Jesus to save them. Understand?

"What you have in mind won't work. The White people are too far gone. They don't understand discipline, sacrifice, pulling together for a common goal. They're too weak, too timid, too spoiled, too selfish, too undisciplined. Hitler's SS legions were the last White force on earth which had a chance of doing what you want to do, and there just weren't enough of them to pull it off. The rabble smothered them with sheer numbers. And the rabble would smother you a thousand times faster. Do you think my Agency is the only armed force in this country? The Army would be called out against you, and it would smother you, no matter how much higher your racial quality or how much better your discipline."

There was silence in the cabin while the two men stared at each other. Finally Ryan glanced down at his watch, and Oscar spoke, his voice husky with emotion. "No doubt there's much truth in what you say. No doubt we would be facing a desperate and risky struggle. But we *must* chance it, Ryan. We *must* interrupt the current trends. We *must* at least give our people a chance to save themselves and make a fresh start. We *can't* permit ourselves to be locked into a new stasis, with the Jews continuing to control the media. That would be inevitably lethal. Order and stability are good things, when the situation is progressive, when a people is embued with a constructive spirit and is building a better future for its progeny. But when the situation is regressive, then order and stability become the enemies of life, the enemies of true progress."

Ryan snorted with impatience as he replied. "I'll tell you what we *must* do, Yeager. We must terminate this useless debate now. I've wasted more than an hour with you tonight. You'd better forget your dream and accept the fact that there *will be* order in this country. You can either be a part of that order or not. If you want to be part of it then you're going to get rid of Rogers for me pronto, with no more slipups. If you don't want to be part of it, I can fix that for you right now."

Ryan glanced to his right and reached for the pistol on the cushion beside him. At that instant Oscar squeezed hard on the pocket clip of the pen he had pulled from his shirt pocket some minutes ago and had been idly toying with as the two men talked. There was a faint popping sound, and a thin stream of liquid spurted from the end of the pen which was pointed directly toward Ryan, diverging into a narrow cone of mist as it approached its target. Ryan gasped, emitted a strangled oath, and stumbled halfway to his feet, upsetting the coffee table.

While Ryan, momentarily blinded by the tear gas, groped on the couch for his pistol, choking and gasping for breath, Oscar sprang. He knocked Ryan aside and seized the pistol, then whirled and fired two quick shots as the other man lunged toward him. Ryan clutched his midsection, groaned once, and dropped to the floor. Oscar kneeled beside him and felt his pulse. Ryan was still alive.

"Sorry about that, Ryan. I really hated to do it. I really wanted to keep working with you. I think we would have had a much better chance with you running the Agency, if only you could have shifted your priorities and put the race ahead of order."

"Then why?" the mortally wounded Ryan gasped weakly.

Oscar thought for a minute before answering. "I guess that, behind all the arguments about what's realistic and what isn't, I did it for that 14-year-old Klansman's daughter you told me about, Ryan."

Oscar rose to his feet, pointed the pistol carefully at the back of Ryan's head, and administered the *coup de grace*. Then he gathered up his own pistol and slipped out into the night.

XXXIX

The faked assassination attempt on Saul had serendipitous consequences. Two days later—the morning after Oscar had killed Ryan—the FBI announced the arrest of the leader and three other members of the Zionist Defense League and charged them with conspiracy in the bombing of Saul's car.

Apparently the militant Jewish group had been talking for several weeks about killing Saul, and an informer in the group had been reporting the discussions to the FBI. Whether the members' talk of assassination had been serious or not it was difficult to say with certainty, but the group had a long record of violence which included a number of bombings of persons who had spoken out against U.S. support for Israel. A search of the leader's home turned up a large cache of explosives and illegal weapons, and that was enough to convince the FBI of the group's responsibility for the attempt on Saul's life.

That evening, with the news full of reports of the Jews' arrests and the demands for retribution by Saul's Fundamentalist followers, Ryan's body was found on his yacht. Although there was not the slightest hint of Jewish involvement in Ryan's death, the timing was unfortunate for the Jews. The Agency chief had been especially popular with the law-and-order elements who made up a sizable portion of Saul's following, and rumors that the Jews had killed him were irrepressible. Synagogues were burned and Jewish department stores were ransacked in a dozen cities in the Bible Belt.

Another effect of these rumors was the President's choice of a Gentile as Ryan's successor, despite the heavy lobbying behind the scenes for the post to go to a Jew. Hedges and his advisers were afraid that the appointment of the Jews' candidate, Sherman Davidson, would confirm the rumors in many minds and turn the wrath of Saul's followers against the Hedges Administration. So the new Agency chief was George Carruthers, who had been Ryan's second in command. Carruthers was an excellent administrator and a skilful diplomat and negotiator, but he utterly lacked Ryan's Praetorian qualities. His habit was to act only after careful deliberation and prolonged consultation with advisory committees, never with the boldness or intuition which had guided Ryan. It was Oscar's guess that the man shared Ryan's views on the Jews, or Ryan would not have chosen him as his deputy. How Carruthers would fare in putting down the anticipated Black rebellion remained to be seen, but Oscar suspected he would have a much rougher time of it.

Oscar had enough faith in Ryan's forecast to make it the subject of Saul's next sermon. Saul gave his own prediction of the rebellion a cryptic treatment, with the aim of avoiding charges of "racism" which might jeopardize the ongoing fight to remain on the air—and also to minimize the likelihood of forestalling the predicted event. He allowed Jesus to speak through him again, halo and all, and Jesus' exact words were: "Behold, my enemies have deceived you and confused you and led you into the folly of taking a great beast into your midst. They have told you to give your children to the beast and to lie with the beast, as a woman lies with a man, and to accept all manner of evil from the beast. They have blinded you, so that you see not what the beast does to you. And now my enemies have told the beast to rise up against you and slay you. And the beast shall rise up, and it shall destroy your cities and ravish your women and defile your children, and it shall slay many of you. And your blood shall run in the streets of your cities because of your folly and because of the hatred which my enemies bear for you.

"And, behold, all of these things shall come to pass very soon. But my father shall have mercy on you, and he shall rally you in the midst of your tribulations, and he shall lead you against the beast and against my enemies, who have brought this evil upon you. And you shall slay them, both the beast and my enemies, and you shall triumph over them, and you shall cleanse the earth of their presence until not even a memory of them remains."

This prophecy generated much speculation among the faithful as to its meaning—for the next 15 days; then it suddenly became clear beyond the slightest shadow of a doubt, as the Black rebellion began with the Day of the Long Knives. White losses on that first day were really substantial only in the largest urban areas. More than 12,000 were killed in New York, a little less than 3,000 in Boston, nearly 4,000 in Washington, 2,000 in Atlanta, 5,500 in Chicago, 9,000 in the Los Angeles area—about 58,000 for the whole country. Although the numbers were not large—a little more than were killed in automobile crashes each year, or a sixth as many as were killed by cigarettes—the psychological impact was enormous.

When Black employees in offices, shops, and factories all across the country pulled weapons from their clothing at exactly noon, Eastern Daylight Time, and began attacking their White co-workers on that first Monday of the rebellion, the White reaction was panic and terror. The weapons in many cases were handguns—sometimes even sawed-off rifles or shotguns—instead of knives, to be sure, but the image which remained in the minds of most Whites who witnessed the rebellion was of blood-spattered Blacks with blood-dripping knives, ice picks, cleavers, or hatchets in their hands, running from desk to desk, from counter to counter, from work station to work station, stabbing, hacking, slicing, chopping, amid the screams and groans of their victims.

In a few instances, mostly in blue-collar locations, White workers defended themselves vigorously, disarming their Black attackers and administering summary justice. As a rule, however, Whites were easy victims. Brainwashed by decades of guilt-inducing "brotherhood" propaganda, they were morally disarmed and incapable of defending themselves. When the Blacks began their deadly work, some Whites scrambled to get out of their way, but others could only watch and wait, paralyzed with fear. The bizarre and horrible scenes witnessed on that day were many.

In the offices of a large law firm in Boston, in which only four Blacks and more than 50 Whites were employed, two of the Blacks—a secretary and a junior attorney—were nationalists. At noon these two produced weapons and herded everyone else, except a dozen or so Whites who already had left for lunch, into a large conference room and ordered them to kneel on the floor. While the junior attorney waved a pistol and ranted about "White racism" and "injustice," the Black secretary went methodically from one kneeling White to another, slitting the throat of each with a straight razor. The Whites merely awaited their turns, some silent, some sobbing. An eyewitness account was given by one of the two Blacks who did not participate in the killings.

In Washington a few minutes after noon Blacks blocked one end of a highway tunnel running under Capitol Hill by parking cars across the roadway. Terrified White government workers attempting to flee the city quickly had the tunnel full of backed-up traffic. Starting at the blocked end a gang of about two dozen young Black males armed with machetes and axes began pulling White drivers and passengers from their vehicles and butchering them. As the Blacks worked their way further into the tunnel, most Whites remained in their cars, watching in horror as the Whites in front of them were dragged screaming through smashed windshields and dispatched with savage machete blows. A few Whites ran back through the tunnel to an exit ramp and attempted to summon the police, but the police all were busy elsewhere. The slaughter in the tunnel continued for nearly four hours, until the Black killers were too exhausted to kill more. More than 300 Whites died in the tunnel during those four hours.

Overall, only a small percentage of America's Blacks were involved in the initial violence—fewer than 40,000 for the entire country. Those were the ones who were members of one or another of the militant nationalist organizations, the ones who had been steeped in the rhetoric of self-pity and hatred for the "White oppressor" for years, who had been preparing themselves for a rebellion for months, and who had been told the time of the uprising and given their final instructions 24 hours beforehand. It was a wonder that, with the "secret" shared by so many, the Agency was the only arm of the government which had a detailed foreknowledge of the rebellion.

The majority of the Black militants were young males, although a surprisingly large number of females also were involved. Many were college educated; in these resentment had reached its greatest pressure. Given endless assurances of their "equality" by the media, by college recruiters, and by their guilt-ridden White classmates and co-workers, they had, more than their humbler brethren, come up with a humiliating jolt against their inherent limitations.

After the first day, however, many other Blacks had, in effect, joined the rebellion. The entire Black underclass—the street gangs, the chronically unemployed, the ones who always were ready for any activity which promised an opportunity for loot, for getting in a blow against "Whitey," for raising a little hell—although not formally affiliated with any of the nationalist organizations or taking orders from them, served the cause quite well by participating independently in the looting and destruction.

The militants did succeed in formally recruiting many Blacks to their cause during the first weeks of fighting, however: some joined because they were intimidated, and some had sympathies or resentments which already had predisposed them toward Black nationalism. As the White reaction began to take shape, with the accompanying manifestations of anti-Black feeling, the polarization between the races grew, and many Blacks who had hoped to avoid the conflict were forced to choose sides.

To Oscar the rebellion seemed a godsend, almost too good to be true. Far from sharing Ryan's antipathy toward the Black nationalists, he hoped that they would emerge from the rebellion with even more influence over their own race than before. But the fate of the Blacks was only a minor issue. The real value of the rebellion lay in three things. First, it did more to raise the racial consciousness and the receptivity of the still-healthy segment of the White population than ten years of preaching with all the media at their disposal could have done. Second, it greatly strengthened Saul's grip on his particular segment of the White population: not only had he firmly established his credentials as an authentic, divinely inspired prophet by serving as Jesus' mouthpiece for an unequivocal prediction of the rebellion, but he had been preaching about the importance of race, even if somewhat obliquely, for months beforehand, while the other supposed minions of Jehovah had been attacking him for his efforts. And third, the rebellion did irreparable damage to the prestige and credibility of the established authorities: principally the government, the controlled media, and the mainline churches, all of which were perceived as sharing the blame for it.

On the evening of the second day of the rebellion, the Washington-area leadership cadre of the National League held an emergency meeting in the Kellers' basement to plan strategy. "Have any trouble getting here?" Harry asked as Oscar and Adelaide entered the room ten minutes late. The President had declared a state of emergency and imposed martial law on the capital area that afternoon. There was a 6:00 PM curfew, and military patrols were roaming the streets to enforce it. In addition there was the danger from the Blacks in many areas.

"Not really," Oscar replied. "We would have been here before curfew time if I hadn't run into a roadblock on Washington Boulevard. In order to get around it I used the side streets. Unfortunately, the route I chose took me through a Black neighborhood, and somebody took a couple of shots at the car. A rifle bullet came in the back window and went out the windshield. That was a bit exciting. I'd just as soon not try to go back the same way tonight. Anyway, we brought our sleeping bags with us, and I hope you've got some free space on your floor for us."

The discussion centered on strategies for using the rebellion to further their own cause, while coping with the government's ban on publications or activities which might incite disorder. Kevin Linden held up the current edition of the *Washington Post*. The principal headline was "Blacks Respond to White Racism with Violence." Under that, in slightly smaller type, was "Government Must Redress Black Grievances, Prevent White Backlash."

"It's pretty clear from this what the Jews' line will be on the rebellion," Kevin laughed. "Until this, I thought they were siding with the Agency to keep the Blacks in line. Now their main concern seems to be keeping *us* in line. They're playing down the atrocities committed by the rebels and even making excuses for them, just the way they did before the Agency was created. They aren't even making much of a fuss about the fact that the Blacks seem to be especially targeting Jewish businesses for looting and burning."

"That's a little misleading," Bill Carpenter spoke up. "I'm on pretty good terms with a secretary in the big Jewish firm down the hall from my office, Abramowitz and Cohen. She said that Jewish businessmen were calling frantically all day yesterday and today, and that Abramowitz was telling them not to worry, that the government would more than cover all their losses under one of the provisions of the Horowitz Act. I looked up the law, and sure enough there's a clause in it which stipulates triple reimbursement of all losses suffered by any member of an identifiable minority group as a result of a 'racist act.' Ordinarily the reimbursement is made from the confiscated assets of the perpetrator of the act, but whenever the perpetrator is unknown or for any other reason cannot be made to pay the government pays the victim instead. Abramowitz was assuring his callers that the fix was in, that all losses suffered by Jews would be attributed to the deliberate 'racist' targeting of Jews by the rebels, that they would qualify as members of an identifiable minority, and that they would get triple reimbursement. The funny thing, the secretary told me, was that when the Jews heard this from Abramowitz some of them became even more upset. One wailed that he had just filed inventory figures for his jewelry store last week. If he had known the rebellion was coming he would have placed at least twice the valuation on his stock. He was inconsolable. Another was moaning that the Blacks had only smashed the display windows of his clothing store and grabbed a few coats, instead of burning the place down. And he was afraid to go back and torch the place himself."

"Excellent!" Oscar exclaimed. "One could hardly ask for a more invidious scenario. Imagine how the White businessmen will feel when their Jewish competitors get triply reimbursed from the Federal treasury, while most of them won't get a dime, even from their insurance companies, because their policies exclude losses due to war or insurrection.

"I'm still surprised, though," he continued. "I had a reliable source of information inside the Agency who told me that the Jews were very worried about the likelihood that they would be targeted if there were a Black uprising, and that this worry would lead them to back the Agency in such an eventuality. It looks like the Jews had things figured a little differently than he thought. At least, they certainly were more prepared for what has happened than they let on to my source, and not half so worried. It looks like they were all set to jump in whichever direction seemed most advantageous to them. It must have been clear to them by the time today's *Washington Post* went to press late last night that this uprising will be no real threat to them in itself and that so long as the Whites don't get too unruly they can safely resume their policy of using the Blacks and other non-Whites as their principal weapon to destroy what's left of White resistance to their rule. Whether the Black nationalists hate their guts or not really doesn't matter a bit to them."

"Always being prepared to jump in the most advantageous direction has been the cornerstone of Jewish survivability for thou-

sands of years," Harry cut in. "The thing to remember about them
is that they never, but *never*, take any interests but their own into
consideration in their planning. More than one politician or bureau-
crat who thought he had an alliance with them has found that out,
to his sorrow. And you can be sure that they've thought about the
public relations consequences of profiting from this Black uprising
and will have their asses covered. First they'll have the media create
the impression that they're practically the only ones who've suffered
any losses; then, when anybody starts complaining about the pref-
erential compensation they're getting from the government, they'll
have their stooges in the Congress and in the Christian churches
cluck-clucking about the awful 'anti-Semitism.' Believe me,
there'll be very few businessmen who'll have the guts to complain
publicly, no matter how much it galls them privately."

"Okay, folks. So much for the anecdotes and theories," Kevin
said brusquely. "Our job tonight is to figure out what we have to do
to upset the Jews' calculations and get the greatest advantage we
can from the current disorder, both during the next few days while
it's going on and then in the months afterward."

The discussion went on until the early morning hours. The
general conclusions reached were that the government probably
would have the rebellion under control within a week or two, even
considering the fact that a number of Army units seemed to be
presently unable to cope with the mutinies by Blacks which had
broken out in their own ranks; that an open appeal to Whites by the
League would lead to immediate governmental suppression of the
League; and that the time had come for the League to shift most of
its resources into clandestine, or "underground," action.

The one exception to this last conclusion was Saul's program.
Oscar and Saul argued successfully that Saul should remain on the
air as long as he could, continuing to bring his viewers around to
positions on which the League could later capitalize. Saul could
even strengthen his position in relation to the government at the
same time by throwing a heavy dose of "render unto Caesar" and
other law-and-order rhetoric into his sermons for the next week or
so, when the government would be grateful for all the support it
could get.

Aside from that, however, their planned activities would hardly
endear them to the nation's political leaders and law-enforcement
authorities. They would use every means available to them to alert
the White population of the country, not so much to the racial aspects
of the present rebellion, which were more or less self-evident
anyway, as to the less-evident Jewish aspects. They would, in other
words, propagate essentially the same message Saul was propagat-

ing, but via other media, without the Christian trappings, and in even more forceful language. They would use pirate radio transmitters, air-dropped leaflets, painted signs on highway overpasses, and aerial balloons to rouse as much feeling as possible against the government's racial policies and to lay the blame for those policies squarely on the Jewish control of the news and entertainment media. It would be a sharp break with the League's previous policy of strict legality, but it was unanimously agreed that the opportunity presented by the rebellion had to be seized by all available means, legal or not. For the next few weeks the government undoubtedly would have its hands full trying to pacify the Blacks anyway, and so moderate discretion in the conduct of their activities should suffice to minimize their risk.

Oscar's own area of responsibility, in addition to continuing his management of Saul's programs, would be to set up a mobile pirate broadcasting station powerful enough to blanket the Washington metropolitan area and reach deep into the adjoining states. Before retiring to his sleeping bag that night he began making a list of equipment Harry would need to obtain for him the next day. He estimated that he should be able to be on the air within three days, if everything were available.

Later, as he and Adelaide lay on the floor in their sleeping bags in a corner of the darkened room, she said to him, "We were too busy for me to mention it earlier, but while you were out this afternoon my mother called. She's been seeing some of the news about the rebellion in this area and was worried about me. I asked her about conditions in Iowa, and she said things are pretty peaceful there. She had heard some radio reports of shootings by Blacks in Davenport and Cedar Rapids, but there wasn't anything about them in this morning's newspaper. Some of the neighbors are talking about buying more guns and ammunition, but Reverend Malone has been phoning everyone telling them to stay calm and don't do anything rash. There's been talk in the past about burning down a Vietnamese resettlement camp the government built just down the road from us two years ago, and he's worried that someone will do it now."

"Just what should be expected of the good reverend!" Oscar snorted. "It's hard to say now just how the folks in Iowa and the other parts of the country which aren't being affected much by the rebellion will react to it, but I'll bet they won't learn much from it. As long as the Jews control the television they watch and the newspapers they read—and as long as the Jews' accomplices, like the Reverend Malone, are permitted to do their work—the sheep will keep ambling along toward the slaughterhouse."

"Well, there are some things that would stir up the people I know back in Iowa," Adelaide replied, "besides having gangs of armed Blacks roaming the countryside. They're not really all that fond of the government here in Washington. There are many things they don't approve of. But as long as there's food in the refrigerator, gas in the car, and something to watch on the screen, they won't do anything. My grandpa isn't the only one in our county who feels the way he does; he's just the only one who isn't afraid of what Reverend Malone will say, and so he speaks up while the others remain silent. But if there weren't any electricity for a few weeks, as an example, so that all of the food in the refrigerators spoiled and the TV screens were blank, grandpa would have plenty of company. He might even be able to drum up a fair-sized lynching party and go after Reverend Malone. A lot of people are still simmering about Malone's getting Washington to resettle those Viets in the county."

"I hope you're right, sweetheart," Oscar replied. "I'd like to believe there's still a little fight left in our race. Better get some sleep now."

He kissed her and then settled himself more comfortably into his sleeping bag, but he did not fall asleep immediately. Instead he thought about the new situation which would confront him and his comrades in the aftermath of the Black rebellion. It was too bad, he reflected, that the Blacks had planned their uprising so poorly. Slicing up a few thousand honkies would gain them little in the long run, not when there were 150 million more. They should have gone after the country's economic infrastructure instead: power plants, dams, factories, transportation hubs, reservoirs, things that could be burned or blasted or flooded or poisoned and would disrupt the flow of commerce, halt the production of goods, pull the plugs on the country's refrigerators, and make its TV screens go dark. Then they might have brought America to a real state of civil war; they might have seriously disrupted the Jews' mechanism of mind control and the government's mechanism of enforcement; they might have kept Whitey off balance long enough to gain some real leverage for their demands.

And, really, that's exactly what the League should do, not just react to the uprising with a momentary burst of new propaganda. He had hoped to be able to give up his one-man commando raids, with the risk they entailed, and devote himself to safer and less violent activity, such as guiding Saul's programs. But he also had made his choice, when forced by Ryan to do so, for flux instead of stasis. Acting alone he could not hope to accomplish the massive damage to the economic infrastructure which 40,000 or so organized and highly motivated Black nationalists might have accomplished, but there were other things he could do. By killing Ryan he had substantially increased the potential for flux. There certainly must be other men in key positions whose deaths also would influence the course of events. Both the worsening economy and the Black uprising would lead to a more unsettled climate in the country, the sort of climate which he ought to do everything in his power to exacerbate. Only in such a climate could the League hope to begin competing effectively with the Jews for the hearts and minds of the White public.

He sighed. Well, he would be very busy during the next few days discharging responsibilities he already had incurred. But after that it would be time to do some more hunting.

Large catalog of Politically Incorrect books available from the publisher of *Hunter* and *The Turner Diaries*.

NATIONAL VANGUARD BOOKS CATALOG No. 17

Many books that are interesting and important to Whites are not available through conventional booksellers because their publishers are not listed in *Books in Print*, and they are not carried by wholesalers or distributors. In some case they come from "underground" publishers. National Vanguard Books carries over 600 hard-to-find books and tapes, including *White Power* by George Lincoln Rockwell, *The Talmud Unmasked, You Gentiles, The Secret Relationship Between Blacks and Jews, Gun Control in Germany, Stuka Pilot, Knights of the Reich, Protocols of the Learned Elders of Zion, Did Six Million Really Die?, The Secret of the Runes, Mein Kampf, The Immigration Mystique, Rising Tide of Color*, and *The Reconstruction Trilogy.*

We have books on the Celts, Vikings, and other European peoples; on the myths, religions, and philosophies of Europeans; on WW II from the German perspective; on National Socialism; on the American pioneers; on survival. We also have children's books and many, many books on race, the Jews, and communism. The 72-page *National Vanguard Books Catalog* alone is $2.00. It comes free with the purchase any book.

NATIONAL VANGUARD BOOKS
Dept H
POB 330 Hillsboro WV 24946

George Lincoln Rockwell Speaks

In the 1960s, as race riots and degeneracy engulfed America, a deco-
rated Navy flier— inspired by the example of Hitler and his National Socialist German Workers' Party—launched his National Socialist White People's
Party to restore America to sanity and White rule. George Lincoln Rockwell took the most public stand of any patriot since WW II.

Just before his assassination he wrote *White Power* to alert Americans and to demand that preoccupied and cowardly Whites stand up for
their people. He attacks the Big Lie—that race differences do not exist. It's
the lie that can destroy us. The media take an unrelenting and well-de-
served beating from Rockwell. Here's an excerpt:

"In one TV show after another, whenever there is some rotten, depraved
character in a scene, nine times out of ten they make him an ignorant, foul-
mouthed, tobacco-chewing, scraggly-bearded, cruel, Southern, White, Protestant Anglo-Saxon of the lowest and vilest sort. Just observe how many
times the villain in a TV show has a Southern — or a German — accent."

Rockwell wrote that thirty years ago. He crafts a case that the very
survival of our race is at stake. *White Power* builds steadily until Rockwell
calls for "White Revolution." If you have any interest in the White race, you
must read Rockwell's *White Power*.

ISBN 0-937944-10-2 White Power 466 pp soft cover $12.95 postpaid

NATIONAL VANGUARD BOOKS
Dept H
POB 330 Hillsboro WV 24946